Counseling Women

COUNSELING WOMEN

Kinship Against Violence in India

Julia Kowalski

PENN

UNIVERSITY OF PENNSYLVANIA PRESS

PHILADELPHIA

Published by
University of Pennsylvania Press
Philadelphia, Pennsylvania 19104-4112
www.upenn.edu/pennpress

Printed in the United States of America on acid-free paper
10 9 8 7 6 5 4 3 2 1

Hardcover ISBN 9781512822854
Paperback ISBN 9781512822847
Ebook ISBN 9781512822830
A Cataloging-in-Publication record is
available from the Library of Congress.

To my parents

CONTENTS

NOTE ON TRANSLITERATION

Hindi is a living language that continues to transform as people deploy it across diverse scripts and transliteration systems, from literary publications to WhatsApp messages. In order to provide readability for readers who may be completely unfamiliar with South Asian languages (as well as readers who may be intimately familiar with South Asian languages, but less familiar with the formal transliteration systems used by scholars), in this book I made the decision to use simplified phonetic spellings for Hindi language terms, rather than a diacritic-based transliteration system. I hope this gains in readability what might be lost in precision, as some distinctions between long and short vowels, or retroflex and dental consonants, are lost.

There is one exception to this pattern. For verbs where a long vowel is the meaningful distinction between the intransitive and transitive versions of the word, I use doubled vowels to help the reader visually distinguish between the paired verbs (such as *samajhna/samjhaana,* to understand/to explain).

Introduction

"What's the way forward?"

Indu, a family counselor in her late twenties, asked this question in the midst of engaging with a young couple, Prema and Gopal. Next to Indu sat Hema, her senior colleague, who had been working as a counselor since the 1980s, when the family counseling center, Source of Strength, was founded to support women facing harm, conflict, and neglect in their families, based in Jaipur, the capital city of Rajasthan.[1] Source of Strength was partially funded by a federal agency devoted to social welfare, and was run by an organization that was highly active in advocating for women's rights in northern India. Between the counselors and the couple were piles of case files, rulers, paper clips, paperweights, and clipboards holding forms and blank sheets of paper waiting for Hema and Indu's notes. I sat kitty-corner to the counselors, squeezed behind a second desk stacked with ledgers, the counselors' lunch tiffins, and Indu's motor scooter helmet. A tiny ceiling fan hung from the low ceiling over our heads. Just out of view through the open door, Prema's brother and father sat in the small courtyard around which the center's four small rooms clustered. Indu and Hema had been talking to Prema, Gopal, and members of their families for several days, and this particular session had already been churning along for a number of hours.

Indu's question—"What's the way forward?"—underscored the goals of counseling, which focused on helping female clients navigate a path (*rasta*) to an improved future in the face of family conflict and harm. Yet Indu's tone was slightly exasperated, suggesting that there may be no easy answer. She provided a list of the dilemmas that had emerged in the case, obscuring both the path itself and the futures to which it might lead: "There's the matter of his drinking, the matter of earning, the tension."

Initially, Prema had, like many clients, approached Source of Strength complaining of harassment (*pareshani*) from her husband. These issues had driven Prema, in her early twenties and pregnant with her first child, to leave the multi-generational household where she had been living with Gopal, his paternal grandparents, and at least one of his brothers. At present, she was living in a women's hostel attached to the hospital where she was training to work in nursing. Over the course of her intake interview with Hema and Indu, she explained the multiple causes of conflict in the household. The couple had been fighting over money and where to live; Prema wanted to move to a better neighborhood. Gopal had been drinking, a habit that harmed both his behavior and his bank account. Prema was also concerned about Gopal's relationships with his extended family, as he diverted both financial resources and, Prema worried, romantic affections, to his uncle's young wife. In the heat of their arguments about these topics, Gopal had slapped Prema. She wanted, she told counselors, to return to her marriage with Gopal, but on better material and emotional terms.

As in every counseling case I observed at the two centers where I observed cases and spoke with counselors, their bosses, and other staff, Hema and Indu did not seek to teach Prema, or her family, the label "violence" (*himsa*), nor did they focus exclusively on the presence of physical violence in the household. Rather than diagnosing and condemning violence, they contextualized Prema's experience within multiple dilemmas resulting from the contradictory expectations surrounding family relations that bore down on Prema and Gopal. From Hema and Indu's perspective, these were dilemmas of interdependence, situations in which people are caught between contradictory messages about how one ought to depend on others. The physical harm Prema experienced was one among numerous symptoms that such dilemmas had disordered relations in her marital household. In order for Prema to return home on improved terms, it was necessary to, as Indu put it, find a way forward through these dilemmas. The process of doing so began with investigating not only Prema's perspective on the conflict, but those of her kin.

When Hema and Indu spoke with Gopal at a later session, they learned more about the contours of these dilemmas. Gopal, only in his mid-twenties, was alone among his brothers in having a relatively stable source of income, from a custodial job in a government office. He felt pressure to provide support for his brothers, for his grandparents, and for other uncles, whose collective needs exceeded his income. Gopal's brother had been ill and needed expensive medical care; Gopal carried a loan taken out to help pay for a sister's wedding. On top of these pressures (perhaps because of them), Gopal drank, an expensive habit that made his fights with Prema worse. Prema struggled to settle into life in the small house that Gopal had rented in a fast-growing squatter colony that clung to a major highway running between Jaipur's old city and the Aravilli hills. To move from this neighborhood to a smaller flat in a higher rent area would mean either sacrificing a multi-generational household, which Gopal did not want to do, or accepting that Prema would work outside the home, which troubled his extended family, because it appeared to violate the norms of gendered behavior that marked families as honorable in their community. Hema summed up these issues as follows: "Your problems are a problem of *roti* [bread]—by *roti*, I mean *palna* [nurturing]."

Like the activist organizers who ran the organization that hired her, and like the transnational scholars and activists who lobby international bodies and governments to define and prosecute domestic violence, Hema connected the problems in Prema's home with the kinship system that structured ideas about social reproduction, gendered difference, and intergenerational support. Global women's rights discourse would interpret those problems of harassment, conflict, and harm as the result of patriarchal kinship norms. Hema, however, interpreted these problems in terms of a breakdown in the mutually reciprocal relationships that were meant to sustain Prema, Gopal, and the wider family network within which they were building a life. Counselors like Hema sought to resolve such household violence, in turn, by deepening and improving kin relations. To do so, they drew on relatedness as a heterogeneous set of practices that help women make claims on and through their interdependent relations with others.

Women like Prema have growing access to institutional support developed in dialogue with transnational projects framing women's rights as human rights, an overwhelming array of institutional venues run by community groups, nongovernmental organizations, and the state. Over the past twenty years, the issue of gender violence has become a topic of intense engagement for both women's organizations and the government in India, as a global focus on gender violence and women's human rights has intersected with longstanding movements addressing violence against women in India via social welfare, progressive social justice movements, and state policy. The intersection of these forces has led to innovative legislation, state-NGO partnerships, and fierce debates about what kind of a problem gender violence represents and how, in turn, to effectively address it. As a result, when women like Prema face household harm and conflict, they have the option to pursue criminal cases, civil legal action, or a variety of informal mediation processes, including those hosted by the state, by NGOs, and by religious and caste-based organizations. In turn, each of these interventions will put them in the position of deciding whether to reform the families where they live or to build their lives separately. For most women, this bureaucratically complex institutional landscape is bewildering, a "problem of plenitude" rather than lack (Basu 2015, 208). Increasingly, women's groups in northern India help women navigate these options by hiring mid-level staff to serve as social worker, legal adviser, and emotional support. This category of frontline worker is often labeled "counselor."

Family counseling, or *parivar paramarsh* in Hindi, is one of a variety of counseling and mediation strategies that women's rights NGOs in India and around the world have come to rely upon as they address gender violence, and plays a central role within the larger network of women's rights organizations in Jaipur, a network that extends from Jaipur to Delhi to the transnational human rights stage. Such strategies have been especially attractive in northern India, where both lay people and women's rights activists describe the legal system as sexist, inefficient, and too easily corrupted by financial and social capital. Women's rights organizations rely on counselors to help women navigate the complex world of legal protections that support their rights, while simultaneously protecting vulnerable women from further harm at the hands of courts and police. As a result, family counseling centers are key sites where frontline workers—counselors—come together with clients and families on one hand and activist-organizers on the other, in order to address what is widely recognized as a crisis in gender violence in northern India.

At Source of Strength, counselors like Hema performed triage for clients like Prema, who were struggling with family conflict that had resulted in material, physical, and emotional harm. Such conflicts were rarely contained within the bounds of married couples. Like Prema, many married women in Jaipur lived in some configuration of a multi-generational family, and house-hold conflicts often involved mothers- and sisters-in-law, brothers-in-law, and natal kin. In some cases, the legal system offered "a way forward" to protect women facing extreme physical threats or to help them exit marriages. In rare cases, medical or psychiatric expertise was warranted. But most clients arrived at counseling centers seeking safer, more sustaining relationships with their families—and the material and emotional dynamics of care, harm, neglect, authority, and future desires within families were just as complex and bewildering as the legal and peri-legal institutions that might provide women with support. Questions of how best to organize multi-generational networks of interdependent kin dominated the conversations of counselors and clients. Counselors treated these desires as continuous with the stated goal of expanding women's rights that motivated the organizations where they worked. Because of the central role family played in understandings of good lives and good persons, such representations were powerful tools in advocating for more just relations with family members. As a result, counseling interactions focused not on diagnosing moments of violence, but instead focused on tracing the practices of care that ought to sustain relations—examining issues of *palna*, nurturing, as Hema said to Gopal.[2]

This book explores why, in the face of globally powerful representations of domestic violence as a pathology of patriarchal kinship systems, family counselors in Jaipur relied on kinship as a *solution to* violent household conflict. I argue that counselors focused on kinship and family because they saw violence as a symptom of powerful dilemmas of interdependence, situations in which people are caught between contradictory messages of what it means to depend on and be depended on by others. Counselors helped women confront household violence by helping them navigate the impacts of such dilemmas on themselves, their households, and society more broadly. While global women's rights discourse has long portrayed gender violence as a problem of inequality, counselors saw violence as a problem of interdependence. Rather than presenting rights as a means for women to become independent, counselors helped women cultivate stronger relations of interdependence with their families. As they did so, they reimagined what it means to have agency and what constitutes violence.

Anti–gender violence advocates frequently suggest that in order to end intimate violence, it is necessary to dismantle the grip of patriarchal kinship systems on both individuals and on state institutions. Such concerns frame gender violence as a problem of kinship and family norms that rely upon and reproduce unequal relations between male and female kin. Observers of counseling and mediation activities in India and elsewhere worry that counselors push women to go "back" to their families, reconciling them with kin who have harmed them and prioritizing family harmony over the individual well-being of kin. When middle-class counselors like Hema focus on activities rooted in care and mutual sustenance, the relatively elite activist-organizers who run women's rights organizations worry that the counselors do not view domestic violence as a violation of women's rights.

Yet this focus on counseling outcomes assumes that "the family" is a static, unchanging container. Such analyses overlook the fact that counseling occurs through interactive practices designed to act on the family as a dynamic, complex set of relations that are made and remade over time. I use the phrase "interactive practice" to describe structured social activities designed to both reflect and act on the world through interaction, including speech and textual activities, such as producing and signing documents. By analyzing counseling as an interactive practice, I demonstrate that counselors carefully—in all senses of the word—engaged with kinship as a fertile ground for reimagining and remaking the future, precisely through underscoring the generative power of sustaining interdependence. They did so by building on the very precarity of kinship that led women to seek counseling in the first place. Their strategies were designed to foster families that were mutually sustaining, forward looking, and continually regenerated through interactions with kin that were ordered by care and support. Counselors differed from mainstream women's rights activists not in their definition of violence, but in their models of how speech addresses and acts on violence, drawing on an understanding of how language acts on relations that emphasizes the power of spoken interaction to generate valued persons and relations. Family counseling reflects thorny questions within anti-violence interventions and the wider ideologies about gender equality and development that they reflect. These include questions about how the way that people speak reflects who they are, what they believe in, and how they relate to others—and how, in turn, those relations orient them toward past, present, and future. By exploring these divergent models of how language acts on the world, I demonstrate that kinship serves as a dynamic resource through which people imagine and act on new familial futures.

In focusing on how counseling operates as an interactive practice, I draw on theories of practice that analyze structure and agency as co-constitutive, ever emergent in social interaction, and generative of both continuity and transformation.[3] Such theories analyze interaction and sociolinguistic activity as the building blocks of personhood, relations, and social life. By attending to how counseling casework unfolds via interactive practices, I show that counseling strategies reflect fundamental questions about what it means to act on the world, to have a voice in social transformation, and to depend on others. These questions are also central to scholarly analyses of human rights discourse, development, and gender inequality.

As an interactive practice, counseling is profoundly shaped by contradictory institutional demands. Counselors worked in a context shaped by longstanding ambiguities about the role of both the family and of women in Indian modernity, as well as tensions in global women's rights discourse about the role of cultural difference. To create social change through the family, organizers who ran counseling centers imagined a future where family dynamics were transformed. Yet supporting vulnerable women in immediate crisis, in a context with few other forms of social welfare, required calling upon and enforcing seemingly "traditional" ideas about gender, generation, and household hierarchy. Such strategies also required counselors to continually reference expectations that arose within, and supported, patriarchal kinship norms.

The many questions that circulate around the role and impact of counseling suggest that we need a richer set of theories for understanding the relationship between kinship and agency, progress, and development, three key themes in efforts to extend the reach of women's rights into the everyday lives of women around the world. Yet, because women's rights are typically represented as tools to liberate women from oppressive kinship structures, activities supporting kinship and family are often excluded from scholarly considerations of women's rights practices. How can we theorize these findings about kinship in terms of how they produce social transformation or contribute to understandings of change? To do so, it is necessary to move beyond the assumption that independent individuals must be liberated from kinship in order to become fully equal political subjects—a deeply held assumption that shapes women's rights and human rights projects around the world. Kinship in India, as everywhere, has long been shaped by, and served as grounds for, political contestations about progress, equality, and belonging. Far from being an outside to the realm of debates about socio-political transformation, claims on, about, and through kinship represent a site of what Anna Tsing calls "contaminated diversity," where diverse representations of kinship interact to produce new interpretations of inequality and interdependence (Tsing 2015, 29–30).[4] Yet, in spite of the intertwined nature of kinship and gender violence, few studies of gender violence interventions have explored how such interventions reshape how people understand themselves as kin. In counseling centers in Jaipur, however, kinship and rights operated alongside each other as counselors helped women make their way through the dilemmas of interdependence they faced. Because of this, counseling practices offer a unique opportunity to reexamine the role of kinship and interdependence in gender violence, at a historical moment when both individual rights and interdependent kinship serve as powerful and precarious sites for desire and belonging.

Analyzing Family Counseling: Mediating in
a Complex Institutional Landscape

Counselors work in a context where the harmful effects of gender inequality are well-documented. Jaipur, a city of around 3 million people, is the capital of the northwestern state of Rajasthan. Along with other northern states, Rajasthan scores poorly on indexes of gender equality. Women in the state face high rates of gender violence, low rates of literacy, low rates of participation in formal employment, low rates of property ownership, and a highly skewed gender ratio that reflects a preference for sons (International Institute for Population Sciences and Macro International 2008). In India, 33 percent of women who have been married report having experienced physical, sexual, or emotional violence at the hands of their spouses at some point in the marriage (IIPS 2008). When studies measure domestic violence at the hands of not only husbands but other family members, such as various in-laws in multi-generational households, reported rates of domestic violence increase (Kalokhe et al. 2017).

Acts of spectacular gendered violence, such as dowry murder and brutal sexual assaults, have long shaped the history of women's activism in northern India, often attracting widespread national media coverage. Much of the activism surrounding women's well-being has focused, in turn, on securing women's rights in order to help them stand independently of these structures of patriarchy. Here, women's movements in India intersect with global anti–gender violence activism. Gender violence emerged, beginning in the mid-1990s, as the central platform of global efforts to reframe women's rights as human rights (Grewal 1999; Keck and Sikkink 1998; Merry 2006). In India, this transnational focus on violence against women provided new energy and resources to a multitude of movements that had begun addressing violence against women through a variety of both grassroots and state-based initiatives, stretching back to the 1970s. These diverse movements were drawn into transnational processes of "NGOization," as institutions worked to professionalize interventions in the service of seeking funding and lobbying the state to pass and effectively implement laws addressing gender violence (Bernal and Grewal 2014a; Lang 1997; Sangatin Writers Collective and Nagar 2006). Throughout the same period, the Indian government passed multiple anti-violence laws in response to social movements, beginning with criminal laws addressing "cruelty" and dowry demand, and extending to civil laws addressing domestic violence (Agnes 1992; Khullar 2005; Kumar 1997; Loomba and Lukose 2012).

As women's movements in India institutionalized over the 1980s and 1990s, a diverse array of interactive practices, ranging from radical attempts to remake the terms of development knowledge production to everyday strategies of conflict resolution and advice giving, were drawn together and pressed into the service of helping women both access and avoid the legal system. Counseling interventions seemed to spring up at the margins of each new wave of anti-violence efforts by the state. "Women's" police stations (*mahila thana*), for example, were supposed to offer a supportive environment for women facing conflict at home. As multiple activists in Jaipur told me, however, such stations were subject to the same pressures to lodge or settle cases that regular police stations were, leading, in turn, to the establishment of counseling centers associated with *mahila thana*. In a similar manner, the family court system was meant to support women by fast-tracking cases related to certain family laws, helping women avoid the overburdened central court system. But, because family courts did away with lawyers to help women more quickly access legal support, they too sprouted counseling offices, to which court magistrates, in turn, occasionally diverted women. As a result, counselors operated at a range of institutional venues, including *mahila thanas*, courts, and NGOs of a wide variety of stripes.

My ethnographic research focused on two free-standing counseling centers affiliated with women's rights organizations, which I call Source of Strength and Center for Advice and Protection. I selected these two sites because they were well known centers in the city and were run by organizations with explicit commitments to framing domestic violence as a violation of women's rights. At the same time, they represented two distinct moments in the history of counseling in the region. Women's organizations began offering counseling, directed at addressing violent family conflicts, in the wake of the rise of the autonomous women's movement, in the late 1970s. Efforts to provide venues to support women and families came from a range of voluntary women's organizations, as well as from the state, in various waves. The Central Social Welfare Board, a body in the central government, started a funding scheme to support counseling centers in the 1980s. Source of Strength was primarily funded by this program, framing its mission as mending "broken and scattered families" (*tutte-bikhre parivar*). Center for Advice and Protection, on the other hand, was one of multiple centers funded with the support of the state police, and was located on the property of a district police station. Such centers, established in a number of Indian states, are designed to support women who seek help at police stations but may not be well-served by the adversarial framing of criminal cases. It framed its goals in terms of "advice and protection" for women (*salah evam surakshan*).

However, counselors at both sites relied on similar interactive strategies as they worked with women and their families. The interactive activities of advising, supporting, and discussing that are grouped under "counseling" have multiple antecedents in both institutional and everyday life. Some arise from long-standing efforts to build communicative connections between different classes of women in building solidarity, such as the well-known Women's Development Programme, which was created with the express purpose of facilitating collective dialogue across differences of class and education, in order to bring women's struggles to the state's attention (Mathur 1999; A. Sharma 2008; Unnithan and Heitmeyer 2012). Others emerged in pedagogical efforts to develop women and families, with roots in family planning projects in mid-century India, where counseling-like activities were deployed as a non-coercive tool to convince couples to conceive fewer children (Chatterjee and Riley 2001; Tarlo 2003).

I base this analysis on observing counseling sessions at Source of Strength and Center for Advice and Protection over 12 months in 2010. I spent additional months interviewing counselors at other centers in 2007, 2010, and 2017, as well as conducting open-ended interviews with people throughout Jaipur about their thoughts on family and social transformation, observing meetings and training sessions hosted by the parent organizations that ran counseling centers, interviewing various activists, organizers, and scholars of gender violence, and occasionally accompanied counselors when they traveled to other institutional sites. In this book, I focus, in particular, on cases from Source of Strength, where counselors had a slightly lower case load and thus more time to talk to me about their interpretations of cases, but my analysis is drawn from cases I observed at both sites, as well as interviews with other counselors around the city, including four other counseling centers or programs. By exploring a few cases in depth, I aim to share the often confusing, beat-by-beat narratives through which counselors navigated household conflict, neglect, and harm.

I first learned about family counseling centers when I was exploring the possibility of researching how people in northern India saw rapid economic and social transformation intersecting with desires for (and criticisms of) joint family life. Given the fact that people kept telling me that multi-generational family relations were increasingly strained, I began asking people I knew in Jaipur where families went if they needed outside support with conflict.

Many people told me that no one would *ever* deliberately expose their family conflicts to outside eyes. But several people I knew were connected with the women's rights groups that ran counseling centers, and facilitated introductions and site visits. After a few introductory interviews, I was filled with questions. It was immediately clear that this "counseling" activity was neither the psychodynamic family therapy I was familiar with in the United States. But nor was it a straightforward enactment of women's rights ideas about independence and empowerment that were powerful among women's movements in Jaipur.

Counseling cases took place with open doors, many participants, and a constant stream of interruptions—from other staff, from other cases, from various site visitors, and from the volunteer activist-organizers who ran counseling centers and the wider organizations of which they were a part. Counselors referred to these organizers, their bosses, as "ma'ams," a term of respect, as most of these organizers were older and more socially prominent. A steady stream of researchers and trainees observed cases, though the organizers at Source of Strength expressed surprised at the length of time I spent observing. As I explain further in Chapter 2, what counselors and their bosses valued was not privacy, but neutrality—a transparency and openness in negotiations that distinguished counseling from other interventions. Visiting foreigners (of whom I was but the most recent) helped underscore the professionalism and neutrality of the site. Indeed, clients rarely asked about my presence, seeming to accept it as part of the background of the counseling center. Counselors at both sites explained my presence as though I were a trainee, seeking to learn how to counsel. Later in my fieldwork, Indu began explaining that I was studying how counseling worked, so that I could teach people back in the United States how to do it. Both of these explanations positioned the counseling centers as leaders in their field. Counselors and ma'ams knew that I was a student, conducting thesis research. As I was in my late twenties when I conducted much of this research (and, as a visitor making sense of new social norms, people expressed surprise at my age, telling me I seemed much younger), it was easy to slot me into a role as a trainee and a learner, rather than an evaluator of either clients or counselors. At the same time, counselors immediately asked about my own family life, and the fact that I was already married meant, they told me more than once, that it was acceptable to talk about issues—and make jokes—pertaining to sexuality around me.[5]

In observing cases, I carefully followed the lead of counselors and ma'ams, who occasionally either asked me to leave or encouraged me to spend time helping staff with other activities, like typing information from ledgers or addressing envelopes. Because of this complex situation, and because I was interested in counseling interactions in their own right, I never approached clients for interviews. It would have been very difficult to distinguish my own questions and interviewing from those of the counseling center. As I show over the course of this book, the mere interactive act of asking for information is framed, in the context of counseling, as a substantial intervention into household relations. Given the complex and careful interactive strategies counselors used, I did not want to complicate family conflict further or impose on clients and their families in the midst of crisis.

Counselors asked me not to audio record or photograph sessions when clients were present, and I complied with their requests. During sessions and staff meetings, I kept careful jottings in a notebook (much as counselors kept case notes). I paid special attention to turns of phrase and discussions of language, seeking to capture as much verbatim language as I could.[6] At home, I typed these jottings into fieldnotes, spending many hours each week writing detailed accounts of the cases I witnessed as well as other elements of daily working life at counseling centers. Attempting to write coherent narratives of the cases I observed often required me to follow up with counselors the next day, to fill in gaps in my understanding. I found these follow-up conversations were often the most illuminating, as I learned that counselors were often far less concerned about the specific factual details of a case than I was, focusing instead on interactive patterns and behavior they observed in the session.[7] Cases unfolded unpredictably, and I augmented my understanding by reading case notes the counselors kept. I also conducted a survey of the past year of case files (organized in a ledger) for counseling cases, as well as cases lodged under the Protection of Women Against Domestic Violence Act at Source of Strength (see Chapter 3).[8]

Clients came from a range of social backgrounds, all complaining of some form of harassment or neglect from husbands, in-laws, and occasionally siblings, parents, or adult children. In seeking outside help for private household problems, clients risked deepening the disorder in their homes, causing permanent rifts with kin, alienating possible sources of support, and embroiling their family in expensive, lengthy legal proceedings over which they might have little control. Counselors were trained to work within these constraints, strategically deploying the threat of state-based legal processes like court cases or police involvement, while working to resolve household problems without legal intervention when possible. They were trained to guide clients to appropriate legal support when necessary, calling police stations on behalf of women facing severe physical violence, directing them to sympathetic lawyers and free legal aid, and providing necessary paperwork. Importantly, counselors first assessed whether potential clients were facing serious physical harm. Rather than encouraging such women to pursue counseling, they connected these women to the police, sympathetic lawyers, or locally prominent activists.

Activists and scholars in India both held great hope for counseling and mediation processes. However, as a form of intervention, counseling also provoked controversy about its nature as a form of expertise: was it non-therapeutic "advice," expert social work, or expert therapy? Was it focused on helping women or helping families? Scholars in feminist counseling and social work in India debate whether counseling is a therapeutic activity, requiring counselors to acquire psychological training, or a subfield of social work (Gupte 2016; Kashyap 2009). Such experts worry that counselors offer "simply advice, with hardly any therapeutic element" (Kashyap 2009, 137). City-wide organizational meetings that I attended featured intense debates about what counseling was and who was qualified to practice it.[9] In interviews with me, leaders in Jaipur's women's rights network expressed worry that counselors who worked for pay might not be adequately "sensitized" to or "interested" in women's rights.

Behind these concerns about expertise and training lies a deeper worry: that counselors will prioritize family unity over gender equality, undermining the very political projects that they are meant to enact. In her work on family courts and marriage mediation in India, Srimati Basu suggests that while feminist organizations around the world look to alternate dispute resolution tools, like counseling and mediation, to escape the inefficiency and sexism of the state, such interactive venues risk smuggling in community norms and expectations about power, interaction, and gender, confusing institutional "efficiency with justice" (2015, 10–12). In northern India, such concerns about counseling interactions reproducing gender inequality pepper training materials, scholarly investigations of counseling practices, and white papers about best practices. Indeed, scholarly research on various marriage mediation practices in India consistently demonstrates that practitioners of all kinds do organize their interventions into household violence around restoring family ties (Basu 2012; Lemons 2016; Vatuk 2017). In regional and national evaluations of counseling centers, this emphasis on familial "reconciliation" is read as a sign that counselors and organizers at a site need further training and gender sensitization. Experts worry that counseling remains "directed at 'restoring order' by attempting reconciliations without explicitly locating domestic abuse as being unacceptable" (Bhate-Beosthali, Rege, and Prakash 2013, 7).[10]

These critiques of counseling practices rely on an oppositional framework: *either* counselors recognize that gender violence is a violation of women's rights as individuals, *or* they seek to reconcile women with their families. Under this framework of reconciliation or recognition, practitioners who seek to sustain kin relations are read as ignoring—or worse, tacitly endorsing—gender violence. "Reconciliation," is assumed to represent a return to the status quo, sending women back to the household, rather than engaging in the progressive work of labeling violence as a rights violation. The reconciliation/recognition binary frames counselors' focus on sustaining kin relations as a failure to act, because such interactive activities do not explicitly center ending gender violence at individual or social scales.[11] Yet such interventions were enormously active, reflecting counselor and clients' desires to act on the future through acting on kin relations. While harmful kin relations drive women to seek outside help, their ability to access that help is often facilitated by other supportive family members; in turn, women often seek help directed at sustaining those relations (Grover 2009; Nagaraj 2010). Building on these findings, Suneetha and Nagaraj have suggested that we must shift our angle of inquiry to better interpret how people rely on kinship, "rather than ignoring women's appeals to family, kinship, community for alleviation of suffering caused by violence" (2010, 474).

Concerns about counselors reconciling women to their families arise within a context where most scholarly observers view frontline workers like counselors as mediating on two fronts: first, between women and their families, and second, between women and the rights and resources they can access from the state. This approach casts frontline workers like counselors as institutional gatekeepers, figures who stand between women experiencing violence and state support and determining the forms of support women access. Yet, as other scholars have shown, even gatekeeping interactions involve interactive activities that generate models of self and relation, beyond the explicit institutional goal of accessing state-based rights (Trinch 2001; 2007; see also Briggs 1997; Ochs 2004; Wortham 2001).

Counselors frequently described their roles in mediating terms: finding a path forward, showing clients a mirror, collecting both sides of a story, making all sides of conflict understand one another. Yet they contextualized these mediating actions in a wider set of institutional contradictions and dilemmas. In a visit with counselor Indu in 2017, several years after I observed her speaking with Prema, she told me about her struggles to mediate between her training as a family counselor and her own role as a family member. "You can criticize in a government office, you can criticize in laws, but you can't criticize in the family. You have to take a middle way." She had been developing this point over multiple conversations on our visit: it is one thing to argue for women's rights in venues designed to implement them. It's another in the household, where different expectations about power, relationality, and recognition take hold. What's liberating to claim in one venue can be crushing and alienating in another, as Indu's own experience of trying to connect these worlds had taught her. In the moment, it wasn't clear if she was speaking to me as an expert in counseling or as a frustrated family member. But of course, counselors *are* family members. After work, they walk to the corner bus stop so that their husband can collect them on his way home from work. They rush to pack up their motor scooter to get home, assuaging a worried mother-in-law anxious about driving after dusk. They ask each other for advice about their own struggles at home, measuring the conflicts they face at home against those described by their clients. They navigate transitions in their own families, arranging marriages for children or learning that they are pregnant, picking up sonogram prints on their lunch breaks. About a third of the counselors I came to know over the course of this project had faced significant familial breakdowns in their own lives. One young, unmarried counselor I interviewed pulled me aside after our interview. "Don't tell ma'am," she said, referring to her boss, "but after seeing all this, I don't believe in marriage anymore."

Counselors, in other words, lived out the contradictions that structured the institutions that hired them. For both their clients and for themselves, counselors balance a commitment to supporting the family as a source of support, and a desire to cultivate agentive, rights-bearing individuals. Since the goal of treating women as autonomous means taking seriously their desires to return to families who may harm them, these goals often come into direct contradiction. Counselors mediate between contradictory demands of creating safety for their clients, spurring social development, helping clients cultivate modern personalities, promoting gender equality, and protecting families. Each of these projects, in turn, come with complex institutional and ideological histories. Counselors worked in the context of class hierarchies; inter-institutional tensions; competing ideologies about language, gender, and violence; and long-standing struggles to provide social welfare in the service of development in India. They mediated between women's diverse desires, not all of which fit easily into expected narratives about abuse and empowerment. They strategized around resilient beliefs about women's behavior and reputations that they could not transform.

As frontline workers, counselors found themselves caught in a classic dilemma of social work, caught between "social engineering" goals and "client-facing" goals (Lipsky 2010). In the case of counseling, social engineering goals led toward legal reforms and institutional venues that transformed kinship systems by pathologizing domestic violence and discouraged families from participating in practices that reproduce unequal gender norms, such as dowry demand. Yet, in the present, clients often needed support in facing family conflict—support most readily available within kin networks and in ideas about relatedness. When Hema tells Gopal that the problem in his family is a problem of *roti* and support, she is articulating a set of dilemmas he faces as he strives to sustain interdependent relations with both his wife, Prema, and his other kin, under materially constrained circumstances. This is a moral and ethical dilemma that cannot be fully addressed by recognizing Prema's rights, nor by reconciling Prema and Gopal. Such dilemmas are the arenas within which counselors translate policies and institutional goals into interactions with clients, absorbing the wider contradictions within which they work (Brodwin 2013; Carr 2015).

Counseling was a terrain on which people—from angry family members to experts seeking to professionalize the field to counselors themselves—debated how to define, discipline, and problematize two concepts at the heart of efforts to generate gender equality in India: *family* and *violence*. Rather than treating these two terms as labels that transparently reference phenomena in the world, I trace how both serve as hotly contested ground in contemporary northern India, arenas where people reimagined what it means to be a person engaged in morally rightful relations with others.

From Reconciliation to Regeneration: Kinship and Relatedness

Seen from the counseling office, these discussions of family life are not about reconciliation, but instead about regeneration. I take the verb "regenerate" from Cole and Durham, who suggest that "while '(social) reproduction' has been used more to suggest the re-creation of particular social forms over time . . . 'regeneration' signal[s] a more dynamic approach, one that is attentive to process" (2007, 17; see also Weiner 1980). In particular, a focus on regeneration illuminates how multiple intersecting, shifting modes of inequality shape relationships within and beyond families, including not only gender but generational difference. As people confront an ever-changing world, they do so through these relations. Such relations, in turn, require on-going generative labor to sustain persons and institutions (Buch 2018). Such labor is vital to reproducing selves and social structures in arenas shaped by power and inequality, where "mutuality and connection do not imply an erasure of difference or hierarchy" (Govindrajan 2018, 4).

Indeed, as counselors draw on familial forms of support and care to confront household violence, they do so in terms of the intergenerational family norms that are prevalent in northern India. In this sense, they are indeed disciplining their clients into a world ordered by unequal kin relations, teaching "kinwork," just as activists and scholars worry they do (Lemons 2016). The counselors I knew best saw gender violence as a product of dilemmas of interdependence, and sought to address those dilemmas by asking who depends on whom, why, how, and with what moral authority. In these conversations, the patriarchal kinship systems that informed household life offered hope and harm, precarity and possibility.

As gendered violence has become central to the global platform of women's rights as human rights, activists and policymakers face an especially overt set of questions about kinship's role in social progress (Keck and Sikkink 1998; Merry 2006; Suneetha and Nagaraj 2010; Wies and Haldane 2011). In India, as around the world, women's rights movements debate what high rates of gender violence mean about the social norms that shape gendered difference and family life (Oldenburg 2002; Roychowdhury 2016; Visweswaran 2004). As they participate in efforts to regenerate families, counselors confront widespread questions about the value and meaning of kinship. Is kinship a harmful, constraining tradition that primarily subordinates women? Or is kinship a means for understanding, contesting, and creating relatedness as a social process that sustains people and relations alike?

Women's rights discourse has a clear answer to those questions. Global women's rights discourse draws on classic liberal models of social progress and modernity that rely upon representations of kinship as a discrete domain to make claims about social development: individual rights come "after" kinship has retreated from organizing public and political life (Carsten 2004; see also McKinnon 2001; Povinelli 2006; Trautmann 1987). As McKinnon and Cannell write, "understandings about the place of kinship in the modern world . . . relate to myths of . . . how modern social life is different from, and differently structured than the past" (2013a, 8). Such representations of kinship are central to how liberal political theory imagines social progress, where individuals are liberated from the constraints of social roles (or "status," in the language of early liberal theory), free to enter the social contract using their independent reason (Povinelli 2006). In this account of liberal personhood, modern persons confine kin-based social obligations to the private sphere. Free of dependency on others, they rationally choose social and political affiliations (Borovoy and Ghodsee 2012; Yanagisako 2015). When the demands of kin relations, rather than independent choice, appear to determine behavior, such political theory imagines individuals to be both less modern and less free. Such narratives use kinship's role in social life to distinguish between societies as a whole (such as modern states and primitive social groups), as well as between types of person who depend on kin ties (men and women, rich and poor, adults and children, white Euro-Americans and people of color, etc.) (Fraser and Gordon 1994; Povinelli 2006; Strathern 1992). This linear narrative of social progress is behind fears that counselors counsel women "back" to the family, as well as representations of kinship practices as "backwards," a common term in Indian English. Through such narratives, the presence or absence of kinship in overtly structuring social life comes to stand as a sign of civilizational distinction, reproducing a hierarchy between more- and less-civilized persons, relations, and societies (Kowalski 2021).

The transnational women's rights movement, like the human rights movements it draws upon, relies on such narratives about modernity and social progress as it addresses gender violence. Women's rights projects reproduce a "liberal discourse of generic personhood," which imagines that individual autonomy requires independence (Brown 1995, 141). In doing so, they reproduce longstanding assumptions about what constitutes civilization, how civilized persons act, and what kinds of phenomena are legible as meaningful social action (see Asad 2003; Englund 2006; Ferguson 2013; Mahmood 2001).[12] Scholars of domestic violence often follow women's rights activists by asking whether material dependence leaves women vulnerable to abuse by diminishing their options for support outside the family (Adelman 2004; Wies and Haldane 2011, 7). When scholars evaluate the effects of anti-violence interventions, they frequently project a telos of increasing material independence and autonomy that underwrites a growing consciousness of rights. By decreasing women's material dependence on others, the argument goes, women's rights organizations can foster agentive personhood, empowering women to separate from their abusers by transforming how they understand themselves in relation to their kin-based obligations. For example, in an article on the challenges that "rights talk" poses to feminine selfhood in Hawaii, Sally Engle Merry describes a "rights-bearing subject" as one who, in her autonomy, is at odds with a subject "defined by family, kin, and work relationships" (2003, 344–45).

Yet the effects of dependence are historically and socially contingent (Brown 1995; Fraser and Gordon 1994), and attempts to present independence as a solution to gender violence can often deepen vulnerability to harm. The ethnographic literature on violence against women demonstrates that dependence can not only generate vulnerability to harm but also offer protections, depending on expectations surrounding kin relations, whether people can fulfill those expectations, and shifting social policies (Adelman 2004; Collier 1997; Van Vleet 2008). In her exploration of anti-violence interventions in Brazil, for example, Sarah Hautzinger demonstrates that when women are materially dependent on their husbands, they may struggle to separate from abusers. Yet, by pursuing material independence, women sometimes experience intensified familial violence, because their independence threatens local models of masculinity (2007).

India, in particular, offers a number of challenges to models that connect women's vulnerability to harm with their material dependence on kin. When scholars and activists construe dependence as primarily material and incompatible with rights-based interventions and individual autonomy, they produce a model that maps poorly onto the terrain of northern Indian household life, which is built on a complex system of competing interdependencies, wherein husband and wife alike may depend on an adult brother's income, or an elderly mother may depend on her adult son. These crosscutting ties of interdependence produce obligations, entitlements, and rights that are not easy to distinguish from legal frameworks, as models of the ideal family tangled together with official family law over India's long engagement with colonialism (Agnes 2000).

These interdependent ties were, indeed, organized by patriarchal logics. The ideal, multi-generational joint family, represented in popular culture and long treated as a pillar of national culture, is organized around brothers, their wives and children, governed by an elder father and mother, and living together in a single household.[13] Sons stay. Daughters marry and leave. Wives enter. Research on everything from birth order to childhood nutrition to educational access in northern India has long suggested that this core kin dynamic animates gender inequality. Many women in Jaipur, as throughout northern India, live in some configuration of a multi-generational household organized around their husband's families. Many residents of Jaipur move through differing configurations of joint and nuclear households over their lives, and these transitions are frequently marked by ambivalence and conflict, particularly for young female in-laws. Any viewer of Hindi TV serials and films knows well the potential for conflict between mother-in-law and daughter-in-law, *sas* and *bahu*, between elder and younger sisters-in-law by marriage, *jethani* and *devrani*. In real life, these difficult relationships were often at the heart of counseling cases, dwarfing conflicts between husbands and wives.

In turn, resolutions to conflict involved many kin. Gopal's participation in counseling was facilitated by advice from his uncles to "solve" his family matter, as well as pressure from Prema's father, who called him repeatedly to get him to come to the center. And the dilemmas that Gopal and Prema faced arose from economic and material demands shaped by logics that saw material and moral relations oriented around ties of descent between male kin. Gopal felt reciprocal obligations to grandparents who raised him and relied on his income to care for one of his brothers; a substantial part of his income was spent paying off a loan he had taken out to facilitate his sister's marriage, based on expectations that the family of the bride will pay for the wedding and offer gifts and even dowry to the groom's family. This complex world of obligations was clearly overwhelming Gopal, but his role in it went unquestioned by counselors. In fact, they saw his efforts to sustain all these ties as signs of his moral worth. Prema's relationship with her natal family was also vital to the counseling process—both her father and brother accompanied her to counseling sessions—but these relations were also called into question by counselors and Gopal's family as potentially inappropriate "interference," reflecting expectations that women's kin ties should exert less pressure in their married lives than those of their husbands.

These dynamics also shaped the horizon of possibilities for women outside the family. International women's rights activists often echo Western feminist movements in seeing an exit from the family as an ideal resolution to household violence. Yet such options are limited for most women in Jaipur, both practically and ideologically.[14] Women can and do live independently in India. However, as Sarah Pinto writes, "in north India, for most but the upper classes, living alone signifies abandonment and impropriety more than freedom, involving social threat and the emptiness of life beyond the embrace of kin, especially for women of a marriageable age" (2011, 389). Single women, especially those known to be married or have been married, are open to assumptions about sexual availability, sexual activity, and insinuations about moral failure that can make life in neighborhoods difficult for women and their children, and can strain ties with natal kin.[15] Beyond these external constraints, women desired "belonging" in families—horizons of desire that bent toward a life crafted together with kin, even if such a life featured conflict or difficult relations (Lamb 2018; see also V. Das 2010; Govindrajan 2018; Maunaguru 2019). In most cases, the path toward such belonging ran through marriage (Basu 2015). In this context, living "independently" was neither a desirable nor a legible outcome of counseling cases. When women did separate from husbands and in-laws, it was either to return to natal homes with parents or married brothers, or, in a very small number of cases, to temporarily live in a "short stay home" or shelter, highly institutionalized spaces with locked gates and wardens. Counselors constantly pointed out the risks of life with natal kin, reminding women that no matter how supportive their parents or brother may be in the present, their position would be vulnerable. They knew Prema, who came from a working-class family, would face difficulties in trying to live alone in the long term, or in returning to her natal home. By helping Prema, Gopal, and their kin sustain the possibility of a relational future, counselors held open the possibility for Prema to act on that future. Their goal was not to reconcile her to a family system that harmed her, but to regenerate that system in terms that sustained Prema, Gopal, and their many relatives.

Research on domestic violence often assumes that family is unchanging, a space that holds women and culture alike, and that the expectations around relations that shape families are necessarily conservative. Yet research on kinship in contemporary anthropology complicates such assumptions. In approaching counseling as a process that is regenerative, rather than merely reconciliatory, I build on this body of research and, in particular, its emphasis on kinship as a domain of creativity and practice, rather than structure and constraint. Rather than beginning with the question of what kinship is, such research examines kinship as a material-semiotic process, a system of meaning and doing intertwined with other categories and social domains shot through with contradictions, fissures, and gaps (Ball 2018; Bear 2013; Carsten 2004; 2017; Franklin and McKinnon 2001; K. Goldfarb 2016; McKinnon 2016; Povinelli 2002; 2006; Ramberg 2013; Shever 2008; Yanagisako 2002; Yanagisako and Collier 1987). Such research shifts from an emphasis on kinship as a set of systemic structures to a collection of practices (Bourdieu 1977; Collier et al. 1992; V. Das 1976; Schneider 1984; Strathern 1992; Trawick 1990; Wadley 1994; Yanagisako 1975).

Many scholars have marked this shift by turning from analyzing systems of kinship to exploring practices of relatedness (Carsten 2000). "Not located within an individual or lodged in static structures," Krista Van Vleet writes, "relatedness emerges in between embodied individuals in joint performances that act upon the situation at hand but that may not directly reference 'relatedness' at all" (2008, 12). Practices of relatedness both spark new understandings of how society might be organized and, paradoxically, work to domesticate those potential changes back to a legible grid of relations, drawing in human and non-human actors alike (Ahearn 2010; Cole 2014; Collier 1997; Govindrajan 2018). Far from a set of private concerns rooted in domestic life, scholars show us that this dialectic of transformation and reproduction is crucial to understanding how seemingly "global" processes take shape (Bear et al. 2015; Cole and Durham 2007; Yanagisako 2015). Such research exploded the notion that there was a singular domain of social life shaped by kinship, and instead explored how ideas about relatedness and relationality shaped everything from the construction of houses to capitalist factory systems to the production of scientific knowledge (Bear 2013; Carsten and Hugh-Jones 1995; Yanagisako and Collier 1987; Haraway 1981; Yanagisako and Delaney 1995; Yanagisako 2002). Diverse ideas about relatedness, for example, pull migrant workers from around the world to provide in-home care for children and older people in the United States, where family norms prize care at home over institutional care, even as "home" is reshaped by the demands of labor markets. Other notions of relatedness, in turn, inform the flows of remittances that these migrants send back to their own kin (Hochschild 2000; Parreñas 2008; Yarris 2017; Wright 2020). By exploring the social processes that naturalize kinship's place in the private sphere and the distant past, such scholars question narratives of civilizational hierarchy, modern development, and gendered difference (Silverstein and Lewin 2016).

By shifting from *kinship* as a (constraining) system to *relatedness* as a set of material and interpretive practices that organize the interdependent relations at the core of social reproduction, this research helps reframe anthropological research on domestic violence and anti-violence interventions. Much of this body of research has examined how anti-violence interventions are limited by what Mindie Lazarus-Black calls "cultures of reconciliation:" "Cultures of reconciliation include precepts and practices about who is included in family, what rights and duties those roles entail, and how gender is organized. . . . The culture of reconciliation assumes that gender hierarchy is natural. It urges compromise, which often translates into women conforming to men's demands" (2007, 8). Contrasting reconciliation with the recognition of state-based rights and protections, Lazarus-Black, like many anthropologists of anti-violence interventions, frames this culture of reconciliation as an impediment to change. Cultures of reconciliation are "barriers" (2007, 8), sites of conservative resistance to change or patriarchal bargains, often taking the form of obligations and commitments to family (Grover 2011; Kandiyoti 1988; 1998; Parson 2010; Plesset 2006). Activists and scholars are both acutely aware that changing legislation alone cannot end violence against women in the absence of wider cultural transformation—and that such transformation, in turn, must take place in dialogue with the distinct ways that intimate violence manifests in specific social and historical contexts (Counts, Brown, and Campbell 1999; Donna Goldstein 2003; McClusky 2001; Van Vleet 2008).

In framing "family" as an impediment to change, however, such research misses an opportunity to more deeply examine how such transformation might take shape (hooks 2015). By approaching counselors' investment in family as regenerative, rather than merely reconciliatory, this book explores the complex ways that people imagine their relations with others to act on and transform the future, treating practices of relatedness as instances of moral imagination through which people envision a future worth living together (Clarke 2018; Livingston 2005; Robbins 2020; TallBear 2019). Such imagination is vitally necessary to remake relations that sustain, rather than harm, whether at the scale of the household, the institution, the state, or beyond.

And yet. As Ruha Benjamin writes, "bonds of relation may *bind* us even as they promise to—and do—buttress us" (2018, 50; emphasis in original). Concerns about how cultures of reconciliation, shaped by desires for familial solidarity, bind women to harmful kinship systems are well founded. In India, criminal laws addressing dowry violence and civil laws addressing domestic violence were undermined by precedent-setting high court rulings that undercut the elements of the law most important to ensuring their ability to recognize women's equal rights, often through reference to "common sense" about women's role in their families and ownership of common property (Lawyers Collective 2013). Even in the face of sustained efforts to train and sensitize, activists in Jaipur told me that police officers, magistrates, and lawmakers often suggest their role is to help women "adjust" to the very households where they are experiencing violence. How are we to reconcile the powerful conservative force of family values with the generative potential of relatedness?

Awkward Kinship: Care and Generative Agency

I address this tension by treating kinship as awkward, building on Marilyn Strathern's classic description of the awkward relationship between feminism and anthropology—another relation charged with both potential and conflict (1987). Here, I play on an old meaning of the term, where *awkward* serves as a sibling to the terms *forward* and *backward*—key words in the linear understandings of social progress on which women's rights rhetoric depends. *Awkward* suggests motion that does not follow this temporal line, that may fold back on itself, perhaps reproducing unequal gender norms, perhaps regenerating relations in new terms, perhaps turning up, uninvited. Anti-violence interventions reveal the awkward continuing presence of kinship in spaces—such as the state or the public sphere—where liberal narratives of progress say it should be absent. The unpredictable demands of the generative labor at the heart of relatedness sit awkwardly with progress narratives, reminding us that the forward momentum of women's rights rhetoric is a useful fiction but not a certain promise. Anthropological concepts of relatedness can help us stand in this awkward space, considering the difficult labors of reproduction and regeneration while recognizing the precarity of kin ties (Pinto 2014).

Such unpredictable, awkward motion echoes the uncertainty of care as a category of practice and of analysis. As a category of practice in Jaipur, acts of care—often glossed by counselors and clients as *seva*, service/respect—were the connective tissue that linked everyday practices of sustaining kin, households, and social worlds to morally valued futures, by implicating people in reciprocal ties of service and obligation. *Seva* was at the core of generative labor at home, while also shaping how counselors and activists understood their interventions. Yet changing circumstances meant that one never knew if one's *seva* would be reciprocated over time. *Seva* resonates with recent efforts to theorize care as an analytic in anthropology, which has approached care as a messy form of uncertain tinkering that exceeds logics of choice or control (Mol 2008). Rejecting arguments that "care" is antipolitical, scholars in this conversation have instead theorized care as a tool for thinking "beyond dualisms" like freedom/constraint or active/passive (Stevenson 2014, 177–79; see Ticktin 2011 on care as antipolitical). Seen from this perspective, the politics of care arise from "a patience for the possible, which draws on the hope that relations could change with time" (Han 2012, 31; see also Bornstein 2012; Aulino 2016). Such patience is highly active. As people collaborate to regenerate valued social worlds, their caring labor both sustains and recognizes others, even as that labor also reproduces social inequality and even harm (Buch 2018; Garcia 2010; Mulla 2014; Sufrin 2017). Seen from the perspective of rights-based approaches to violence, the uncertain outcomes of care make it a poor candidate for resolving violence. But in the hands of counselors, such uncertainty becomes a tool.

I argue that counselors draw upon the precarity and possibility of relatedness to facilitate generative agency for their clients. Anthropological scholarship on agency approaches agency as the "socially and culturally mediated capacity to act" (Ahearn 2001, 112). This approach has revealed that "modes of being, responsibility, and effectivity" (Mahmood 2005, 15) are always mediated by socially specific understandings of gender, age, embodiment, and other salient categories (Ahearn 2001; Berman 2019; Ferguson 2013; Hodžić 2016; Jarrín 2017; Keane 1997). Agency, in other words, always emerges via relations with others, rather than in resistance to those relations (Enfield 2017). This approach to understanding social structure and social action as mutually constituted helps us avoid treating our interlocuters as "dupes . . . or irrational actors" who embrace social positions that from the outside may appear to harm them (Jarrín 2017, 7; see also Madhok 2012).

Yet the relational features of agency are erased in the mainstream liberal political theory that informs development and rights-based projects around the world. Under this model, agency is understood as an individual possession, something individuals "have" that is most easily legible in doing and acting on the world, particularly in the form of resistance to socially imposed constraints (Wardlow 2006; K. Wilson 2013). As Saba Mahmood argued: "Agency, in this form of analysis, is understood as the capacity to realize one's own interests against the weight of custom, tradition, transcendent will, or other obstacles (whether individual or collective). Thus the humanist desire for autonomy and self-expression constitute the substrate, the slumbering ember that can spark to flame in the form of an act of resistance when conditions permit" (2001, 206). From this perspective, "agency"—often glossed as "empowerment" or "capacity"—is legible when people act *against* the strictures of kinship. When people act within kinship, on the other hand, they are read as lacking in agency; the relational demands of kinship smother the slumbering ember of Mahmood's account.

Mahmood's account of participants in Islamist piety movements focuses on what she calls "docile agency" that arises via submission to morally valued norms (2001). In treating the modalities of agency at play in counseling as "generative," rather than docile, I build on Mahmood's call to provincialize definitions of agency that read agency only in resistance to social structure by incorporating a closer focus on the structure and meaning of relatedness in shaping agency. Generative agency is a product of the vulnerability of norms to change as relations shifted over the course of social reproduction, as people fulfill and incur obligations to those on whom they depend.[16] This model of agency recognized that personhood was continually remade via relations with others, and that who one was and how one acted on the world came about through those relations (see Lamb 2000; Trawick 1990). Building on Mahmood, then, these findings suggest that we also must provincialize scholarly definitions of agency as primarily centered within individuals, rather than relations. Generative agency treats relatedness as a source of meaningful social action that arises as people engage in—often subordinating themselves to—relations in terms that indicate involvement in and a commitment to sustaining those relations into the future. In kin worlds, people's roles and authority shift over time, as young people grow older and authoritative; as new married kin are incorporated into family life, growing more central to the life of households; and as powerful kin grow older and weaker. Generative agency thus treats the reciprocal, cyclical nature of social reproduction linked to kinship as a source of action rather than constraint, emphasizing the constant regeneration of social reproduction that kinship norms seek to order. Such agency is "provisional," to build on Beatrice Jauregui's concept of "provisional agency" as "a moral virtue that reflects qualities of both temporary necessity and social-material capability," arising within "the contingencies of social interactions and the shiftiness of social positions" (2014, 82–84). As a strategy for living well with others, generative agency enabled clients to simultaneously transform and sustain interdependent relationships with kin.

Counselors cultivated generative agency through encouraging clients to attend to the dynamics of their spoken interactions with kin. When counselors urged clients to think of their families, to adjust, and to speak with care, they encouraged clients to act on their families by disciplining themselves, regenerating kin relations through an awareness of the delicate dynamics of speech, action, and power in the household. A compromise in the present might reflect the moral capacity to be a good family member, with the promise of better interdependent relations in the future. When Hema described the goal of counseling to visitors as "taking broken and scattered families and joining them together," she described generative agency: a mode of calling a valued future into being by joining, sustaining, and investing in interdependent relations, such that the complex interdependent ties of northern Indian kinship became a platform for agency. Acting, speaking, and caring as if one were already supported by those with a moral obligation to support one might in fact call those supportive ties into existence.[17]

Generative agency sits uncomfortably with the logics that underwrite women's rights projects. While transnational women's rights discourse sees domestic violence as a problem of kinship systems that ratify unequal gender relations, counselors see it as a problem of relatedness. Where women's rights discourse seeks to remove vulnerable women from relations of dependence on others, counselors shared, with their clients, a desire to resolve dilemmas of interdependence by deepening and strengthening those relations. In seeing kinship as awkward, rather than seeking to locate it on a line of "forward/backward," I mean to capture the discomfort such analysis provokes—in myself and, I suspect, in many readers of this book. Family counseling practices do not make for easy categorization. I respected and admired the counselors I knew, empathizing with their efforts to manage dilemmas in both families and in the institutions where they worked. I grew frustrated that their expertise was under-recognized in the wider professional environment where they operated, in large part due to the socioeconomic hierarchies of their workplaces. At the same time, I watched counselors tell young women to adjust to mothers-in-law who hurled abuse in their direction, or advise clients to avoid the legal system because it would be ineffective. In discussions with counselors, in watching sessions unfold, and in interviewing the activist organizers who ran counseling centers, I learned such advice was both helpful, in the sense that it accurately reflected the world clients occupied, and also harmful, in that it pushed women into relying on the strategies that socialized them into patriarchal family expectations: just adjust. Be flexible. You are strong enough to bear this. Counselors and clients also appeared to experience this advice as simultaneously helpful and harmful, as I show through this book.

It would be easy to dismiss counseling strategies as conservative patriarchal bargains foisted by middle-class women poorly "sensitized" to feminist politics, as results of poorly resourced institutions gripped by neoliberal logics, or as mindless bureaucratic efforts to "settle" as many cases as possible. Yet dwelling in the awkward nature of kinship allows us to stay with the trouble of interdependent ties (Haraway 2016). Normative models of the independent individual merely erase, rather than overcome, our inter-dependent relations with others (Buch 2018; Kittay 2013; Tronto 2014). Just as counselors taught their clients to see dilemmas of interdependence as sites of generative possibility, I treat the awkwardness of kinship as generative for thinking through key questions of agency by helping us rethink interdependence: How can people organize interdependence in terms that are mutually sustaining, rather than coercive or exploitative? When someone depends on someone else, is such dependence rightful or wrongful? Morally correct or exploitative? Age-appropriate or a sign of immaturity? To answer such questions, people draw on a "chain of signifying practices" that weave together kinship and gender, making kin relations central to the reproduction of intersecting hierarchies of gender, sexuality, race, class, and caste (Borneman 1997, 574; see also Ball 2018; Rubin 1975). To answer such questions requires moving from the question "Are you independent yet?" to the question of whether people are able to appropriately depend on others.

Careful Speech: Interactive Practices, Language Ideologies, and Anti-Violence Interventions

In approaching violence as a problem of interdependence, and offering gen-erative agency as a solution, counselors participate in a global interpretive project focused on gender violence. Movements that frame conflict and harm as gender violence raise challenging interpretive questions, because they reframe and reinterpret what such violence signifies about relations and per-sons (Moore 1994). The many institutional venues that have emerged to diag-nose and address gender violence offer novel spaces for interactions targeting violence. In spite of anxieties about counselors promoting reconciliation, the organizations where counselors work deliberately cultivate institutional spaces that are not constrained by the rigid interactive norms that govern court rooms and police stations. Sometimes referred to as alternate dispute resolution, such interactive institutions connect to a global set of efforts to generate social transformation by teaching people how to talk to each other differently, linking the interpersonal to the socio-structural (Ellison 2018).[18]

In analyzing these processes, scholars point to the substantial role of "talk" in contemporary NGOs working in the field of development and human rights. "Human rights talk" is a substantial enough element of human rights practices that scholars suggest analyzing it separately from "human rights law" (R. Wilson 2007; see also Madhok 2010). In the face of amorphous goals, NGOs produce "technologies of talk" premised on training and deploying speech as an easily measured technocratic outcome (Watkins, Swidler, and Hannan 2012).[19] Such discussions of talk often carry a whiff of concern that "talk" might amount to *mere* talk in lieu of action. In India, as across the world, such projects build on—some scholars suggest co-opt—social movements that experiment with interaction to remake society. These range from Freirean consciousness-raising to "people's courts" and "customary" dispute resolution practices (Ellison 2018; Madhok 2012; A. Sharma 2008). In Rajasthan, for example, organizers of counseling centers often came up through state-wide projects that built on rural processes for collective decision-making to cultivate grassroots solidarity within the women's movement (Unnithan and Heitmeyer 2012). Such spaces, by design, bring together diverse ways of understanding how speech reflects and generates personhood, relations, and social orders. Scholars of women's rights and human rights have carefully studied such variation in terms of how key concepts, such as "rights" and "violence," are translated as they circulate globally, asking what is gained and what is lost when such concepts are made local, or "vernacularized" (Englund 2006; Gal 2003; Gal, Kowalski, and Moore 2015; Daniel Goldstein 2013; Goodale 2006; Levitt and Merry 2009; Madhok 2015; Merry 2006; Morreira 2016; Riles 2006; Stephen 1995; Unnithan and Heitmeyer 2014).

But projects that address gender violence do not only deploy conceptual categories, such as "rights" or "violence." They also reshape ideas about how language acts on the world. In spite of this close attention to the role of talk and the friction that results when key universalizing categories are translated, few studies of anti–gender violence interventions examine how practitioners in these linguistically diverse spaces conceptualize the role of interaction itself in addressing violence. As linguistic anthropologists have long argued, interactive practices constitute, rather than merely label, the social world, linking structure and action via practices of meaning making and interpretation (Agha 2007; Silverstein and Urban 1996). When counselors interact with clients, bosses, and each other, they both reference and reshape the contexts of family and institution alike.[20] Generative agency relies upon strategies, in turn, for remaking families via spoken interaction. These strategies rely on what linguistic anthropologists refer to as language ideologies. Linguistic anthropologists show that all people hold multiple views about what language use reflects about types of person, interaction, context, and the social world, referring to such views as language ideologies (Irvine and Gal 2000).

Language ideologies are overt and covert "system[s] of ideas about social and linguistic relationships, together with their loading of moral and political interests" (Irvine 1989, 255).

The chapters that follow build on analysis of interactive practices to demonstrate that counselors draw on language ideologies that differ from those animating transnational women's rights activism around gender violence. They agree that household violence represents a serious moral and material problem. But they mobilize a different understanding of how spoken interaction acts on household violence and conflict. While organizers and activists in Jaipur, as around the world, centered the interactive act of labeling violence in order to condemn it, counselors sought to order interdependent relations through careful speech. Careful speech was a strategy that both demonstrated care for others and, in so doing, suggested that the speaker was involved in and working to sustain interdependent relations. Careful speech was a method for practicing and reflecting on generative agency, by encouraging people to see the capacity of interactive practices to regenerate relationships. Via careful speech, counselors emphasized the multiple interpretive frameworks that actions might invoke and the multiple futures they might produce. In this way, practices of relatedness offered an interpretive framework to domesticate change, to explain and overcome differences between family members, and to order households that had been disordered by dilemmas of interdependence. Careful speech was a strategy that enabled counselors to sustain the investments of both their clients and their institutions in "good Indian families," even as they tinkered with the relations that sustained those families in order to enable women to become autonomous, speaking kin.

Yet, as an interactive strategy, careful speech is at odds with the heavy emphasis on diagnosing, labeling, and condemning violence that animates global anti-violence activism. In bringing together diverse experiences of harm under a single label that categorizes such experiences as a violation of women's humanity, women's movements around the world sought to politicize what was seen as personal and to pathologize what had been seen as normal modes of intimate conflict. Indeed, the reclassification of once socially accepted forms of discipline and coercion as legally and morally unacceptable violence was, and continues to be, a major political victory for the women's rights movement around the world. On an everyday basis, use of the label "violence" has thus come to stand for whether a practitioner occupies a stance on women, autonomy, and social progress that aligns with the politics of transnational and local women's rights activism (Bumiller 2008).[21]

In tracing counselor strategies of careful speech, I build on an alternate approach to language and violence in anthropology. Scholars have argued that even as social movements seek to name gender violence, efforts to define violence produce unpredictable effects. Veena Das suggests that anthropologists take such instabilities as their ethnographic objects in exploring intimate violence (2008, 284). Interpretations of violence are fluid, shifting for different audiences, and subject to complex negotiations around meaning—not only around the meaning of violence itself, but around what that violence indicates about the relations, institutions, and structures of authority within which it takes place (Berman 2018; El Ouardani 2018). Sometimes, as Das and others show, people respond to violence by "folding" it into everyday life and relations (2007, 8; see also Donna Goldstein 2003). Such responses do not reflect a refusal to name violence, but a different way of linking violence to meaning-making. Not all everyday analyses of violence, in other words, begin with the impulse to name and label.

At the same time, efforts to address intimate violence by explicitly defining it and linking it to symptoms and treatments can create new forms of harm and do not necessarily guarantee justice for survivors. Official interpretive frameworks for addressing violence—what Das calls "collective scripts"—often erase other potential strategies for engaging violence (2008, 290). Sameena Mulla, for example, demonstrates how forensic nurses diagnose sexual assault in anticipation of a future court case, and in doing so foreclose more structural analyses of the cases they confront, restricting their gaze to the individual body before them (2014, 227). In the context of institutions that engage violence, actors draw upon language ideologies to both illuminate and obscure violence. Gregory Matoesian shows how American defense lawyers use an interactive practice that they call "nailing down an answer" to undermine plaintiffs in sexual assault cases. By drawing plaintiffs into repetitive question and answer interactions that play on shared cultural understandings of the relationship between verbal consistency and honesty, lawyers are able to cultivate doubt about their narratives (2005). In this case, defense lawyers play upon widely shared American language ideology about how consistent speech reflects truth-telling. Many studies of language ideologies in legal spaces demonstrate how unspoken ideologies about how language references the world can marginalize speakers who are not, for various reasons, able to narrate their stories in these terms (Briggs 1997; Blommaert 2001; Richland 2007; Trinch 2001).

From the perspective of careful speech, labels like "violence" could remove alternate future paths for women in their kin networks. Pulling women out of kin relations to enable independence could foreclose potential sources of support, care, and meaning. In other words, even as labeling violence offers tools to name and condemn the violence of kinship, such strategies risk removing the possibilities of generative agency. In enacting generative agency through careful speech, counselors did not abandon a rights-based definition of domestic violence. Instead, they offered a model of intervention that did not center labeling as the orienting task of anti-violence interactions.

Plan of the Book

Counseling centers were sites where counselors, their bosses, and their clients work together to simultaneously support clients by sustaining their families, while transforming family dynamics to lessen gender inequality and modernize the nation. This book explores how counselors engaged the dilemmas of interdependence that are provoked and deepened by discourses about women's rights and gender violence. As counselors debated how women should depend on others, why, and with what effects, they connected relating to kin with generating agency. In exploring counselors' strategies, this book challenges conventional academic wisdom about the role of so-called traditional kinship values in naturalizing gender violence. As the title of this book suggests, counselors and their clients turn kinship desires, practices, and relations *against* violence, relying on ideas about speech and interaction that are shaped by the complex, cross-cutting ties of multi-generational family life in northern India. To demonstrate the sophisticated interactive strategies counselors relied upon, *Counseling Women* follows several paradigmatic cases as they unfolded. This approach makes visible the beat-by-beat interactive practices that counselors relied upon to support clients, practices that are concealed when cases are narrated in terms of problem and outcome.

Counselors described their expertise as "neutral." Chapter 1 explores how counselors' understanding of the meaning and value of "neutrality" was shaped by a long history of policies that draw kinship and state together in the service of national development. Such policies strive to simultaneously address gendered inequality while sustaining the family as a source of social and national stability. As a result, counselors are called upon to help families with the goal of enhancing social order, while intervening in women's lives to interrupt the structural violence inherent to that social order. Counselors focused on the family not because they were invested in traditionalism, but as a result of how their expertise was shaped by institutional histories that yoked family and gender inequality together.

Chapter 2 returns to Prema and Gopal's case, in order to show how counselors elevated a seemingly simple, everyday interactive practice, "explaining" (*samjhaana*), from an everyday means to overcome misunderstandings to an institutional tool for familial and social transformation. *Samjhaana* served as an interactive tool to manage contradictory voices from families and counseling center staff. *Samjhaana* allowed multiple voices—whether of family members or of the diverse perspectives that counselors and organizers themselves brought to casework—to coexist without coercing one another, modeling a form of relational dialogue that allowed counselors to sustain family relations, even as they worked to transform them.

Chapter 3 examines what happens when the multiple voices cultivated in counseling are disciplined into a single voice, speaking in a legal setting. Counselors at Source of Strength supported India's domestic violence legislation as service providers, offering domestic incident reports to support plaintiffs' cases in court. Counseling expertise drew counselors into the service of the law, yet the anticipatory structure of a future court case restricted their ability to draw on the multi-vocal strategies of counseling. Chapter 3 examines the institutional life of the label "violence," and follows the case of Simran, a plaintiff seeking a domestic incident report to support her court case, to show that beneath a shared focus on "sensitive" interactions with plaintiffs and clients lurked two distinct models of how spoken interaction might address violence.

Chapter 4 explores how counselors understood the relationship between family, violence, and spoken interaction, situating strategies of careful speech in ideologies about how speech sustains relations. Counselors believed that good family relations were made, broken, and repaired through everyday spoken interactions that reflected northern Indian understandings of good families organized around *seva*, reciprocal practices of service, care, and support. Such interactive strategies reflected values around careful speech— speech that is cautious in recognizing its impact on others, as well as reflecting relations ordered by care and support. Subtly reframing or interrupting how clients deployed careful speech, counselors identified disordering dynamics while helping women navigate the complexities of patriarchal kinship as interdependent, yet autonomous, speakers. By cultivating strategies of careful speech, clients could bring about ordered, supportive homes in which they were speaking members.

Yet such strategies set counselors at odds with the dynamics of transnational women's rights activism, where institutional interventions were meant to label violence, not to cultivate careful speech. Strategies of careful speech often led counselors to avoid diagnostic labels, focusing instead on fixing—in both the sense of repairing as well as holding fast—kinship systems as tools to address violence. Exploring cases where counselors directly confronted physical violence, Chapter 5 argues that careful speech enabled counselors to both sustain and transform families in the service of women's rights by referencing, rather than replacing, kinship norms.

As an institutional practice that draws together counselors, clients, organizers, transnational rhetoric about rights, and Indian women's movements' debates about violence and solidarity, counseling produces family as a valorized good, a promise that isn't yet achieved but remains possible, perfectible as a source of support and meaning. At the same time, it produces the promise of women's rights as a similarly valorized good, a promise not yet achieved but evermore possible as a source of support. In juggling these two goals, counseling centers navigate the contradictions in ideas about families and individuals in contemporary India.

CHAPTER 1

Neutral Experts: Counseling between the Family and the State

In late summer of 2019, a story from the north Indian town of Meerut appeared on multiple news and content aggregator websites based in India. "Man Seeks Divorce from Wife, Thanks to a Diet of 'Tantrik Laddoos' & This Happens Only in India," one site headlined the piece. Laddoos are a round, palm-sized sweet, often offered to deities and then consumed by worshippers or distributed to celebrate an auspicious event. The *Odissa Post* wrote,

> A resident of Uttar Pradesh's Meerut district has sought divorce on grounds that his wife, under the influence of a "tantrik" (shaman), was giving him only "laddoos" to eat.
>
> The man approached a family court where he said that on the instructions of the "tantrik," his wife gave him four laddoos to eat in the morning and four in the evening. He was not given or allowed to eat anything else in between.
>
> The couple has been married for 10 years and has three children.
>
> The man said that he had been ailing for some time and his wife approached the "tantrik" who asked her to make her husband eat only the laddoos. Officials at the family counselling centre were puzzled over the pretext for seeking divorce.
>
> "We can call the couple for counselling, but we cannot treat the woman for being superstitious. She firmly believes that the laddoos will cure her husband and is unwilling to accept otherwise," said a counsellor. (Post News Network 2019)

The hook of the story, linking something as mundane as laddoos to something as serious as divorce, leads to an intriguing narrative structure reproduced in all of the descriptions of the story online. The main characters of the story quietly shift venue as they seek support. After seeking advice from a ritual expert (the "tantrik" or "shaman" mentioned in the story), they approach a "family court" to seek divorce. Yet the pronouncement we hear is not from a magistrate but from someone identified as a family counselor. At some point, the couple's dispute left the official legal realm and was transferred to a counseling center. And, rather than resolving the dispute, the counselor and "officials" only diagnose the impasse the couple has arrived at. "We can call the couple for counseling," they tell us, but they cannot change the wife's firm beliefs (or "superstitions"), or force her to "accept" that her efforts to care for her husband may be harming him.

The counseling expertise described in this article initially seems puzzling. Counselors can invite clients to participate, identify problems (superstition, an unwillingness to change) and potentially counsel "couples." Yet they claim they cannot "treat" a family member by changing their beliefs. Even in its brief description, this article suggests a mode of expertise that dances delicately between sustaining relations, working toward transformation, and respecting the autonomy of family members' distinct perspectives and desires.

When I observed Hema, the senior-most counselor at Source of Strength, explaining the counseling process to new clients, she gave this type of expertise a label: "We aren't a police station, we aren't a court, we're an NGO. We do counseling, we listen to both sides. We're a family counseling center; here we try to make compromises [*samjhaish*]. We're completely neutral," she'd say in a practiced tone, using the English loan word "neutral" in her Hindi sentences. I heard Hema give versions of this presentation over the phone and in person many times, always including the label "neutral." As I observed cases, spoke to counselors and activists, and read about counseling's role in addressing household conflict, I came to hear *neutral* as a statement about what made counseling distinctive as an institutional space, as an interactive practice, and as a response to a long history of addressing gendered inequality by acting both on and through the family in India. When Hema explained that counseling was neutral, she revealed the careful positioning of counseling centers with regard to state interventions, family values, and articulations of women's rights.

This chapter builds off of Hema's description of counseling in order to show how counseling practices are shaped by a long history of pressing the family into projects of national identity and development—and the contradictions regarding family, gender equality, and the autonomy of individual family members that ensued. Such projects long figured the family in contradictory terms: as a tool to tame rapid social transformation, as a source of social support and solidarity profoundly threatened by transformation, and as an impediment to social transformation, particularly for women. As a result, the concept of the traditional Indian family offers a site for debating continuity and change, seeing in household life a reflection of order across scales, from the mental health of individuals to the cohesiveness of the nation. From India's central government to various women's rights projects to films and on television, such representations laminate family order onto national order (Mankekar 1999; Uberoi 1998). In this context, many people draw connections between broader societal disintegration and the behavior of kin towards one another (Cohen 1998). The actions of the argumentative daughter-in-law or insensitive mother-in-law can be read as destructive on a scale much larger than the household.

The complex histories behind these representations of the family create dilemmas for counselors, organizers, and clients alike. Is the project of family counseling a project of reforming and supporting families for the sake of family cohesion? Or is the project a tool to support women as individuals by cultivating their voices and teaching them to condemn violence? Experts involved in running and evaluating counseling centers, from Jaipur to major centers of social work in Delhi and Mumbai, debate this question. On one hand, counseling is meant to help women articulate themselves against their families, ideally leading to changed norms about gender and family roles over time. However, because women's well-being is strongly connected to the stability of their households and kin networks, counseling is also meant to help specific families. These contradictory representations of family reflect a dynamic familiar to scholars of social work: tensions between what Michael Lipsky calls "client-centered" and "social engineering" goals (Lipsky 2010, 41). Counselors sought to triage individual women's situations of harm and crisis; this client-centered goal sometimes meant propping up a household by encouraging a client to better play her role as a subordinate junior family member, hewing to expectations about good wives and daughters-in-law. Yet the institutions where counselors worked held larger goals of reforming families and society as a whole to be more gender equal—"social engineering" goals directed at larger transformation over time. Like social workers elsewhere, counselors manage these tensions even as their work generates fierce debates among the activists and organizers who manage them about what constitutes their expertise, and in what terms their strategies are effective (Abbott 1995; Brodwin 2013; Carr 2015).

Such dilemmas appear even in the case of the "laddoo divorce." The wife's care, an uncanny echo of so-called traditional wifely worship, is also neglect. Like a deity at a temple, her husband is given only sweets to consume. To ask the wife to cease feeding him laddoos is, from her perspective, to ask her to give up her role as a good wife, seeking to support her husband. Counselors are in a double bind—sustaining the relationship requires pushing family members to "accept otherwise," a change that the counseling staff quoted in the article are unwilling to force on husband or wife. Hema's description of "neutral" interactions followed a similar logic: accommodating differing perspectives and desires without, ideally, forcing any specific family member to have to change their deeply held values. This approach built on longstanding representations of the ideal Indian family as a space where differences between kin were ordered through cooperative, shared efforts, rather than coercive force—a representation, as this chapter will go on to show, that connects to representations of India as a nation-state unified in diversity. In practice, this neutrality produces impasses of the variety on display in the laddoo divorce case: cases that reveal contradictions within models of the ideal family itself.

Yet in their role as social workers, counselors are never working on the family in the abstract. Instead, they engage specific families, carefully tracing connections between concepts often treated as distinct, or even contradictory: care and violence, individual and community, submission and agency, coercion and consent, independence and interdependence. By exploring how counselors understand themselves as experts in family and in counseling, this chapter traces the institutional and historical contexts within which counseling took place, first tracing Jaipur's larger cartography of institutional support, and then situating family counseling in a larger historical context of national development and women's movements over the course of the twentieth century.

Counselors produced neutrality, a kind of "tactical wisdom," as they balanced the contradictory demands of the institutions where they worked with regards to the value and meaning of "family" (see Brodwin 2013). A stance of neutrality reflects an ethics of intervention that seeks to sustain "rival horizons of possibility" (Pandian and Ali 2010, 7) for kin, for families, and for institutional actors alike—horizons where women are protected *from* families and also where they are sustained *by* families. Rather than resolving those rival horizons, counselors worked—sometimes against the stated goals of their own institutions—to sustain space for "moral striving" toward diverse ends within and beyond household life (V. Das 2010). In claiming that they and their institutions were "neutral," counselors connected their work to the interactive projects of cultivating women's voices and helping them claim rights and support that arose from the transnational women's rights movement while still engaging intersecting histories of development, rights claims, and institutional practices that clustered around the trope of the traditional Indian family.

Jaipur's Cartography of Care

When Hema reassured clients by saying, "we're not the police, we're not a court," she projected a cartography of sites that supported vulnerable women in Jaipur. One facet of neutrality arose from how counseling centers distinguished themselves from both state and familial interventions. Counselors frequently described the differences between sites for clients in terms of whose voice would be heard and whose perspective would be honored, which institutions could remake families and which might further deepen conflict. Counselors and clients both described these differences through a language of "spoiled" homes (*bigre hue ghar*). According to promotional materials at Source of Strength, counseling took broken, scattered families (*tutte-bikhre parivar*) and joined them back together (*jorna*).

When things went wrong in Jaipuri households, women sought help from venues ranging from their extended kin networks to caste organizations to the courts and police. Most clients at Center for Advice and Protection and Source of Strength had either already sought help from one of these sites, or needed help navigating between them. Counselors and clients both frequently worried that the wrong kind of institutional intervention might make household conflict permanent, breaking the family rather than remaking it. Women who sought help outside of their home for family issues proceeded carefully. Clients frequently told counselors that a family member had instructed them not to seek outside help because it would spoil their homes.

Women who were experiencing conflict, particularly disputes over property (such as jewelry) and household maintenance, or conflict involving physical violence, often pursued support from the police or from the court system. Many organizers in Jaipur told me that women also often sought help at police stations because police stations are among the most visible sites at which to seek support. Yet police are trained to focus on crime. As a result, women often found themselves either dismissively returned to their families if their troubles didn't seem to warrant registering a criminal case, or drawn into a divisive case that quickly spiraled out of their control. Police constables were believed to exert pressure on women, either because they over-prioritized the family, or because the constraints of their own professional obligations impelled them to do so. Another option for distressed women and families was to lodge a court case under one of India's women-focused family laws. These range from criminal laws addressing household "cruelty" and dowry abuse (particularly section 498a of the Indian penal code), to family law surrounding maintenance, inheritance, conjugal rights, and property division, to the relatively recent Protection of Women from Domestic Violence Act (PWDVA), a civil law guaranteeing women rights to family support in the face of violence. Efforts to promote police sensitivity in order to support such cases also led to the development of *mahila thanas*, women's police stations, where mostly female constables worked solely to register women's complaints about family issues.[1]

Laws like the PWDVA, *mahila thanas*, special fast track family courts, and counseling centers all emerged in response to concerns that the adversarial framing of criminal and court cases were imperfect tools for addressing household conflict (Basu 2015; Mathur 2004). For example, the pressures on police stations to register and then resolve cases meant that a visit to the police station might push a woman into a criminal case against in-laws, or lead to pressure to drop the complaint all together. A court case might financially ruin a family through lawyer fees and time lost at work, as it worked through India's notoriously slow courts. Any attempt to seek help outside the home might lead to anger from family members and scathing judgment from neighbors and acquaintances.

Yet women who approached the counseling centers for help had typically also reached the limits of emotional and material support available to them through their extended families. In addition to trying to solve problems on their own, within their households, women also often sought help from their natal families, from extended family members, and even from sympathetic members of their marital households (for example, wives struggling with a mother-in-law were sometimes accompanied to counseling by their husbands, and vice versa). Such support sometimes included seeking help and mediation through a caste organization, called *jati samaj, caste panchayat*, or caste society, supporting local members of the particular caste that a family belonged to.[2] The role played by such caste organizations in adjudicating familial disputes reflects the centrality of marriage and family-making activities to sustaining caste identities and distinctions, as marriage and gendered comportment are often central to caste identity, and caste background is often central to arranging marriages (Chowdhry 2009; Fuller and Narasimhan 2008; Gilbertson 2018; Mishra 2013). As a result, both family members and caste organizations brought their own stakes to conflicts, and often wielded material and emotional influence that dwarfed that of the woman seeking help.

If kin networks and caste-based organizations were biased with regards to outcome, the police and judiciary had the opposite problem: while (ostensibly) unbiased, they were also insensitive to women's complex interdependent relationships with kin. In distinguishing Source of Strength from courts and police stations, in listening to "both sides," Hema underscored these distinctions. In the midst of these different venues, the claim "we are neutral" also marks counselors as beyond the reach of material influence. While in theory state spaces were unbiased, in practice they were vulnerable to bribes and corruption.

In spite of these differences, clients and their families frequently expressed initial confusion about whether counseling centers were courts or police stations. Superficially, all of these sites look remarkably similar: slightly run-down, with identical pieces of furniture, down to the same brands of plastic chairs and metal cabinets; heaps of ledgers and carbon copy paper; the same file folders heaped in corners, case numbers scrawled on the covers. Many counseling centers in Jaipur are on the grounds of police stations. Furthermore, other institutional sites were shaped by the same impulses to reform families and support women.

Counseling, however, differed in terms of the interactive practices relied upon by counselors and ma'ams, the activist-organizers who ran the organizations that hosted counseling centers. Jaipur's family court, for example, was meant to be responsive to women's needs because cases do not officially require a lawyer, and cases move through relatively quickly. However, the experience of being at a counseling center is profoundly different from being at family court. When I visited Jaipur district's family court with a legal aid NGO, we found the hallway was crammed with families waiting for a part of their case to be heard, listening for their names to be shouted roughly by one of the magistrate's clerks. The doors to the "court" itself stand open; families who were about to have their cases heard stood in the corners while cases currently on the docket stand before the magistrates and clerks, who sat on a raised dais behind a partition. There were no other chairs or benches in the space. It was noisy and difficult for individuals to make themselves

heard; other cases occasionally elbowed in to ask a question of the magistrates, who scolded in response. Magistrates appeared stern, busy, and impatient. In comparison, the counseling centers were relatively calm spaces, even
when crammed with clients and family members. While counseling was a
structured process, it allowed for long narratives, exploration of context, and
experiments with strategies to elicit dialogue from quiet clients, to shame mis-
behaving kin, or to repeatedly reframe narratives in light of new information.

These institutional differences and similarities facilitated counselors'
performances of neutrality by allowing counselors and ma'ams to calibrate
their presentation of counseling centers based on a client's needs and concerns: to tentative female clients, they might downplay their connection to the
state, while for recalcitrant male kin, they might emphasize it, stressing their
government funding and the ma'ams' social connections. Even as Source of
Strength and Center for Advice and Protection distinguished themselves from
these state institutions, they also highlighted their state funding.[3] By plaster-
ing the phrase "Funded by the Central Social Welfare Board" across its offices
and literature, Source of Strength worked to broadcast its financial independence from any political groups, on one hand, and any religious organizations, on the other—to offer "transparency," in the words of the ma'ams.[4] The
ma'ams also used the slightly shabby built environment of Source of Strength
to demonstrate that the organization was "poor but honest," as I was told more
than once.[5] Center for Advice and Protection marked its neutrality somewhat
differently. Being on the grounds of the police station itself, it was difficult to
emphasize its complete independence from the criminal justice system. However, the significant differences between the process of counseling and the
process of lodging a case report were powerfully clear to clients. The station
was manned by uniformed officers; police duty jeeps sat outside its door. The
atmosphere in Center for Advice and Protection itself felt, in contrast, significantly more informal and comfortable. In coming to Center for Advice and
Protection, clients and families literally bypassed the police, walking past the
station on their way to the small outbuilding that held the counseling center.

Neutrality as Interactive Expertise

Positioned between official state venues and complex kin networks, counseling offered distinct interactive possibilities. Counselors could hear women
as intimates, but were not biased by the politics of household intimacies.

They recognized how dependence shaped the narratives, needs, and limits of family members, yet had nothing at stake in enforcing or unraveling those dependencies. Counselors Hema, Indu, Gita and others all occasionally cajoled reticent clients by saying, "We're all friends here!" or, "Treat us like we're your aunties [or *mausi*, in Hindi—maternal aunt]." Clients marked this ambiguity in their terms of address, shifting between respectful familial forms of address, like *didi* (elder sister) and *bhabhi* (sister-in-law), and terms of more official respect, like ma'am. These interactive strategies were central to counselor expertise.

Yet counseling practices were not always seen as expert by ma'ams, program evaluators, or other observers. Anthropologists emphasize that expertise is "something people do rather than something people have or hold," something that people must "enact" before an audience, drawing on shared understandings of what makes experts expert in particular contexts (Carr 2010a, 18). As people enact expertise, they distinguish between different types of venues, translate ideas between different social arenas, assign value to resources in the world around them, and offer frameworks through which others should understand the objects of their expertise. Counselors, for example, teach clients about differences between counseling centers and other legal and familial sites of conflict resolution; they take ideas about rights, family, and gender from sensitization sessions they attend to interactions with recalcitrant parents-in-law; and they offer ideas about how different styles of interaction might repair damaged relations and sustain household life. When counselors enact their expertise in family life, they reference shared representations of talk, family, and good kin; in citing such representations, they reproduce and transform them.[6] Yet expertise can also be contested, and counselors' neutral expertise was often interpreted by women's rights activists in the region as an attempt to promote the importance of family *over* women's needs as individuals, as an inexpert refusal to fully implement the goals of the larger women's movement by prioritizing reconciliation over recognizing women as equal rights bearing subjects.

In distinguishing themselves from formal legal settings, counselors suggested that they were capable of properly attending to how women's status within the family shaped their ability to ask for help within and beyond the household. In addressing individuals' suffering, struggles, or vulnerabilities by acting on the family, counselors drew on widespread understandings of individual well-being as a product of supportive social relations. Across India, communities often interpret individual struggles, mental health crises, or ill-health as manifestations of familial neglect or conflict, as "signifier[s] of relations elsewhere, between others" (Cohen 1998, 178; see also Chua 2012; V. Das and Addlakha 2001; Marrow 2013; Pinto 2011). As experts in local institutions, counselors could translate clients' needs and claims across different modalities and institutional sites. Counselors reframed long narrative complaints into pithy sentences on a form; reframed angry outbursts as concrete requests for resources; and offered clients language they could use with lawyers, police, mothers-in-law, and ma'ams.

Throughout these negotiations, counselors framed their interventions as rooted in compromises that respected the diverse needs and desires of kin. These dynamics emerged particularly clearly when helping clients navigate the dissolution of a relationship—splitting a joint household into nuclear households, or ending a marriage. Even in these contexts, counselors focused on structuring interactions around compromise rather than coercion or conflict. For example, a long-running case between Pooja and Kishan Das, a middle-class, fairly conservative couple in their late fifties, reflected counseling urges to compromise, even when negotiating conflict, as well as demonstrating the often painfully iterative nature of counseling casework. Counselors were helping the couple organize a mutual divorce. Pooja and Kishan Das had married later in life, after both their previous spouses had passed away. In spite of the goal of the marriage being a less lonely old age, both were deeply unhappy and frequently fought. The case dragged on because of friction between two counseling impulses. First, counselors wanted to help Pooja articulate her wants and desires as a female family member—a difficult project, as Pooja alternated between a keen desire to leave Kishan Das and panic about supporting herself after a lifetime of being materially dependent on family members. As a result, Pooja frequently revised her requests for support, always upward. This led to additional conflict with Kishan Das, who explained that he saw these changing requests as efforts to bleed him and his family dry. Counselors wanted to support Pooja's developing articulations of needs and desires. But they also wanted to avoid resolving the case through conflict or force. They wanted the divorce to be truly mutual.

After one long talk with the counselors about the minutiae of how much money one needed to survive in Jaipur, Pooja muttered, angrily, that she'd fight for what she needed to get by. Hema interrupted her, and said, "Decisions shouldn't be made through fighting. They should be made with conversation" (*faisle larai se karna nahi hona chahiye. batchit se karna chahiye*). Another day, Hema walked Kishan Das through a list of Pooja's recent requests: a fan, a TV, an air cooler, a gas cylinder for cooking. As she did so, Indu reminded him, "There should be no fighting [about this decision]; there should be no tension." Kishan Das groaned that the decision was being "forced" on him (*zabardasti se*). Indu urgently corrected him: "It is not! It should not be!"

The case illustrated both the promise and limits of counseling neutrality: Keeping the divorce case out of the courts gave Pooja a greater degree of control over the process, giving her the time and space to feel her way through what she would need to live independently. But that very process created ever greater friction with Kishan Das. Preserving both interactive neutrality (no fighting) and institutional neutrality (not the courts, not the family) was painstaking, time-consuming, and lacked a clear temporal trajectory. Pooja and Kishan Das's case began almost a year before I arrived, with no resolution in sight when I left, the longest case on active file at Source of Strength. Hema and Indu themselves had grown weary of the couple and became visibly impatient when Pooja or Kishan Das called. As Pooja's case makes clear, neutrality was not about disengaging from household conflict. Instead, it described a mode of engaging conflict through balanced interactions.

In spite of the often frustrating paths such neutrality led down, counselors maintained a fierce commitment to this model of incremental, careful change that resulted when family members debated and voiced their diverse opinions openly, compromising with one another. Such incremental change, they suggested, was potentially more effective than the pressure that might come from police, or from magistrates enacting the law. It was more effective than counselors or kin directly pressuring men on behalf of women, or than family members wielding what they called "emotional blackmail" to achieve their ends. By positioning themselves as neutral, counselors marked their interventions as cooperative rather than coerced, domesticating social transformation. Counseling outcomes ideally came through balanced interaction, not through corruption, nor legal demands, nor physical or juridical coercion, nor excessive pressure.

Counseling in Historical Context: The Joint Family and National Development

As counselors distinguished between "fighting" and "conversation," between "force" and compromise, between venues where people "listen" and venues where they do not, they centered their expertise in both their own interactive skills as well as their ability to evaluate interactive practices in families and in other institutional sites. Counselors sketched a cartography of institutional care for their clients within the context of a long history of projects that sought to promote democratic development through persuasive talk targeted at social reproduction and family life. In particular, the concept of "family" they engaged with has been shaped by contemporary debates about what the goals of social development should be, goals that in turn shape how people engage with ideas about women, rights, and the nation itself. Although the "traditional" family is often represented as a timeless foil to modernity and progress, both in India and abroad, such links between Indian identity and a distinctive family form are products of historical shifts across the twentieth century (I. Chatterjee 2004; Majumdar 2007; Newbigin 2010; Sturman 2012; Uberoi 2005). Counselors drew on this complex history as they navigated questions of whether to focus on individual clients or families as a whole, and as they sought to create change in individual homes without reproducing coercive family dynamics. If the joint family was fundamentally hierarchical, how might it be used to help women access their rights as equal citizens? Would changing ideals around family support leave women vulnerable to neglect? Because of the role of family in debates about development, modernity, and the nation, these dilemmas were not only about women's status at home, but always were shaped by long-standing debates about what kind of society and nation India was and would be. Beginning with anti-colonial debates about social reform, policy makers, activists, and scholars all debated how to encourage people to transform the intimate practices of household life—often reflecting deeply held moral beliefs—without resorting to direct coercion. The stakes of such reforms were high, as both the treatment of women and the structure and internal dynamics of family life were treated as signs of civilizational progress as well as cultural continuity (P. Chatterjee 1993; I. Chatterjee 2004; Uberoi 2005).

The challenge of reforming behavior while emphasizing individual autonomy and freedom generated sophisticated interactive interventions, training, educating, and motivating people into consenting to participate in development (N. Chatterjee and Riley 2001; Hull 2011). Such challenges were reflected in one of the texts that various training courses assigned in Jaipur. In *Counselling and Guidance*, author S. Narayana Rao locates counseling firmly in the present moment, as a response to rapid social transformation, while also pointing to a number of continuities between counseling and earlier forms of advice-giving. Rao suggests that the present moment is defined by increasing civilizational "complexity" marked by growing individual autonomy in the face of decreasing "cultural conventions" (2002, 1). This combination of increasing complexity and greater freedom to navigate it leads, he suggests, to a demand for a professional field of advice-givers.[7] Rao locates the need for counseling within the context of societal development where people are faced with a bewildering array of choices, departing from models that connect counseling either to individual development ("young people need help with decisions because they are still learning how to make them") or to individual pathology ("some people need extra help because they are facing extraordinary challenges and/or lack the tools to cope with challenges"). Counseling can help people "adjust," Rao argues, to wider social changes; in the face of social upheaval everyone is like the new daughter-in-law who must adjust to novel conditions out of her control.[8]

In naming contrasts between social connections and individual choice, between some uncorrupted past and a list of modernizing transformations, Rao echoes a number of distinctions at the heart of the classic social science study of South Asia. India is, according to these arguments, collectivist rather than individualist; hierarchical rather than egalitarian; traditional rather than modern. In this context, modernization comes as a disruptive force that demands some kind of clinical intervention. Anthropologists, historians, sociologists, and other social scientists have long argued against this simplistic version of Indian tradition versus modernity. Yet Rao's text demonstrates that such arguments have saturated expertise surrounding, in particular, family life and the place of the family within development, and shape people's interpretations of both familial conflict and institutional interventions.

As one such interactive practice, counseling is shaped by these histories, particularly as they link the concept of a unique Indian family with questions of social welfare. India became officially independent on August 15, 1947. Immediately, the government faced a series of crises of social welfare, crises that required both debate about the form and meaning of the nation, as well as immediate practical interventions. The Partition of what had been British India into India and what was then East and West Pakistan occasioned flows of migration on a massive scale. Millions of Hindus left what was now Pakistan for India, and millions of Muslims moved in the opposite direction. As people crossed the new borders between the two nations, violence exploded at the borders and in cities and towns across the subcontinent. The disruption of Partition followed on the heels of serious famine in the eastern part of the country, generated by British demands for raw materials and grain during the war. These crises lent urgency to the demands of postcolonial development (Sen 2018). India negotiated these crises in the context of a policy of non-alignment within the growing tensions of the Cold War, carefully balancing a commitment to a planned, centralized economy, resonant with the Soviet model, with a commitment to full adult franchise in a parliamentary democracy (Nikhil Menon 2021; Sherman 2018). Such planning efforts also took place in the context of global panics about a population explosion, directing development energies to practices of intimate life and sexuality. These concerns provoked dilemmas that appear throughout planning documents at the time: How can you encourage people to change their intimate practices in the service of development while continuing to maintain your status as a democratic, rather than authoritarian, state (Connelly 2006; Sreenivas 2021; Rook-Koepsel 2021)? The figure of the family loomed large in these efforts, as both a figure of authoritarian threat and a potential model for ordered, cooperative difference.

Representations of the joint family have long offered frames for imagining how to organize difference and dissent into an ordered, coherent whole with minimal coercion. Family has served as a means to make sense of perceived tensions between tradition and modernity across a range of sites, from domestic life to institutional practices to public policy (Basu 2015; I. Chatterjee 2004; Cohen 1998; Majumdar 2009; Newbigin 2013; Pinto 2014; Raychaudhuri 2000; Sreenivas 2008; Sreenivasan 2004; Sturman 2012; Uberoi 1993; Vatuk 1975). In mid-twentieth-century social science representations of "traditional Hindu India," the multi-generational, patrilocal joint family, along with the village and the caste system, was a central token of what made India culturally distinct, though experts debated and continue to debate what such distinctions mean for both India as a nation and for Indian families. Multi-generational, patriarchal, with property held in common across male kin, the joint family was depicted as both foundational to Indian society, and a sign of India's difference from the West.[9] This perspective persisted through the mid-twentieth century, as modernization theorists predicted the joint family's decline, debating whether the joint family was an impediment to Indian development (for example Madan 1962; Shah 1968; Goode 1963).[10]

Simultaneously, the family became the site for debates over what to prioritize in the difficult years after Independence. During debates about how to reform Hindu inheritance laws to include women as equal coparceners in their fathers' estates, for example, policy makers shifted from focusing on women's rights to addressing concerns about economic development. Law-makers worried that by extending the field of possible inheritors of land and property, already miniscule landholdings would become so divided as to no longer be productive for agricultural and economic development (Majumdar 2007; Newbigin 2010). At the same time, the joint family was also taken up by the state as a "welfare delivery system" (Uberoi 2005, 382). Crises of vulnerability are thus often interpreted in India as crises of the family, as opposed to crises of the state. For example, in 2007, the Indian government passed the Maintenance and Welfare of Parents and Senior Citizens Act, an act akin to child abuse laws in the United States, that allows the state to prosecute adult children who fail to support their aging parents (Lamb 2009).

For contemporary India, a massive, diverse democracy, questions of how to order difference are central to how the nation and its relation to the state are imagined. After Independence, Indian sociologists and anthropologists hunted for some form of social structure that unified the new nation in the face of differences of socio-economic class, caste, religion, region, and ethnicity. The problem of cultural difference was highly visible in the decades after Independence, with language riots leading to the redrawing of state lines along linguistic-cultural boundaries. Kinship systems also varied dramatically along both north–south and east–west axes (Karve 1965). Beneath these cultural and linguistic differences, Indian social scientists argued, Indian families of all languages, castes, and religions were unified by the joint family structure (Karve 1965; Kapadia 1955; see Uberoi 2005 for further analysis of this intellectual project). The joint family provided both concrete evidence of a shared national culture, as well as a set of metaphors for imagining non-coercive, ordered socio-cultural difference.

For example, in his 1944 *Discovery of India*, India's future first prime minister, Jawaharlal Nehru, asked the question the joint family answers: "How to combine these utterly different groups in one social system, each group co-operating with the whole and yet retaining its own freedom to live its own life and develop itself?" (2004, 269).[11] Although the traditional Indian family, along with two other "pillars" of Indian society, caste and village, were profoundly hierarchical, Nehru echoed other mid-century thinkers in arguing that they also harbored the seeds of democracy, promoting both group solidarity as well as resources for individual rights claims (2004, 271). The joint family offered a model of a social system in which differences are recognized and yet overcome, supporting everyone equally—a picture that resonated with the model of centralized socialist economic development buttressed by decentralized autonomous communities that Nehru shared with many proponents of social and economic development in India (Sherman 2018):

> The joint property [of the family] was supposed to provide for the needs of all the members of the family, workers or non-workers. Inevitably this meant a guaranteed minimum for all of them, rather than high rewards for some. It was a kind of insurance for all, including even the subnormal and the physically or mentally deficient. Thus while there was security for all, there was a certain leveling down of the standard of service demanded as well as of the recompense given. Emphasis was not laid on personal advantages or ambition but on that of the group, that is the family. The fact of growing up and living in a large family minimized the egocentric attitude of the child and tended to develop an aptitude for socialization. All this is the very opposite of what happens in the highly individualistic civilization of the West and more especially of America, where personal ambition is encouraged and personal advantage is the almost universal aim, where all the plums go to the bright and pushing, and the weak, timid, or second rate go to the wall. The joint family system is rapidly breaking up in India. (Nehru 2004, 274–75)

In this passage, Nehru articulates both the promise and perils of the joint family. The joint family is group-focused, not individual-focused; it allows for a particular kind of subject formation. It offers security—and yet that very security contains the threat of a "leveling down." Most importantly, this description of the family cannot operate without a contrastive comparison with the West: the joint family is not only distinctly Indian, but is the "very opposite" of the West. And yet this token of distinct Indian social organization is "rapidly breaking up."

Politicians, policy makers, and scholars continue to rely on the joint family as a metaphor for discussing the challenges of promoting social transformation while protecting cultural continuity and diversity. The joint family frequently provides the framework for imagining how to assimilate difference in a manner that is conflict-free, ordered, and non-coercive. Again and again, the joint family appears in nationalist treatises as a model for creating cooperative order out of overwhelming differences. The joint family has remained a resource for talking about managing a nation of differences as it faces an uncertain future up through the present. While I was in the field, bookstores were promoting a book published in 2008 by former Indian president and nuclear scientist A. P. J. Abdul Kalam and revered Jain religious figure Acharya Mahapragya called *The Family and the Nation* (tellingly rendered in Hindi as *Happy Family, Prosperous Nation*). Kalam and Mahapragya, like Nehru, treat the joint family as both model and means for a uniquely Indian form of social and economic development. The authors draw a parallel between the challenges of everyday family life and the challenges of nation-building. The authors describe the family as "the blossoming of oneness in diversity. If there are ten members in a family, they will have their ten different modes of thinking and varying styles of working. . . . A family is all about living amicably in such a diverse environment and coexisting peacefully" (Mahapragya and Kalam 2008, 134–35). In fact, "variety brings connectivity to the family" (135). Kalam and Mahapragya suggest that the joint family is a model for bringing multiple "cultures" together without making any particular group "submit" to the values of another, generating a shared identity without coercing any particular subgroup into following the majority's mores or beliefs, all the while reproducing "ethnic identification" within the space of the household itself (195). The challenge, the authors argue, is allowing each family member/citizen the space to be distinct and unique, while still supporting and being supported by others: to live without too much autonomy or too much restriction. In order to respect these limits, they suggest that family members must devote "close association, attention, and care" to preserve the love that brought them together in the first place (160). For Kalam and Mahapragya, the family is a metaphor for nation-building. Yet nation-building is also a metaphor for making a family. The stakes are high: the book is introduced as an effort to generate a "system of peace" to balance India's new nuclear military capacity (ix). Baldly put: the joint family is what will keep India safe from nuclear war.

In Jaipur, when people talk about ideal family life, they are often discussing social transformation and continuity, from the scale of kin relations to the scale of society as a whole. As counselors, activists, clients, and other residents of Jaipur imagined the role of kin relations in linking past, present, and future, they drew ideological distinctions not only between tradition and modernity, but between ordered and disordered relations of difference. Because the joint family is taken up as a model for how to organize difference into ordered wholes, concerns about household disorder are never contained by the domestic. In a context where joint family values are also values of national order, a daughter-in-law's ability to "adjust" to the norms of her marital family comes to seem like a confirmation that differences can be ordered and overcome.

Women's Rights Activism and Counseling Controversies

In counseling women in the context of their families, family counselors in Jaipur had to position themselves between protecting the Indian joint family as a means to order society, and suggesting that practices and beliefs associated with the joint family may be harmful for women. Even as the joint family was presented as a model for ordered, distinctly Indian democratic development over the second half of the twentieth century, women's rights activists and feminists have continually pointed out that that model was profoundly patriarchal. The so-called ill-treatment of Indian women at the hands of their families was central to the colonizing mission. In turn, efforts to reform women's position in society were central to early anti-colonial nationalism (P. Chatterjee 1993; Mani 1998; Sarkar 2000; Sinha 2006). From nineteenth-century reformers who attacked child marriage, sati, and widow remarriage to more recent activism organized around inter-caste marriage, sex-selective abortion, and dowry abuse, women's rights activism in India has long focused on culturally particular kinship practices as sites for political mobilization. In this portrayal, India's distinctive family system harms women from conception, where they are at risk from female feticide; to girlhood, where they are at risk from child marriage and differential access to nutrition; to young adulthood, where they are at risk from dowry pressures and domestic abuse; to motherhood, where they face retaliation for producing daughters instead of sons; to widowhood, when they are systemically excluded from social life.

After Independence, however, "women's issues" were submerged in concerns about economic development and poverty alleviation, despite gender equality being a central tenet in India's new constitution (Khullar 2005; R. Kumar 1997; Majumdar 2007; Newbigin 2013). When issues specific to women, and frequently children, were addressed, it was typically in terms of welfare. For example, the Central Social Welfare Board, which was a federal funding body that supported Source of Strength's operating expenses through grants, was founded in 1953 to organize and fund voluntary organizations of women involved in social work, but did not itself explicitly address questions of women's rights or needs (Sherman 2021).[12]

In the 1970s, the women's movement reemerged as a major social movement in India. In 1974, *Towards Equality*, a report documenting the failures of the state to fulfill the constitutional promise of gender equality, measured the continued inequalities that marked women's relationships to development in India (K. Sharma and Sujaya 2012).[13] By 1980, the government had included "women in development" as a distinct topic in its sixth Five-Year Plan, addressing women's issues explicitly for the first time since Independence. The plan also added cells to existing government programs to specifically interact with women. Such changes were driven by the emergence of the autonomous women's movement, composed of women's groups unaffiliated with other formal organizations such as state ministries or political parties (Burte 2016; Kapur 2012; R. Kumar 1997; Madhok 2010). As the 1980s and 1990s progressed, representations of the role of the family changed: while the family continued to be represented as both a locus and vector for development, women's rights activists and scholars increasingly discussed women's relations with family in terms of conflict, ranging from antagonistic bargaining to overt violence (see for example classic pieces by Agarwal 1994; Kandiyoti 1988; Karlekar 1998).

At this same moment, women's movements began to draw national and international attention to events of catastrophic violence against women rooted in kinship practices. In Jaipur, for example, the senior-most activists active in 2010 had founded organizations during this time, building on mobilizations to address dramatic cases of dowry violence as well as the 1987 sati of rural Rajasthani widow Roop Kanwar, events that brought national attention to patriarchal Rajasthani kinship practices (R. Kumar 1997).[14] The women's movement began to look toward kinship beliefs and family practices to think about how these forms of violent disorder were generated and naturalized by patriarchal values, revealing the many ways that the very values that organized family life harmed or exploited individual women.

These concerns mean that counseling's role in women's rights activism generates controversies about whether counselors should generate change or enforce family norms. Scholars of marriage mediation in India question counseling's focus on settlement, adjustment, and compromise. Such goals, scholars worry, pressure women to conform to the norms of patriarchal kinship.[15] Experts and activists tend to frame these questions in binary terms: either counselors help women recognize and seek recognition for their rights as individuals, *or* counselors encourage women to reconcile with their families, prioritizing the family over the client. In the words of scholar-activist

Manishe Gupte, organizers worry that counseling centers risk becoming "pro-family but anti-woman" (2016, 73), with interventions coming "at the cost of" larger social transformation:

> With feminist critiques pointing towards the family as the primary site through which patriarchy operates, the very concept of counselling in the event of domestic violence comes up repeatedly for questioning among feminists. Do we *merely defuse conflict or reduce the extent* of our interventions merely to placate the situation in individual homes, *at the cost of ignoring* the structural violence that generates violence against women? Besides, counselling in domestic violence is not limited to any one kind of interpretation or method. . . . Cohabitation with the husband, labelled as "reconciliation," is considered to be the hallmark of the successful "case" in many counselling centres. (2016, 73; emphasis added)

Gupte encapsulates a tension expressed by other counseling experts I spoke with, as well as activists and ma'ams in Jaipur: that counselors and other frontline workers might encourage women to reconcile with families (presumably while accepting gender violence as normal and acceptable) *instead of* recognizing women as rights-bearing subjects. In this binary framework of recognition versus reconciliation, counselors' strategies of neutrality are often interpreted as reconciliation, as Gupte describes the term in the passage above. In conversations with scholars of counseling and activists in Jaipur, I found this recognition/reconciliation binary drove efforts to train counselors, distinguish different organizations from one another, and authorize the expertise of activists and organizers, who frequently use similar language of "merely" to describe strategies targeting families rather than women. Activists in charge of more recently founded counseling programs in Jaipur distinguished their programs from Source of Strength precisely by insisting that their centers focused more on the female client than the family (although in my observations, I found counselors at such centers also focused deeply on family relations in practice). Social work scholars who evaluate the national programs to fund counseling centers consistently worry that counselors overprioritize family.

Counselors in Jaipur, however, were quick to point out the deep connections between family cohesion and the well-being of women in the home.

Counselors and ma'ams told me that the label of "family" helped them draw family members to the center in the first place, protecting their reputation as a neutral and unbiased site for resolving family disputes . As Hema often told clients, the goal of counseling was to mend broken families. Her explanation echoed longstanding language used by the federal-level Central Social Welfare Board, which funded Source of Strength. Going back to the 1970s, leaders at the CSWB framed women's well-being as continuous with that of their families, advocating for addressing violence, cruelty, and dowry pressure directed at women by preventing "broken homes and splintered families" (Varadappan 1975, 106). The clients who sought out counseling centers like Source of Strength frequently did so precisely because they faced problems that did not easily fit into the agonistic roles necessary for civil or criminal court cases. Indeed, the need to slot family members into such roles in legal cases could itself break families. Counseling was an alternative to these venues precisely because it did not insist that kin take on such roles, keeping control of the narrative in the hands of family members themselves.

These tensions between reconciliation and recognition mapped onto the sociology of counseling sites, and in particular, on distinctions between counseling staff and the ma'ams who hired and supervised them. Counselors at the centers I observed in Jaipur were all female; the oldest, Hema, was in her mid-fifties, but the rest were in their mid- to late twenties. Between 2010 and 2017, when I last was in the field, a number of these younger counselors left the workforce after they married and had children. By 2017, several had returned. Others were single parents who relied upon counseling to support their families. Some counselors had been recruited by organizers who served as their college professors; others, like Indu, had seen an advertisement for a counseling position in the newspaper and applied. All counselors had at least bachelor's degrees, if not master's degrees, in psychology, political science, or sociology from one of the local colleges. They were also informal experts in family law, differing beliefs about marriage in the region, and in the byzantine institutional structures that had grown up around the state to support women over the past thirty years. They had attended various short training courses and workshops on counseling. Importantly, they also knew how to get the documentation right, a key part of their labor that allowed centers to maintain access to various government funding sources. Counseling was not, however, particularly well-paid, and salaries were often interrupted by delays in grant dispersals.

While counselors were salaried staff, they worked for activist-organizers who managed counseling centers as volunteers, many of whom had been working on issues of gender inequality in the region for decades. Although the ma'ams worked as volunteers, it was clear that they were in charge. Staff stood when they entered; they were often accompanied by drivers carrying their water and bags of paperwork; they were served tea on their visits. When counselors addressed them, or discussed them in the third person, they appended "ma'am" to first names. Ma'ams instructed counselors as to how to spend their time. While counselors worked from around 9 to 5 each day, ma'ams came and went according to their own schedules. While the ma'ams wore carefully starched cotton handloom saris and understated gold jewelry, counselors tended to wear brightly colored synthetic saris and heavy lac bangles. While counselors rode public transit, carpooled with family members, or rode scooters to work, ma'ams arrived in their own cars—sometimes with drivers. In the richly multilingual world of northern India, the ma'ams generally possessed more fluent English skills than counselors, who had typically been educated in Hindi, rather than English, language schools.

These seemingly minor sociological distinctions had major effects in how counselor expertise was imagined and disciplined at counseling centers in Jaipur. Although they were relatively well-educated, the counselors I knew did not have access to the social, cultural, and political capital wielded by their bosses. It was not clear that "counselor" offered a career pathway to "ma'am." The ma'ams had jobs—or had retired from jobs—as professionals in other fields, and several moved between their professions and positions in state ministries. In doing so, they maintained the connections necessary to keep counseling centers open and connected to state-based resources and projects. The ma'ams took care of the difficult administrative work required to run NGOs in India, such as finding below-market-rent office space, cycling funds across loans with banks, and applying for and maintaining the grants that paid counselor salaries. In encouraging reluctant kin to engage in counseling, counselors relied on the prestige of the ma'ams' reputations. While organizers in Jaipur hotly debated what kind of degrees and training were required of staff counselors, similar questions were rarely, if ever, asked of the ma'ams, who frequently sat in on counseling sessions and offered advice to clients meant to progress or conclude active counseling cases. While counselors spent the vast majority of time with clients, it was sessions with the ma'ams that marked a case as officially heard and settled. During the work week, counselors worked to implement the goals and visions of their employers, but were not able to directly control those goals or set the larger policies that informed them.

If counselors located their expertise in neutrality, ma'ams, along with experts and activists across northern India, located their expertise in distinguishing between recognition and reconciliation. In an interview with a scholar active in training and evaluation of counseling centers at the federal level, the scholar expressed frustration, off the record, that the federal government program that funded Source of Strength insisted on calling the scheme a "family counseling scheme," rather than choosing a label that emphasized women. In discussing different women's rights organizations in the city, an activist-scholar working in development in Jaipur described the organization that ran Source of Strength by saying, "Well, they're a little . . ." and pressing her hands together in front of her chest in a stiff gesture of *anjali* while pursing her lips a bit, suggesting a stern, somewhat pious Hindu middle-class moral stance, one potentially at odds with the goal of creating radical change.[16] The leader of an organization that coordinated with several federal and state programs to run counseling centers across the state emphasized the difference between counseling centers that truly focused on women, and those that insisted on family reconciliation. Such concerns frequently erupted in city-wide meetings that I observed, where organizers hotly contested what qualifications were necessary for counselors, as well as in interviews I conducted with ma'ams. Organizers and activists often pointed to counselors' client-facing strategies, which focused on family dynamics, to question counselors' expertise in gender equality.

The counselor Indu, observing all these dynamics as a staff member of Source of Strength, once observed to me that although they worked hard not to show it, the cohort of activist-organizers who founded Source of Strength and these other organizations—the ma'ams—were "like an orange: they had started together but fallen into sections." As I came to learn more about the wider world of women's rights activism in Jaipur, my sense was that such sectioning was driven by conflicting answers to the question of whether to focus on individual women and their families, or so-called larger socio-legal structures, and deepened by the binary framework of recognition/reconciliation, which framed these two options as conflictual. Such dilemmas are the product of the history of women, family, and social reform in Indian modernity. While contemporary women's rights activism frames reconciling families as the opposite of recognizing women's rights and condemning gender violence, the institutional and familial realities that counselors faced were shaped by histories that wove women's well-being and family systems together. As the next chapters will show, within counseling sessions, recognition—of individual differences, needs, and rights—might facilitate reconciliation with kin, and reconciliation with family members might lead to recognition of mutual obligations and entitlements. Whether deliberate or not, counselors' strategies around neutrality worked through the reconciliation/recognition binary presented by women's rights activism, as counselors navigated institutional histories alongside household politics.

Conclusion

Counselors' interactive strategies are contingent solutions to dilemmas arising from longstanding debates about the role of the Indian family in supporting and harming women. In light of these histories, neutrality facilitates both client-centered goals of diminishing harm and creating support together with social engineering goals of transforming families and society as a whole. Counselors in Jaipur did engage in processes of reconciliation—but the reconciliation at stake is reconciliation between contradictory institutional mandates as well as between women and their families. To borrow a turn of phrase from Michael Lipsky's *Street-Level Bureaucracy*: as individuals, counselors represent the hopes of women's rights activists for gender equality, even as they are positioned to see clearly the limitations of institutional interaction and the constraints on social transformation engendered by dilemmas of interdependence (2010, 12).

In suggesting that neutrality represents an enactment of expertise, rather than a refusal to take a position, this chapter has argued that neutrality was a tool for engaging and acting on dilemmas of interdependence that arose in institutional contexts seeking to support women.[17] Such dilemmas may arise from trying to resolve a conflict, like the laddoo divorce, without changing either party's beliefs (even when those beliefs cause harm). They may arise from trying to hold a space open for a client to explore and articulate her needs for support, even as that process further generated conflict with her kin, as with Pooja and Kishan Das. When counselors like Hema say that they are neutral, they enact themselves as experts in confronting such dilemmas, dilemmas rooted in the histories of family and development discussed in this chapter:

between women and family; between economic development and gender equality; between triaging household crises and working for greater social transformation; between psychological and structural approaches to gendered violence; between supporting women's choices and convincing them to pursue different desires. When counselors say, in the face of these dilemmas, that they are neutral, they acknowledge: such dilemmas may not have resolutions, and clients and families may need to find a way to dwell within them.

In counselors' hands, neutrality is an active interactive project. The next chapter turns to the question of how counselors organized their interactions with clients and their families, via an everyday interactive activity: *samjhaana* (to explain). *Samjhaana* builds on the histories described in this chapter: a history of seeing the family as a model and means for unity and diversity, on one hand, and a history of seeking to reduce women's vulnerability and promote gender equality by reforming the family, on the other. Chapter 2 explores what these strategies look like at the scale of counseling interactions themselves.

CHAPTER 2

Adjusting and Explaining:
The Multiple Voices of Counseling

As Hema's invocations of *not a court, not a police station* made clear, counselors were quick to distinguish counseling centers from venues where women might face the full brunt of state power. Rather than relying on coercive, punitive power, counselors drew on interactive strategies that transformed conflicts into communicative impasses that could be navigated through understanding and adjustment. Hema, for example, explained this to the father of a client, Prema. Prema's father had asked her what consequences Source of Strength could bring to bear on Prema's husband, Gopal. He seemed to be under the impression that the institution had legal authority, but Hema was quick to correct him. "We aren't a police station. But we have power" (*hamare pas power hai*). She went on to clarify the distinction between Source of Strength's "power" and the police station: "We try to create compromise with love and affection. Both ought to agree" (*pyar mohabbat se samjhaish karte hain. dono manzur hona chahiye*).

The work of creating compromise through love and affection was achieved via interactive techniques that simultaneously mobilized and transformed familiar activities of explaining—*samjhaana*—and adjustment. By engaging clients and their kin in such interactive techniques, family counselors used ideas about interdependence, hierarchy, and care to create change without coercion at the level of individual families. Yet precisely because these practices required dialogue between speakers and listeners with different perspectives and desires, they invited multiple, often conflicting, voices into counseling center offices. As a result, counseling provided a space within which multiple models of family, gendered difference, and social change came into contact. These models came from many sources: other kin who were not physically present during sessions;

legal sources; expert discourses about family, gender, and social change; and popular narratives about decaying families and modernity. As these different models came into contact, counselors as well as clients found opportunities to reflect carefully on the dilemmas that confronted their families and the nuances of power and affection within which those dilemmas unfolded.

Even though, as Hema put it, the goal was to use love and affection to create compromise, counseling relied upon the "power" of social hierarchies to engage other family members. To get Prema's husband Gopal to turn up for this session, Hema had worked with Prema's father to call Gopal's senior family members and his boss at work, relying on these networks of authority to ensure his participation. Such gently coercive "power" was made possible by the hierarchies that structured everyday life in Jaipur, within and beyond households. These included the socio-economic hierarchies that differentiated staff counselors from organizers, as well as those that distinguished staff counselors, in turn, from many of their working-class clients. They included hierarchies of age, gender, and relatedness in households.

These intersecting hierarchical relations structured the voices at play in counseling sessions. Counseling sessions hummed with these many voices. They were sometimes literally noisy, with multiple kin, counselors, and organizers squeezed together in an office, while other clients waited outside. Beyond the speakers present, multiple voices jostled together in other ways as well. Posters produced by a local NGO used legalistic Hindi to remind viewers that dowry demand is a crime. Counselors moved between official-sounding diagnostic language, intimate gossip, and informal bossy scolding. Across notes, ledgers, and forms, they switched between what they called "spoken Hindi" and official paperwork terminology. In their narratives, clients directly quoted other characters, speaking as other kin, people at other institutional sites, and as other versions of themselves. These multiple voices were a defining feature of counseling sessions. They expanded the walls of Source of Strength's small offices, invoking and bringing together contexts ranging from overcrowded kitchens to the Supreme Court.

Counselors worked to bring these many voices into an equal dialogue. They described these efforts as *samjhaana,* to explain (literally, to cause someone to understand). Through making clients and kin understand, counselors remade the hierarchies of household and public life into communicative challenges that could be addressed via better mutual understanding. *Samjhaana* allowed multiple voices—whether of family members or of the diverse perspectives that counselors and organizers themselves brought to casework—to coexist without coercing one another, modeling a form of relational dialogue that allowed counselors to sustain family relations, even as they worked to transform them. Via *samjhaana,* counselors sustained dialogue across differences in desires, perspectives, and personalities. *Samjhaana* allowed counselors to address family issues non-confrontationally through dialogue, leaving open the possibility for kin to reframe their interpretations of household conflict and reimagine their desires. As a result, they focused on how clients' voices emerged from a larger conversation, literally and metaphorically, within the family.

Samjhaana simultaneously addressed and deepened the paradoxes surrounding coercion and compromise that shaped family counseling. Kin were supposed to work with each other to arrive at a shared understanding of what the future should hold—yet arriving at an understanding required outside guidance and even pressure. Even as counselors worked toward non-coercive change, they relied on potentially coercive forces that arose from the same hierarchies that left women like Prema vulnerable. Precisely because of its non-confrontational, dialogical approach to changing the family, counselors' strategies of *samjhaana* also allowed other voices into the counseling process—voices that referenced models of gendered difference, ideas about social change, and ideas about ideal family life that did not always align with the larger institutional goals of counseling centers. The tensions between compromise and coercion within counseling mirror the tensions between compromise and coercion present in households, where family members were expected to compromise with love and affection, but always within relations shaped by intersecting hierarchies.

Counselor strategies around *samjhaana* resonate with anthropological theories of "voice" as a product of social interaction. Anthropologists who study language and social life approach "voice" as a dialogical object, emerging as people use styles of speech and interactive roles to reference, reproduce, and contest shared understandings of types of persons and the relationships that draw those persons together. In typical conversation—even within a single utterance—speakers draw together multiple voices as they create a relationship between their audience, the context within which they speak, and themselves (Bakhtin 2010; Agha 2005; 2007). The interactive activities that speakers and listeners link to an understanding of "voice" are always mediated by these contexts, including ideas about what distinguishes "speech" from "silence" (Gal 1991; see also Hill 1995; Keane 1999; Kunreuther 2006; Weidman 2014).

Counselors use *samjhaana* to focus on how clients' voices emerge within and act upon a larger conversation, literally and metaphorically, within the family, relying on what Webb Keane has called the "clash" of multiple voices to clarify the moral and material dilemmas that harm female kin (2011, 168). Such efforts do not draw counseling participants toward a single understanding of their household conflict. Instead, they leave the path open for multiple interpretations of household histories and futures to exist in dialogue, in order to offer women options for navigating their futures with their families. Rather than pressuring people to change or adjudicating disputes, counselors taught families how to better explain and understand the diverse behaviors and perspectives of kin. *Samjhaana* reframed inequalities generated by household and social hierarchies as communicative differences to be resolved by careful interactions, where kin might speak on relatively equal interactive terms even though their household roles may be dramatically unequal. In this way, *samjhaana* offered a pathway to generative agency, by opening an interactive space to act on family relations while still acknowledging the hierarchies of family life.

Concepts of voice also play a key role in cosmopolitan debates about addressing household violence, as activists and practitioners often seek to recover and center the voices of victims of gender violence. A focus on recovering the voices of victims shapes both scholarship and interventions. Here, voice is represented "as presence, authenticity, agency, rationality, will, and self or interiority," something inside the individual to be recovered and empowered (Weidman 2014, 39; Kunreuther 2006; Mahmood 2001). In this approach to voice, voices pre-exist dialogue, rather than being facilitated by dialogue. From such a perspective, the many voices invoked in Jaipuri counseling may seem to further drown the "voice" of vulnerable clients in a scrum of arguing kin, rather than recovering it, muddying efforts to condemn and address household violence. Counselors were exposed to this model of voice-as-internal-truth via training sessions facilitated by the activist-organizers who ran their institutions, as well as via discussions of women's rights that circulated in Jaipur more widely. Yet *samjhaana* suggests an approach to recovering voice that sees voices as emergent in dialogue with others, always implicated in shaping relations with others and shaped by those relations.

This strategy of *samjhaana* helped counselors manage institutional demands to both remake northern Indian family norms to better recognize women's rights and voices by cultivating women's consciousness of their status as agentive, desiring, rights-bearing subjects, while sustaining family relations as sources of support for clients. It helped them navigate intersections between discourses of personal and societal development, and the realities of financial constraint faced by growing families. In a social context where people often suggest that kin—particularly female kin—risk disrupting family solidarity when they voice individual needs or desires, these goals sit in direct tension. Such tensions were deepened by the fact that as counselors worked with clients to elicit their desires, those desires frequently took the form of deepening of their relations with kin on better terms, as clients framed household harm and neglect as a failure to fulfill expectations about supportive household behavior. Such contradictions reflect dilemmas of interdependence faced by households and by women's rights organizations, as counselors, clients, and activist-organizers debate what interdependence reflects about selves, relations, and society.

Chapter 2 follows Prema and Gopal's case closely, following it as it unfolded over several sessions. Like many cases, Prema and Gopal engaged briefly and intensely with the counseling center, and then disappeared. Perhaps they sought support from other venues. Perhaps the case eventually found its way into some kind of legal setting—a divorce, a domestic violence case, a court case for restitution of conjugal rights. Perhaps the various conflicts returned from a boil to a simmer. Perhaps Prema would return, in a few months, in a year, to seek support again. Prema and Gopal's case illustrates the themes that shaped counseling practices: tensions between love and power, the difficulties of adjusting to kin in the context of a changing world, and the challenges of interpreting household conflict. Beginning by exploring the interactive tools of *samjhaana*, "making understand," and *adjustment*, the chapter then turns to how these interactive modes unfolded in Prema and Gopal's case. By examining how counselors use techniques of *samjhaana*, this chapter introduces the interactive strategies counselors rely on as they endeavor to transform Jaipuri families, even while they sustain them. By tracing this one case in detail, this chapter demonstrates the subtle movements between recognizing the rights of kin, and reconciling family members that unfolded, beat by beat, as counselors sought to make their clients understand one another, and taught them to use understanding to resolve conflicts.

Samjhaana: Explaining, Understanding, and Compromise

Like many counseling clients, Prema and Gopal were in their first five years of marriage; Prema was pregnant with their first child. She had approached counselors because of conflicts with Gopal over resources and money. The couple lived in a small flat in a rapidly expanding squatter colony, in a multigenerational family together with Gopal's paternal grandparents, as well as one of his brothers. Gopal was the only member of his extended kin network with a steady job, which meant that he provided financial support to a range of kin, including an uncle. Gopal's frequent interactions with that uncle's wife made Prema suspicious about an affair. Gopal drank regularly, an expensive habit that increased the financial pressures in the household. The couple had heated arguments, which sometimes ended with Gopal slapping Prema. Prema had moved to a hostel affiliated with a training program she was completing for nursing assistants. She wanted help figuring out next steps. These details emerged over multiple meetings with Prema, Gopal, and other kin, during which the dilemmas of how to sustain competing ties of interdependence came to the forefront. Hema and Indu would seek to resolve these dilemmas through making Prema and Gopal understand each other.

Prema had asked for help from counselors in improving Gopal's behavior moving forward. Now, Hema was speaking with Gopal about his side of the conflict.

Hema warned Gopal, "Your wife needs to be cared for."

Gopal quickly countered, "I don't want to break the family."

Prema had already expressed to counselors and to Gopal that she hoped to move away from the house where they lived with Gopal's extended family. But for Gopal, this action would cause a break with his household, made up of his grandparents and adult brother. From Gopal's perspective, "caring" for his wife came at the cost of supporting his blood relations: the two demands conflicted. This was a dilemma of interdependence he could not resolve without harming either his wife or his other kin: these ties of "duty," as Gopal referred to them, left him in a position where he had to choose between the desires of his wife and the needs of his kin. Hema would work to help Gopal reframe this problem, seeing his support of Prema and his other kin as complementary rather than contradictory.

Gopal, like so many clients who came to Source of Strength, would conclude this first meeting with Hema by asking her to provide a solution to his family crisis. Yet counselors insisted that providing solutions was not their job. Their job was to help families work together to find a way forward, not to dictate what to do. For example, when Hema told me her plan for counseling Gopal, she suggested that her goal was to help him think more reflectively about the situation. "Think of your home," she said, demonstrating how she would speak to him. "Think of your wife, *think*." When I asked her later what these imperatives accomplish, she thrust her arms forward wildly, as if she were tossing a tray in my direction. "We'll show him a mirror" (*usko aina dikhate hain*). She would reflect Gopal back to himself, so that he would transform his actions. She would make him understand.

The Hindi verb *samjhaana* is most frequently translated as "to explain." But, unlike the English "explain," the verb *samjhaana* has a direct relationship to the verb "understand" (*samajhna*), serving as its causative form ("to cause to understand"). While the English word "explain" has a sense of a speaker making something inside themselves clear, the Hindi *samjhaana* draws our attention to how a speaker creates a change within her listeners. Such interactive labor is inherently relational, premised on forms of speaking and listening that bring speaker and audience into a shared perspective on the world, even if they do not agree. *Samjhaana* was a solution to misunderstandings, maladjustment, interference, communication gaps—the issues that clients and their kin pointed to when discussing household problems. As a solution, *samjhaana* reframed these issues as primarily communicative in nature. To make clients understand, counselors did not need to adjudicate who was right or who was wrong, nor to even arrive at a shared agreement on the source of household problems. Instead, via *samjhaana,* they invited a transformation in perspective, an ability to see household life from multiple points of view. *Samjhaana* was a tool that family members could use to show that their efforts to advocate for themselves across differences of age, education, and gender sustained rather than disrupted interdependent ties. Etymologically related terms were central to counseling processes. Being understanding, *samajhdar,* was a mark of a good family member, and counselors often prompted clients to consider their own quality of understanding, *samajhdari.* Counseling sessions ideally culminated in *samjhaish,* settlement or compromise statements.

In the case of counseling Gopal, *samjhaana* meant inviting Gopal to see himself anew in his relations with others. Importantly, this did not involve directly telling Gopal what to do. For Hema and Indu, counseling primarily consisted of encouraging clients to re-evaluate their relations, then working with clients to suggest paths forward. Such interventions were often subtle. For example, Hema understood one central problem in Prema's home to be Gopal's "alcoholism"—a blanket term that counselors used to refer to men who drank regularly. At other moments, Hema told me that drinking was one of the principal problems in counseling cases; men who drank became careless and violent, spent time away from the family, and the expense of alcohol created strain in economically struggling families. Hema responded to Gopal's fears about breaking his family by inviting him to reflect on how it was his drinking—not Prema's demands—that was causing strain. Hema told Gopal that they didn't want his family to break either. "We're a *family* counseling center," she reminded him. But, she added, "you can't lose sight of your wife."

"I haven't," Gopal insisted.

"Yes! You have!" Hema shot back. "You're not wrong—you're a good boy. It's the alcohol that's the problem. We suggest solutions [*karyavahi*] here, because we're trying to help families." The problem was the interpersonal and financial effects of drinking on Gopal's capacity to support his kin. Hema spelled this out: "It spoils your understanding [*samajhdari*]. It's worth it to quit, right?"

"It's worth it," Gopal agreed, mirroring Hema's words.

"So then," she said. "Change yourself." She gave him some advice about how to taper off; later she'd give him the phone number for a clinic.

This exchange was framed by Hema's claim, "we're a family counseling center," and offers an example of "showing a mirror." Even as Hema assures Gopal that she shares his commitment to his family, she works to shift the frame of that commitment: rather than fighting with Prema, he first needs to "change himself." Drawing on patterns of backchanneling ("worth it . . . right?") and framing their exchange as a "solution" to help his family, Hema guided Gopal into an interactive position where he affirmed and aligned with her perspective on his household problems, while still affirming his value as a family member ("a good boy").

Dilemmas of Adjustment in a Changing World

In guiding Gopal into agreement that he needed to change, without overtly confronting or pressuring him, Hema's "explaining" also offered an example of encouraging what clients and counselors alike referred to as "adjustment." "Adjustment" is a central feature of discussions about family life, in counseling centers and beyond. The English word appears frequently in Hindi language conversations both as a noun, as well as the verb "to adjust" (*adjust karna*).[1] It is also a term used frequently in non-domestic venues. People ask others in cramped quarters on a train to "adjust," to make a little room. People seek to adjust to difficult material conditions, such as heat, or physically demanding labor. They adjust to exigencies of ill-health, as when my landlord told me, after I injured my arm in a scooter accident, that I would have to adjust to life with a weaker arm. Others discuss the need to adjust to aging bodies. People debate how to adjust to social transformation, to changing relations between generations, new economic conditions, and new ideas. And people adjust to those who are, at least at first, "other," particularly new kin via marriage. As people adjust to others, such others become kin. Such adjustment takes time and practice.[2]

Samjhaana and *adjustment* both reflect ambiguities at the heart of repairing fractured family relations. Both are a way to act on relations while also submitting to be disciplined by those relations; both suggest a vision of family life as an ongoing dialogue that unfolds into an uncertain future where change is both inevitable and unpredictable. Through *samjhaana* as an interactive activity, family members could both express the things to which other kin needed to adjust, and also perform their own willingness to adjust. Yet these efforts to adjust always unfolded against what Sarah Pinto calls the "conditions of precariousness [that] are part of what it means, for women especially, to be bound to others" (2014, 261). Desires for adjustment and criticisms when adjustment failed: both reflect a vision of family life that simultaneously acknowledges differences between kin and strives to overcome those differences. These ambivalent engagements with adjustment reflect tensions between trying to build a family around similarities while acknowledging that differences are necessarily present in kin relations. At the same time, debates about adjustment reflect efforts to contain difference to what can be managed within those kin relations, rather than differences that might strain or even destroy relations.

Such issues formed the core of counseling cases, where counselors and clients used adjustment to refer to everything from the ability to adapt to a smaller living space in a different part of town to the ability to handle intense interpersonal conflict with in-laws to the willingness to cooperate with household demands often placed on junior female kin. Yet, in counseling sessions, adjustment issues were always sites of debate about who ought to adjust to whom or what, and about what elements of shared life could be adjusted to. In other words, adjustment issues offered a venue for counselors and their clients to debate what, precisely, was changeable: about individual family members, about kin relations, and about wider social contexts. Does someone's behavior represent a failure to adjust? Or is that person in a situation where adjustment is impossible? Of whom was it was morally or practically appro-priate to request adjustment, and why? Who could be expected to change, on what grounds, and with what pressures? Such debates brought minute details of bodily and emotional behavior together with ideas about national identity, historical transformation, and moral worth. Adjustment was never merely a tool for disciplining kin. It was always, at the same time, a tool for contest-ing and reshaping kin relations, envisioning "rival horizons of possibility" for household futures (Pandian and Ali 2010, 7).

Indu had married into a joint family not long before I met her at the start of fieldwork, and often discussed the meaning and challenges of adjustment. During down time, she frequently sought advice from Hema about her own married life and relationships with not only her husband but her mother-in-law, brother-in-law (*jeth*), and his wife (her *jethani*). During a slow afternoon, I asked Indu to explain adjustment to me, as I'd been hearing counselors and clients use the term frequently. She used a newly married woman as an example. If a new bride—a *bahu,* or daughter-in-law—didn't meet her new family's expectations, then there would be conflict. "It's not just the *bahu*," she went on, "the whole household should make adjustments." But it's hardest on a new bride—she has to adjust to a whole family, while they need only adjust to her. "It's not just in families," she quickly added. "In the neighborhood, in the country—people have to adjust."

She went on to use herself as an example. The household Indu married into practiced *ghunghat*, where female family members kept their heads and occasionally their faces covered with the end of their sari, or *pallu*, in front of senior kin, as well as in public. Indu grew up wearing salwar-kameez, as well as jeans and T-shirts, and her mother had not practiced *ghunghat* at home. The novelty of wearing a sari full time excited her—she and the other staff spent hours talking about sari styles, fabrics, and drape. It also exhausted her. Saris are complex garments; they take time to drape correctly, and must be care-fully pinned to avoid becoming disheveled, particularly when doing things like preparing meals or driving a motor scooter to work. As she explained adjustment to me, she used her experience with *ghungat* as an example. She tried to cooperate with the expectations in her *sasural*, her married home, she told me. But as she learned how to manage chores and interactions while keeping her head covered, she often became impatient: "To hell with this!" she said, switching to English, to describe her attitude in those moments. It was at those moments that her mother-in-law would complain: Indu quoted her mother-in-law, with a sharp-tongued, "She is not adjusting." Indu's use of the third person here suggests an unnamed audience—perhaps her husband or sister-in-law, perhaps neighbors visiting her mother-in-law—silently observing whether Indu was adjusting or not.

As Indu explained adjustment to me, she illustrated its complex ethical power. She moved between telling me how it worked in practice—junior female kin disciplining their bodies and selves—and how it should work, ideally, with kin adjusting equally to one another. At this point, Hema joined our conversation, agreeing that adjustment should be "mutual" among family members. Indu should try her best. But her mother-in-law should be understanding, *samajhdar*, of Indu's efforts and background.

As in Indu's account, adjustment could simultaneously be a sign of productive responses to individual and social change and a sign of powerlessness within relations with others. This is because kinship was an arena in which people sometimes experience a sense of meaning and efficacy in creating continuity in the face of change—or generating change in the face of continuity—and also an arena in which people experienced profound vulnerability. As in Indu's example, adjustment is interactive, a product of how people speak with one another. It is only at the moment when Indu expresses her frustration—"To hell with this!"—that her mother-in-law complains she isn't adjusting. Yet it is also embodied, as with the constant, habituated effort to keep one's sari tidy, and to keep one's *pallu* appropriately over one's head. In this sense, adjustment reflects widespread understandings in India of how habit and attunement to others continually generates both body and self (Kantor 2019; Sargent 2020; Walters 2016). As such, adjustment reflects a wider ethics of self and other, one that acknowledges difference in the service of cultivating morally valued relations (see Pandian 2009).

Such cultivation often required that less powerful people cooperate with and submit to more powerful people. At the same time, adjustment offered a language for contesting such hierarchies. Adjustment is, as Hema said, ideally mutual. Yet the capacity to adjust is unequally distributed, often in paradoxical terms. Many in Jaipur, as across India, argue that young people are more "adjustable" than old people. For example, clients at counseling centers frequently pointed to rising ages at marriage as responsible for increasing family disfunction, as older brides are less able to "adjust" to their in-laws and marital homes. Some suggest that women are inherently more adjustable than men—either by nature or by socialization. One's ability to adjust was also a reflection of your family and how you had been raised. Hema and Indu told me that women raised in "affectionate" (*snehpurn*) families were often able to adjust, but women who had been "pampered" (they used the English term) may not adjust as well—they adjusted their counseling approach differently, as needed. People in Jaipur also suggested that more educated people could be better expected to adjust in some cases, using their ability to reason and explain to carefully compromise with others. Adjustment was a sign of moral authority and power—and at the same time, the pressure on young daughters-in-law, or *bahus,* to adjust and compromise with husbands and in-laws was a sign of their lack of power within the household. Older people across India, including in counseling sessions, used the inversion of this dynamic to emphasize the effects of rapid social transformation: shockingly, in these times it was parents-in-law who had to adjust to their newly assertive daughters-in-law or risk broken relationships with their sons.[3]

At this nexus of gendered and generational difference, the figure of the *bahu* comes to stand for the very possibility of continuity in the face of transformation—the ability of new relations to carry forward the expectations and desires of the past. Such interpretations rely upon and reproduce ideas about gendered difference, where young women are responsible for ensuring the continuity of their husband's family precisely because they are thought to be malleable. This is a significant interpretive burden for women trying to figure out how to salt the dal to their father-in-law's expectations, or how to respectfully assert the needs of their children to mothers-in-law. Indeed, reflecting other studies of counseling, the majority of clients who sought support at the centers I observed in Jaipur were within their first four years of marriage, like Prema (Kashyap 2009). A substantial minority of cases featured women at the other end of the life course, struggling with their relationships with adult children or with second marriages after being widowed later in life—other modalities of adjustment problems, here exacerbated by changing times or lifetimes of habit.

Across counseling casework, case discussions, and institutional meetings, I witnessed debates about whether adjustment cultivates belonging and connection with kin, or disciplines women into sustaining families in which they are subordinated. Such ambiguities were present in professional evaluations of counseling as a practice. Activists and scholars who seek to ensure that counselors work toward gender equality are highly alert to discussions of "adjustment," seeing such discussions as counterproductive and even potentially harmful, arguing that by encouraging women to adjust, people suggest that the power dynamics of Indian family life cannot be changed. In a survey of family counseling programs, counseling expert Lina Kashyap wrote, "even professional interventions have continued to accommodate the implacable entrenched positions men often take in therapy by forcing the socially powerless, resourceless woman to change and adjust to prescribed roles" (2009, 137; see also Basu 2015). For such observers, calls for adjustment reflect an "accommodation" of fixed positions of relatively powerful men by less powerful women. Accounts like Kashyap's suggest that having to adjust to others is a sign of being "resourceless," "powerless" in relations with others.

Yet advocates of counseling also suggest that the value of counseling lies precisely in its ability to help people adjust to a changing world. One training text used by counselors in Jaipur asserted that as social conditions transform, *everyone* needs counseling to help them adjust, echoing a long history of family welfare interventions that worked to sustain families in the face of rapid social transformation (Rao 2002). In such texts, adjustment is a society-wide project, accommodating present, past, and future. When counselors explained the possibilities and limitations of adjustment to their clients, they suggested that a compromise in the present that reflected the moral capacity to be good kin and the promise of better interdependent relations in the future. When women adjusted well, they became integral members of their new families, and could—at least ideally—use these positions to eventually exert influence on other kin. Adjusting in the present offered promises of belonging more substantially in the future.

Seen from this perspective, "adjustment" comes to feel like a tool for moral imagination, a tool, in Julie Livingston's terms, for "those who are marginalized . . . to exercise moral power in certain settings" (Livingston 2005, 21). Here, adjustment is a tool for engaging the precarity of kinship as not just something that risks harm, but that offers possibilities of change—a space for what Veena Das calls "moral striving . . . in everyday labors of caring for the other, even in contexts where a mutual antagonism defines the relation" (2010, 398–99). Indeed, counselors also framed the capacity to adjust as a source of meaning and strength, a capacity exercised even in small encounters. Indu gave another example of this multiple times, when staff brought milk-based sweets like laddoos and barfi to the office to celebrate a birthday or anniversary. Indu would eat her portion with relish, telling us about how before she was married, she hadn't liked milky sweets. But her in-laws liked them, and so she learned not only to eat them but to enjoy them. "And I do!" she said triumphantly. "Now I like them." Indu's discussions of adjustment captures the territory this term covers—from cultivating patience with *ghunghat* (and avoiding a mother-in-law's sharp tongue) to cultivating pleasure, as with the sweets. These discussions reveal that adjustment generates ambivalence, particularly with regard to the changing status of women in their families and in public life.

Adjustment talk danced a fine line, between calls for those with less power to change themselves to sustain relations and, at the same time, for people to set the terms of those relations precisely, through demonstrating their capacity to collectively work towards a morally valued future. Adjustment marked some elements of family life as fixed, but adjustment was also necessary because nothing was fixed and families were always changing. As critics of northern Indian kinship systems are quick to point out, the labor of adjustment is not evenly distributed. It is junior, female kin who are expected to adjust; it is men and elders who are adjusted to, just as one adjusts to bad weather, crowded buses, and other things that can't be changed. But maybe in adjusting to the unchangeable situation, people changed it a little bit even as it changed them, the joy of a new taste for shared sweets reshaping relations alongside the frustrations of *ghungat*. Nevertheless, the risks for failing to adjust fell heavy on women, while they rarely grazed parents-in-law or husbands.

Contesting Adjustment in Counseling Casework

These complex dynamics of adjustment shaped counseling casework. Tropes related to adjustment appeared in diverse combinations—as dignity, as degradation, as a form of self-transformation, as a mutual achievement. Family members often directed complaints about adjustment toward junior, female wives. Yet counselors built on the ambiguities of adjustment as a relational project, reframing complaints about adjustment in terms of the larger network of relationships in the family as a whole. They often disagreed with each other about what adjustment meant and how it connected to familial futures and valued pasts.

Counseling clients faced intersecting challenges that both required adjustment and impeded the ability of kin to adjust. Some of these challenges were rooted in tensions within northern Indian kinship systems. For example, household conflicts often took their most overt form as tensions not between husband and wives, but between wives and mothers- and sisters-in-law. Such dilemmas are familiar from both popular and scholarly representations of northern Indian family dynamics. Sons often represent their mothers' strongest connections to the patriline into which they married; when, in time, those sons marry and potentially shift their primary focus to their wives and nuclear family, tensions sometimes form over a son and husband's loyalties, weaving together concerns about emotional connection with concerns about material issues, such as jointly owned property. Over time, joint families frequently split into separate nuclear households—which then, as sons grow up and marry, may expand back into joint households. Such tensions are structurally endemic to patriarchal, patrilineal kinship structures—the alternative is a single household that grows, within a few generations, to dozens of people descended from a shared male ancestor, difficult for most families to sustain, particularly in urban areas. Yet this process is often experienced as interpersonal conflicts between female kin (see Uberoi 2005; Wadley 1994).

In Jaipur, these systemic dilemmas intersected with changing patterns of consumption, desire, and aspiration, all of which were inflected by shifting expectations about women's education, occupational attainment, and household practices. Clients and their kin narrated the roots of household conflict in the rapid social change they perceived in their community. "Nowadays" (*ajkal*), older women would often begin their discussions, adult children cared less for their elders. Educated, employed women struggled to "adjust" to husbands' families, according to many clients. New technologies like mobile phones opened the household to disruptive "interference" from a young wife's parents and brothers, as well as exposing young women to virulent suspicions about potential affairs. Younger women, who often found themselves as housewives in families with older women with substantially less education, described a mismatch between their own life experience and education and that of their in-laws and elders. They complained about rigid mindsets that prevented their kin from fulfilling their duties as supportive family members. Rising prices and rents, shifting economic winds, and continued commitments to economic ties across extended kin networks meant that these conflicts often took place in straightened circumstances, in homes too small, in crowded neighborhoods.

These shifting grounds had the potential to make joint living difficult, placing clients in excruciating double-binds. One client wept as she told counselors that her husband had once talked of saving, building a new, bigger house in a better neighborhood, and filling it with labor-saving, high status devices like a washing machine. But now, when she reminded him of those plans, her in-laws insulted her, calling her greedy (*lalchi*). "But how can it be greed," she asked counselors, "when these are my dreams?" She faced a dilemma between, on one hand, beliefs that women's tastes and self-presentation reflect the reputation of their family as a whole and, on the other, that good wives adjust to their in-laws' lifestyles. Such tensions were heightened at a moment when both social movements and mass-market consumerism encouraged women to pursue their "dreams"—whether for education and careers, or for better washing machines. Behind this clients' frustrated tears lay a host of unanswerable questions, beginning with the one she asked: Was it greedy to pursue her dreams? On whose behalf was she dreaming? Did her "dreams" represent selfish desires that sowed conflict, or a vision of a better life for her relations? Adjustment problems between kin reflected contested visions of how present actions generated familial futures—as well as differing visions of what those futures might entail.

Such dynamics would emerge clearly in the case of Prema and Gopal. Themes of adjustment wove through counseling sessions with Prema and Gopal, which featured, at different times, Hema, Indu, trainee Trupti, and institutional organizer Neela ma'am. All four used "adjustment" as a diagnosis of the problems in the family. But behind this informal diagnosis clustered competing ideas about how kin should work to make others understand in a changing world. Neela ma'am and Trupti suggested that the problem was that Prema was not adjusting to her role in Gopal's family. Hema and Indu stressed the mutuality of adjustment, modeling reciprocal adjustment in their conversations with Gopal and Prema.

Interpreting and Reinterpreting Household Conflict

Counselors explained their job in terms of *samjhaana* and neutrality, insisting that their job was not to definitively diagnose or assign blame to a single cause (or, frequently, individual) in a household. Yet they still needed to label household problems, in no small part because they had to provide documentation of their work for institutional records. Here, too, they relied on *samjhaana* to guide and engage clients, as well as to elicit multiple interpretations of the causes of household conflict.

Both counselors and clients shifted their interpretations of household conflict frequently over the course of counseling. Once Gopal's initial session with Hema had finished and he had left the center, I asked Hema what she thought about the case. Earlier, before the meeting with Gopal, Hema had told me what she saw as the key problems in the house: drinking, Prema's suspicions about a possible affair between Gopal and his father's brother's

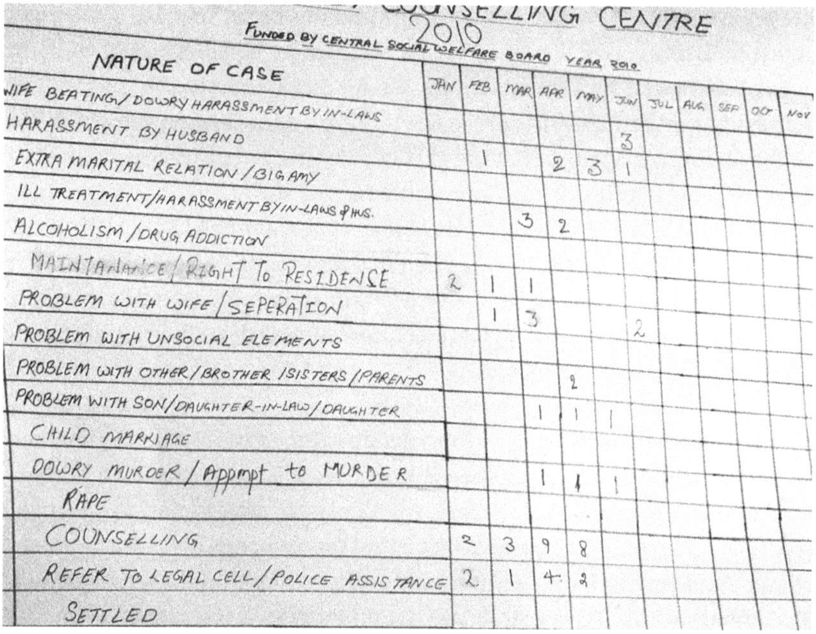

Figure 1. Wall chart of cases, Source of Strength. Photo by author.

wife, and the fact that Gopal had hit Prema. Now, however, she had a slightly different reading, one that contextualized the challenges of adjustment in the household. She added to the list "interference" from Prema's own parents (evidenced by Prema's father's heavy involvement in the case). She also explained the challenges presented by the difference in education between Gopal's family—who Hema referred to as "poor uneducated people"—and Prema, educated up through the tenth standard (the equivalent of a high school degree). With these many challenges, I asked which of the "categories" of case this would fall under. In case ledgers, as well as on a large, hand-drawn English-language poster, counselors logged cases as under a list of multiple categories (figure 1). Although the case featured issues from multiple categories, Hema told me it would be filed as "harassment by husband," because of how Prema had framed her requests for support during intake.

At the same time that they explored dynamics of understanding and adjustment, counselors also engaged in a structured process of logging and organizing cases—a documentation process that was a substantial part of their work. This documentation reflected the institutional pressures on

Source of Strength to keep track of all clients with whom counselors interacted to demonstrate appropriate use of funds. Through this process, the
complex perspectives counselors elicited were transformed into categories
that matched institutional metrics for measuring harm and communicating success. Dynamic relational issues such as adjustment were categorized
in ledgers and paperwork as "harassment by" or "problems with" kin. *Samjhaana* and multiple voices were reframed as "counseling," which was in turn
obliquely referenced with passive verbs like "referred to" or "settled." When
clients arrived at the center, the first people they spoke with were the staff
counselors. Sometimes, clients or their family members would have called
ahead, and so the counselors would ask questions that followed up on that
earlier conversation. They asked prompting questions, for anywhere from a
few minutes to more than an hour. Then, once they had settled on the fact
that the client did, in fact, want to seek counseling, they would begin to pre-
pare intake paperwork.

Counselors and clients worked together to complete a four-page, pre-
printed intake form and a letter that clients wrote (often copying down
counselors' dictation) to request support from Source of Strength's parent
organization. The interactions necessary to complete these documents gave
counselors a guide for exploring what was at stake in a client's case, and
whether counseling was the best path forward. This paperwork was structured to lead clients to answer a deceptively simple question: What do you
want? (*ap kya chahti ho?*).[4] This seemingly straightforward question often
challenged clients—frequently they returned to their narrative of household
disorder without directly responding, prompting counselors to ask again,
often multiple times. Yet this question was central to the counseling process,
because the answer would ensure that the action (*karyavahi*) that followed
pursued the desires of the female client. If she wanted a mutual divorce, counselors would connect her with legal aid to pursue one. If she feared for her
safety, counselors would contact sympathetic police officers on her behalf,
and seek to house her in one of Jaipur's few "short stay homes," shelters for
women. If she wanted to encourage her family members to change how they
interacted with her, counselors would contact her in-laws to discuss further
counseling to resolve household conflicts.

Reaching this answer, however, took intensive interactive work, both to
help clients articulate their desires, as well as to frame those desires in terms
that counseling centers could actually address (no one, for example, could
make a daughter a son, or magically make a working-class family wealthy).

All of the counselors I interviewed discussed the tension between eliciting a client's desires and guiding her to reflect on whether those desires were appropriate and feasible. If clients lacked the literacy skills to manage these forms themselves, counselors would write on their behalf or dictate precisely what they should write, spelling out more difficult words. At the same time, counselors would begin writing their own case notes from the session on a blank sheet of paper. After all of this paperwork was completed—a process that itself could take several hours, as the forms often prompted detailed conversations, and women often struggled with some of the language on the form, written in an elite, bureaucratic register of Hindi—the counselors would give their own notes to the client and any other family members present. The client would read the notes and sign them, the counselors would sign them, and the notes would be hole-punched and put into a case file.

Additionally, counselors had to frame the case in relevant terms for the case register, the next step in officially documenting the case. The case register was a thick notebook with single-line entries for each case, with ledger entries for the client's name, address, and household structure (joint or nuclear), the result of the first meeting, and the type of case. Counselors determined the "type of case" based on what clients wrote on intake forms, drawing from a set list of complaints such as "harassment from husband," "dowry demand," and "harassment by in-laws."

The next step involved contacting other family members with whom a woman was struggling—most often her husband and in-laws—and inviting them to the center. Counselors would describe the goals of the center over the phone. "We have only heard one side of the story," they would say. "Now we need to hear both sides [dono paksh]." They also sent a form letter on letterhead to the family with the same message, saving a carbon copy in their files. I was initially surprised at how frequently other family members complied. Often they would resist a bit over the phone, or miss scheduled meetings, but rarely did they refuse to come at all. Over time, I came to learn that their participation came in part out of the "power" Hema described, in part via pressure from other kin, and in part because things really were rough at home, and everyone wanted a solution. For example, after his first meeting, Gopal missed several scheduled counseling sessions. He returned only after Hema worked with Prema's father, both of them dialing through a dog-eared list of phone numbers in the hopes of contacting someone who would convince Gopal to turn up.

The Conflicting Voices of Samjhaana

When Gopal returned for a joint session with Prema, Hema scolded him for missing his previous sessions: "Didn't you think it was necessary to come fix things?"

Gopal replied by explaining the dilemma he faced: "For me there are both, grandparents, and wife. . . . I'm responsible [*zimmedar*] for them all." This was not an answer to Hema's scolding questions. But Gopal had shifted slightly from his earlier position that supporting Prema would mean "breaking" his family. Here, his claim to be "responsible for them all" echoed the interpretive frame that Hema had urged him toward in their previous session.

Yet Gopal insisted that this responsibility for his kin also meant understanding his family's reticence to let Prema work as a nursing trainee, a responsibility that Prema shared. "Today," he told Hema, "every girl is earning, needs to earn . . . but [my] family doesn't favor it."

Hema responded by reminding him that he shared some of Prema's goals for improving their household: "You don't wish to live in that place [the neighborhood], she doesn't wish to live in that place, so what is the problem? Fine, keep your brothers with you."

Gopal demurred, saying, "One's wife must also take this responsibility . . . we need to do something for my grandparents."

Hema reframed his concerns in a soothing voice, suggesting that these changes would break not the family, but Gopal's own earlier priorities: "Both relationships will strengthen ["family" relationships and his relationship with Prema]—break your priority on your [natal] family."

When, at last, Hema and her fellow counselor Indu were able to gather Gopal, Prema, and their kin all together for a joint session, they were also joined by Trupti, a middle-aged master of social work student observing at Source of Strength for a few weeks, and Neela ma'am, a member of the organization's board who had dropped by with sweets to thank the staff for helping a relative with a research project. Trupti and Neela ma'am both participated in the session by offering their own interpretations of what Prema's case suggested about her, her family, and the larger social world. Although Hema and Indu, I would learn, did not necessarily agree with these interpretations, in the spirit of *samjhaana,* they let these interpretations jostle alongside their own as they worked, both in the service of respecting Neela ma'am and teaching Trupti. The diverse perspectives on the counselors' side joined the many voices of kin (including Gopal's absent grandparents and uncles, who were repeatedly invoked). The presence of these voices allowed counselors to model the process of making diverse perspectives understand each other, even as they counseled understanding and adjustment as the solution to Gopal and Prema's conflicts.

Counselors explicitly invited these voices into sessions. They did so in order to better gain a picture of how such voices interacted in clients' lives. But they also sought to model how clients might manage competing interpretations of conflict at home. For example, while Gopal sat with counselors, waiting for Prema, Hema asked what his grandparents said about the tensions in the house.

"[They say] it's her fault [*uski galti*]," he said.

Hema conceded this, and proceeded with a classic counseling turn, redirecting Gopal away from questions of blame, toward the possibility of future change: "Okay, it's her fault, but both of you will find the way out, right [*raste tum dono niklenge, na*]?"

Gopal built on Hema's point to reassert his own vision of the family's ideal future: that remaining together in a joint family would be better than splitting into a nuclear household. He asserted that three fingers were stronger that one finger, but five fingers were strongest—suggesting that a joint household was more stable, better, than a nuclear household. Hema and Trupti were impressed by this rhetorical turn. It suggested he had the capacity to understand, as Trupti explicitly pointed out: "He's very understanding!" (*bahut samajhdar, voh!*). Here, "understanding" has a sense of rational or sensible— that Gopal understands the larger context within which he operates, that he is able to explain the constraints to others.

Gopal continued to portray Prema as failing to adjust to life with his family. "Even if we moved into the Taj Mahal she wouldn't be happy," he added, another turn of phrase that tickled Hema and Trupti. "If you call a neighborhood a *kacchi basti* [slum], then from the beginning your thoughts about it will be bad." The problem was not the neighborhood but Prema's thoughts and feelings.

At this point, Neela ma'am arrived, on an impromptu casual check-in visit. Hema invited her to hear the case. She took Neela ma'am's interruption as an opportunity to summarize the case. Her summary, simultaneously meant to inform Neela ma'am, reframe the facts for Gopal, and model counseling for Trupti, demonstrates the deftness with which counselors wove together diverse voices to meet multiple institutional aims. The discussion that followed her summary demonstrates how the strategy of *samjhaana* generates clashes between voices—not only the voices of kin, but of diverse counseling interpretations.

Hema's brief description relied upon a clinical register of diagnosis; a scolding, instructional voice; Prema's voice; and a supportive voice that invited Gopal back into the narrative she was unfolding. She chose to tell Neela the following facts, moving back and forth between addressing Neela ma'am and Gopal: Prema was training in a hospital and four months pregnant. "A separation has come between them" (*unke bich separation ho gaya*), she said, offering a diagnosis of the case so far. She then turned back to Gopal with a scolding turn: "Take heed [*dhyan do*]: listen to us because it is easy for her there [at the hostel]." She turned back to Neela ma'am and continued: Gopal had a temporary job at the university as lower-level staff in the library. Neither wants a divorce, a point she made by directly quoting Prema in a loud, emphatic tone: "I don't want to give a divorce!" She concluded by mirroring what Gopal had been saying. "They live in a joint family. Gopal is a good boy, a simple fellow. Right?" she concluded, turning back to Gopal and inviting him to comment.

Hema's deft weaving together of voices framed this particular case as a conflict that could be easily remedied through the character of family members ("a good boy") and through dialogue (which she performed in the narrative itself, voicing Prema and inviting Gopal to elaborate). Yet her dialogue opened the door to competing interpretations from Gopal and from Neela ma'am, both of whom reframed the case in terms of Prema's deficits.

"Ma'am, you aren't listening," Gopal said, insisting that the main problem was Prema's resistance to living with his extended family.

Neela ma'am, who had not yet met Prema, added confidently, "She doesn't want to live in a joint family."

Hema sought to bring the conversation back to her earlier goal, "finding a path" between Gopal and Prema's desires for the future. She asked Gopal to reflect on his role in his family: "What do you want? What is your duty?"

Gopal held firm to his stated desire for a joint family. "What do you consider duty?" Gopal replied. "I want us to live together. If I live with Prema in one room at the hospital, where will my brother sleep?"

Neela ma'am asked why they couldn't rent a two-room flat, and Gopal told her he couldn't manage the cost. Hema suggested that they try and see, reminding Gopal that everything was likely to change once the baby was born. Like Hema, Gopal's discussion of his family problems also incorporated many voices, including kin who were not present. In incorporating these voices, Gopal cast himself as an attentive and respectful family member. When Hema asked why his grandmother hadn't also come to discuss what was happening at home, Gopal explained that his elder sister's husband had advised against bringing his grandparents.

"He told me," Gopal said, assuming a stern, brusque voice, "'It's your matter, so you resolve it.'" Through this brief exchange, Gopal pulled the machinery of kinship that had been working to help interpret and resolve their conflict into the counseling center—including defining who, exactly, was responsible for this issue, who was authorized to act and whose actions constituted interference.

Neela ma'am and Hema both sought to pull Gopal back into focusing on how to better manage these various relations in the future, rather than the past. Neela ma'am interrupted him: "We understand your side of the story. But what do you *want?*"

Gopal was unmoved. "I want to live [together] in a single house," he repeated, and went on to talk about how marriage had disrupted his life, impressing Neela ma'am and Trupti with his sophisticated turns of phrase and self-reflection.

At one point, Neela ma'am even turned to me and said in English, "He is only 20 years old!"

Hema appeared less impressed by the performance, although she listened carefully. She offered something like a diagnosis of what was going wrong with efforts to explain and understand in Gopal's home, suggesting that some voices were louder than they should be. "It sounds," she said, "like there is interference from Prema's parents."

Gopal was not satisfied by these interpretations of his current problems. He repeated, "I don't want to leave my family or her *and* I want everyone to be happy."

Here Neela ma'am turned to Hema, in agreement with Gopal though for different reasons. "It will be tough for them to live independently with family responsibilities," she said, underscoring Gopal's point about financial constraints and referencing, with "family responsibilities," Prema's pregnancy.

"Yes," Hema agreed. She suggested to all present that they counsel Prema, to make her understand that it was necessary to stay with Gopal's grandparents for financial as well as moral reasons. Prema would have to adjust to the situation that she had insisted was unlivable.

Yet Hema did not leave the issue at that. Instead, she reframed the issue of adjustment as family wide, pointing out issues that challenged all of the family members to adjust to their financial situations in new ways, particularly Gopal. She asked Gopal for some details about the house where he lived, and Gopal replied that it had three total rooms, including the kitchen. Hema underscored how challenging this was for the family: "How can you all adjust with so few rooms?" she asked, surprised.

Gopal pushed back, framing the issue of adjustment as Prema's problem. Speaking as Prema, in a petulant tone, he whined, "I don't like this! The area isn't good!" Also, he went on, Prema was frequently absent for work and did not help with the housework as much as she should have. A few times, he'd even had to wash out the pots and pans.

In a teasing tone, Hema reframed this as an opportunity for Gopal to adjust instead of Prema. "And why not? Why shouldn't you wash the pots if your wife is working? If she's learning to work outside the home, then why not work in the home yourself?" This elicited smiles and chuckles from Trupti and Neela ma'am. Or, Hema went on, if it is really a problem, Gopal should adjust his own work, earning enough so Prema wouldn't have to work.

Gopal was not convinced that adjusting his own behaviors would improve Prema's attitude toward his family. He spoke faster and faster, listing his frustrations with Prema, with her parents. He concluded with his own interpretation, using a phrase people often deployed to suggest that adjustment and understanding were impossible: "It's a difference in thought" (*soch ki farak hai*).

Hema, however, resisted this interpretation. Differences in thought led to family breakdowns, a point she made to Gopal. "Don't make enemies," she said, "or your family will break. We have to find out what you want, what she wants, then we will find a path through both of your desires." Again, Hema was reframing Gopal's claim about what was going wrong in his family. Speakers at counseling centers often used the phrase a "difference in thought" to point to seemingly irreconcilable differences between kin, particularly surrounding questions of tradition, modernity, social mobility, tastes, and the role of men and, especially, women. A "difference in thought" was often used as a foundational warrant, a claim that resolution was, potentially, impossible, between kin or factions of family members. A difference in thought meant that adjustment and *samjhaana* might be impossible. Where Gopal suggested an unbridgeable gulf, however, Hema suggested the possibility of a "path through." Where Gopal described set ways of "thought," Hema presented future-oriented "desires."

These careful alignments of adjustment and authority, future and past, duties and desires, would emerge anew once Prema finally arrived and the joint session with Gopal, Neela ma'am, Trupti, Indu, and Hema began. Throughout, Prema only spoke to the counselors, expressing her anger by ignoring Gopal sitting beside her. Like Gopal, she spoke confidently. Counselors asked Prema questions that drew out her distinct perspective on her family.

Indu began by asking Prema, "What do you want, *you*?"

Prema responded, "I can't live in [our neighborhood]." The house was too small.

Hema intervened, explaining to her how difficult a move would be, financially. She and Indu then turned to Gopal to draw him into the counseling conversation. Although Gopal had discussed the ills of drinking already, this time the counselors appeared to engage the topic to demonstrate their support of Prema.

Hema directed a long string of scolding at Gopal: "Drinking will ruin your lungs and your liver and your finances!" She was no longer attempting to engage him in dialogue about the issue. Perhaps sensing that this was, in part, a performance for Prema, Gopal began to grin and then giggle, grimly.

"This is a matter of your life," Indu said sharply, "why would you laugh?" (*life ki matter hai, hans kyon rahe?*)

Prema took advantage of this opening to describe how Gopal brought men over to the house to drink—a violation of social norms in many communities in Jaipur that suggested Gopal was not a responsible husband. Indu echoed her point, telling Gopal, you are married now, you shouldn't bring men over to drink anymore. Gopal denied ever doing so.

Uninterested in his answer, Hema turned to Prema, making clear the purpose of the previous conversation: "Now we are with you [*tumhare sath hain*], to improve [*sudharna*] your situation." To Gopal she said, "Will you stop drinking? Will you?"

This elicited meek promises from Gopal: "*Ji*, ma'am, I'll give it up."

Having laid the groundwork for a conversation where they would elicit multiple voices, while supporting Prema's position, the group turned to a long conversation about the question of the family's budget, and what exactly they could afford to do to compromise around Prema and Gopal's desires. Yet this conversation seemed to only uncover more troubles, rather than the "way forward" Hema had promised.

"There's the drinking matter, the earning matter, the tension—what's the way forward [*kya rasta hai*]?" Indu asked Hema.

At this point, everyone was worn out and counselors had to turn to other tasks. "Think it over" (*soch lo*), Hema told both Prema and Gopal, suggesting another meeting.

"Think seriously," Indu added.

As Gopal thanked the counselors and left, their attention shifted to Prema. At this point, it became clear that even if, as Hema said, the various counselors in the room were standing with Prema to improve things, they had different ideas about what "standing with" might mean.

"Give him another beginning," Hema suggested as Prema stood to leave.

Neela ma'am added, "If you break the relation, it will be very difficult to marry again—you have to try."

They sent her on her way. Indu called after both Prema and Gopal with one final reminder about the power of interaction to remake their family: "Don't quarrel, converse!" (*larna mat, bat karna!*).

The various participants on the counselors' side during the case had a variety of interpretations of how adjustment and understanding featured in the case. According to Trupti, Prema had an "adjustment issue." Both among the counselors, as well as in front of Prema during the session itself, she returned over and over to the modern ills of society: "Today," she said more than once, "society is going bad." "Today's parents are selfish, today women think *my* saris, *my* jewelry." This narrative of moral decline is present in much of daily life in Jaipur and across northern India (Gold 2009). But while Source of Strength's annual reports relied on this narrative framework to describe the importance of the center's work, Trupti was the only counselor I ever heard actually mobilize it in a counseling session. Hema and Indu avoided connecting the details of individual cases to larger frameworks of contemporary moral decay. I would later learn that they were irritated with Trupti's frequent comments along these lines. It indicated, they would tell me, that she wasn't really listening to the client.

Neela ma'am shared Trupti's concern about adjustment but saw it as an issue arising from Prema's position as a *bahu* and young woman. Unlike Hema, who continuously reframed "adjustment" as a family project rather than the job of young wives, she suggested that ultimately Prema would have to adjust. "Actually," she said to Trupti at one point, "parents need to teach their kids to adjust. We shouldn't argue with Gopal—we need to take him into our confidence so that he feels we are working for him." She agreed with Trupti, however, that Gopal seemed very understanding, *samajhdar*.

Yet from her perspective, this meant that it would be difficult to change his behavior.

"For Gopal," she said to the other counselors at one point, "social structures, responsibilities are ingrained." She moved her fingertips in a circle around her temples as she said this, implying that they were literally written on his brain. "So we need to work on the girl's side to get her to agree." Here, Neela ma'am echoed Gopal: the key issue was a difference in thinking. Yet unlike Hema, who reframed "difference" as "desires" through which a couple might together forge a path of compromise, Neela ma'am saw gendered difference itself as offering a solution. Social structure was engrained in Gopal; Prema was malleable. Neela ma'am's comment echoes northern Indian adages that "a woman should be like water, which . . . can take the shape of the vessel into which it is poured"—a phrase I heard Trupti utter more than once during her training period (Raheja and Gold 1994, 77). Ironically, her argument that Prema might be more malleable than Gopal might also arise from Prema's relatively higher level of education; even as Prema learned to stand on her own two feet, her very ability to do so demonstrated a capacity for change that left her open to gendered expectations about her ability to adjust to her in-laws.

Conclusion

Taken together, Neela ma'am, Trupti, Hema, Indu, and Gopal all seemed to be working toward a shared end: a "joint family" where Prema subordinated her own desires—for a job, a sober husband, no more violent fights—to the expectations of Gopal's patriline. Yet closer examination reveals not a single goal but many different voices with subtly different positions on how to reconcile Prema and Gopal—and what their struggles meant about their personalities, their families, and society as a whole. Family counselors like Hema subtly reframed household conflict to draw on clients' investments in interdependence and care to create change without coercion at the level of individual families. As they sought to simultaneously sustain and transform families, they worked within longstanding debates in India about the role of kinship and family in a changing society.

Counselors worked to make these voices understand one another, encouraging reflection, thinking, and discussion. Yet these very strategies also gave the stage to arguments like Neela ma'am's, whose ultimate goal for Prema seemed to be remaining in the marriage, concluding the conversation by reminding Prema that she had to try to patch things up with Gopal because "it will be very difficult to marry again." Hema's advice—"give him a new beginning"—also encouraged Prema to remain in the marriage. But there are subtle distinctions between the two pieces of advice. Hema's advice lacked the compulsion—"you have to try"—that Neela ma'ams statement contained. While these two pieces of advice appear complementary, both oriented towards Prema's relationship with Gopal, Hema positioned Prema as someone in control of the family's future, with a new beginning to give, rather than someone at the mercies of a punitive marriage market. In the nuanced interactive space of counseling sessions, these two voices wove in and out of one another, never directly confronting one another, but never quite resolving. The presence of multiple voices opened the space for Hema to model generative agency for Prema, demonstrating her capacity to harness these inevitable changes to shape her own family through her relationship with Gopal, to offer new beginnings. But these multiple voices also sustained conservative, family-focused tropes, such as Trupti's narrative of moral decay and Neela ma'am's focus on remaining married at all costs.

The Family—patrilocal, multi-generational, structured by hierarchy—felt like it was a fixed feature of life in Jaipur. But individual families were always changing, with babies born, people marrying, elders passing away, people losing jobs, getting promotions, growing closer or further apart through habits cultivated in the everyday rhythms of household life. In between these two facts, counselors guided clients like Prema and Gopal through the dilemmas of interdependence they confronted: to converse rather than quarrel, to find paths through difference rather than deepening it. These strategies were oriented toward futures rooted in family relations, but those family relations were always under construction, in the making through interactions. By both preaching and modeling *samjhaana* as a tool to manage adjustment and change, counselors sought to sustain families structured by multiple, perhaps conflicting, voices.

Because counselors knew how to interpret, manage, and act upon the multiple voices of family life, they were ideal experts to support novel legal interventions into household life, such as India's new civil domestic violence law. Such laws were designed to overcome the narrative inequality that marked most family law cases by sensitizing the state to women's distinctive needs. However, as the next chapter will show, even as legal interventions saw the multi-vocality of counseling as an index of the gender-sensitive nature of counseling centers, they required counselors to elicit and reproduce a single voice of a female plaintiff. Chapter 3 explores the difficult and often frustrating process through which counselors at Source of Strength strove to use *samjhaana*, a fundamentally multi-vocal and future-oriented interactive practice, to ratify a single voice narrating past violence.

It was challenging to track the long-term effects of these interactive strategies. Over the next month, I didn't see Prema or Gopal again. When I asked about what had become of the case, and if it had been settled, Indu told me that Gopal had left Prema "in a lurch," stuck in the middle with no resolution. Such tactics were also difficult to track in case files, where the complex interplay of voices was flattened into fixed labels such as "harassment" and into outcomes like "settled" cases. Over time, however, I came to realize that the documentation of casework still bore traces of this multi-vocalic labor. In her summative case notes for Prema and Gopal's case, Hema wrote: "Heard the case and registered it. Counseled the lady. Called the husband to the center and counseled him as well. Both were made to understand [*samjhaaya gaya*]."

CHAPTER 3

Law's Single Voice: Counseling in the Context of Domestic Violence Legislation

While India has a constitutional commitment to gender equality, as well as a range of criminal and civil laws addressing gender violence, there is a substantial gap between the letter of the law and the implementation of policies. Activists and scholars have long argued that institutional sexism, combined with overburdened legal systems, is the cause of these implementation failures. In particular, women seeking relief from household violence and conflict encounter institutional gatekeeping, whether at the police station or the court, where police officers, magistrates, and other figures frequently see "success" as reconciliation with the family. Activists in Jaipur often described these issues as interactive failures that arise from a lack of gender sensitization, framing this gap between legal promise and the reality as an interactive problem. Given their sophisticated interactive strategies, counselors would seem to be ideal figures to address this major issue in legal efforts to address gender violence in India. One solution to this issue has been to create gender-sensitive institutional mediators to broker between vulnerable women and legal institutions (Basu 2015; Lemons 2016; Roychowdhury 2016). Such efforts focus on sensitizing institutional actors to gender in order to sensitize the state to gender.

These two impulses came together in the Protection of Women from Domestic Violence Act, PWDVA for short, a civil law passed in 2005 and implemented in 2008, not long before I began research at Source of Strength. I came to be aware of the PWDVA because Source of Strength served as an official "service provider" under the law—an existing civil society organization that could "protect the rights and interests of women by any lawful means including providing of legal aid, medical, financial, or other assistance" (Jaising and Sakhrani 2007, 16). Due to the connections of its parent organization,

Source of Strength had managed to register as a service provider by the time I was in the field. Hema, Indu, and other staff had attended several short trainings on how to serve as "service providers" under the auspices of the law, and PWDVA casework took up a substantial part of their working hours. While counseling was one service that the PWDVA suggested service providers might offer, most of Hema's and Indu's PWDVA work consisted of copying, logging, and circulating paperwork necessary to produce documents called Domestic Incident Reports, or DIRs. These documents served as evidence of events of domestic violence, ratifying plaintiffs' claims to material support from their families.

In the language of women's rights activism, counselors appear "sensitive" to the many ways that gender shapes women's ability to access support from the state, particularly the legal system. From this perspective, counselors were capable of listening to vulnerable women while recognizing the complex ways that women's capacity to narrate the conflict and harm they faced might be constrained by hierarchies of power and coercion. Yet PWDVA casework revealed tensions between legalistic and counseling approaches to violence. In my early weeks at Source of Strength, I struggled to distinguish PWDVA casework from counseling casework, as counselors spent long hours in conversation with women and their families. But I soon learned that beneath these superficial similarities were substantial differences in how counselors approached their work *as counselors,* and how they understood their work as *service providers.*

In turn, the intersection between counseling strategies and legal interventions caused friction for counselors as well as for legal experts and activists implementing the PWDVA. Hema and Indu, who conducted the bulk of the work with PWDVA plaintiffs, expressed frustration that they could not offer more nuanced support to plaintiffs, that they did not learn the outcomes of court cases (and thus had no way to know whether the DIRs they created were effective), and that the structure of the DIR asked them to ratify narratives of household violence that they felt they did not fully understand. In evaluations of the law and in regional implementation meetings I observed in Jaipur, activists and legal experts worried about how to ensure that the counseling activities that were part of PWDVA implementation actually served to stop violence and help women access legal rights. They repeatedly expressed concern that, if not properly sensitized to gender concerns, counselors would seek to reconcile women with their families, serving as yet another set of institutional gatekeepers preventing women from accessing their rights.

Through such frictions, counseling strategies come to feel at odds with legalistic understandings of women's rights, even when laws are, like the PWDVA, framed explicitly to recognize the complex terms through which women depend on others and to incorporate interactive expertise that is sensitive to that interdependence. Both counseling and the PWDVA strategize around the intersections between violence, interdependence, and the ability of both families and institutions to hear the voices of vulnerable women. However, they configure these themes profoundly differently. Just as counselors used *samjhaana* as an interactive strategy to engage contradictory goals around sustaining and transforming households, so too did they, along with activist-organizers, legal experts, and transnational institutions, generate complex interactive strategies that marked speakers and institutions as *gender-sensitive*. For counseling casework, note-taking, signed compromise statements, and ledger entries were a means toward an end, which was a home better ordered through the very interactive practices counselors modeled for clients during counseling sessions. For PWDVA casework, the DIR paperwork was the end, and the interactive practices counselors modeled were the means.

Contrasts between PWDVA and counseling casework reveal the multiple anticipatory structures surrounding family, violence, and interaction that coexist at counseling centers. I borrow the phrase anticipatory structure from Sameena Mulla's research on forensic nursing in cases of sexual assault in Baltimore. Anticipatory structures shape interactions in the present by orienting past experience, evidence, and interaction in anticipation of a particular future. Through anticipatory structures, even future outcomes that are unlikely to take place discipline the present. In Mulla's example, forensic nurses are tasked with collecting images and physical traces that can serve as evidence as they treat women who have experienced sexual assault. The intrusive and difficult process of collecting such evidence is structured, and indeed justified, by the anticipation of a trial where it may play a pivotal role for prosecution. In fact, nurses are aware that sexual assault cases are rarely prosecuted, and evidence shows that even successful prosecutions rarely rely on forensic evidence. In spite of this, the anticipatory structure of the future criminal trial profoundly shapes the care nurses are able to offer victims. In turn, such care reinforces the promise of the criminal justice trial as an ideal form of justice for the victim (2014, 30).

The anticipatory structure of a future PWDVA court case similarly distinguished PWDVA case work from counseling. In both cases, counselors drew on similar interactive strategies. Yet DIRs were meant to capture the

single voice of a female plaintiff, narrating her past experiences of violence
"in her own words," and "in simple language," as counselors told me. This
single voice was a complex creation that resulted from dialogue between the
plaintiff, counselors, kin accompanying the plaintiff, and existing paperwork
that had been submitted for the case. Nevertheless, these interactive activities were directed toward framing a single perspective on past events. This
voice was disciplined by what counselors imagined to be the demands of the
court—magistrates alert to potential "manipulation," suspicious of both too
much detail and too little text. Yet, as in Mulla's research on forensic nursing
in the United States, evidence suggests that few PWDVA cases ever see their
day in court (Lawyers Collective 2013). The implementation of the PWDVA
was constrained by a lack of government funding and high court decisions
that undermine the law's central goals (Jhamb 2011; Lawyers Collective
2012). Both the anticipatory structure of the PWDVA case, and the anticipatory structure of counseling, were sustained under the broad umbrella of
gender-sensitive approaches that rely upon interactive expertise to remake
gender relations within and beyond the home.

    This chapter traces the interactions that supported the creation of a DIR
in one particular plaintiff's case, in order to unpack the subtle differences
between how counselors addressed violence in terms of law and in terms of
family. After contextualizing the PWDVA within both Indian and transnational approaches to gender violence, the chapter turns to how counselors
facilitated Domestic Incident Reports, exploring how counselors managed a
plaintiff, Simran, who required a level of counseling support that they could
recognize, but not offer, in their role as PWDVA service providers. Much of
the scholarship on anti–gender violence legislation, in India and elsewhere,
begins with the important question of what institutional and social forces
block women from accessing the legal support to which they are entitled
(e.g. Basu 2012; Lazarus-Black 2007; Lemons 2016; Hautzinger 2007). Here,
however, I shift the angle of analysis to ask how the anticipatory structure of
a court case shapes, and is shaped by, existing interactive strategies within
institutions that are pressed into the service of the state. Rather than focusing
on how those interactive strategies block women's ability to access the state,
I ask how the law shapes the ability of counselors to draw on their existing
interactive expertise.[1] Given the relative lack of successful court cases under
PWDVA, these institutional impacts are arguably the most substantial practical effects of the law. I argue that counselors' interactive strategies under
the PWDVA are shaped not by their beliefs about the value of reconciliation

or rights, but by the tensions between the anticipatory structures of court cases and counseling. In bringing these two anticipatory structures into contact, the PWDVA reveals their distinct visions for how to resolve dilemmas of interdependence via interactive engagement.

Establishing a Gender-Sensitive Anti-Violence Law

Like counseling processes, the PWDVA is sophisticated in how it approaches the intersection between women's dependence on their kin and their vulnerability to violence. In the language of women's rights activism, both counseling and the PWDVA strove to be "gender-sensitive." But "gender-sensitive" can mean many different things (Daly 2005). For transnational bodies like the UN, "gender-sensitive" means first and foremost "not gender-blind." For proponents of the PWDVA and those who monitor its implementation, "gender-sensitive" suggests an awareness of how women's capacity to have their experiences of violence recognized by legal bodies might be curtailed, whether by laws that leave women vulnerable or by counselors who counsel family stability over women's rights. And as Chapter 2 demonstrated, counselors saw themselves as sensitive precisely because they were "neutral," able to recognize and support women's needs *while* protecting the stability of their families. Under the broad label of "sensitivity" were concealed substantial differences in how people understood the role of institutional interactions in supporting women facing violence.

The Protection of Women from Domestic Violence Act was the product of Indian women's movements' long struggle to address gendered violence (Jaising 2009; Lodhia 2009). Beginning in the 1970s, a variety of women's movements in India began to agitate for laws addressing household violence and murder, resulting in criminal laws commonly referred to by the number of their sections in the Indian Penal Code, Section 498A and Section 304B. Section 498A defined and sought to address "cruelty" in the home, while 304B was designed to prosecute cases of violence and murder of women by in-laws seeking to extract larger dowries from their kin (Agnes 1992; Sunder Rajan 2004). While such laws quickly gained prominence and notoriety, they were also limited: judges tended to narrowly interpret the scope of such laws to deal only with dowry-based violence, leaving aside a wide range of other forms of violence that took place in houses, as well as narrowing the scope of potential perpetrators to marital kin. Additionally, criminal laws were poorly

suited for addressing women's desires to improve, rather than sever, connections with their family members; while such laws penalize violence, they often
left women destitute, without support from kin. As a result, beginning in the
1990s, activists began to agitate for a civil law that would specifically define
domestic violence and explicitly address women's needs in the face of such
violence (Roychowdhury 2021).[2] The PWDVA is the result of these efforts.
It draws together longstanding debates about violence against women that
developed within India together with international human rights standards
that began to frame gendered violence as a human rights violation during this
period (Basu 2015; Lawyers Collective 2012).

Because the PWDVA is a civil law, rather than a criminal law, it provided
for a variety of remedies for women facing violence in their homes, emphasizing women's rights within their households. This is an important reframing of
the household, as a private space structured by rights (versus a private space
where civil rights cannot be applied) (Jaising 2009). Rather than directly pun-
ishing violent kin, the law instead articulates the rights of plaintiffs to protection from violence and support from their families, enabling plaintiffs to seek
various forms of relief, ranging from protection orders to monetary support
and shelter from their husbands and in-laws. Because the PWDVA is a civil
law, it is only if a plaintiff's family members violate a court order—failing to
comply with a court order for material support or residence, ignoring a protection order—that criminal procedure comes into play. The law both relies upon
the power of the state to punish offenders while seeking to support women
without fully invoking that punitive authority. Yet to claim these rights to support, women have to demonstrate that they have faced domestic violence.

The PWDVA defines "domestic violence" in very broad terms. This definition includes "physical abuse" and "sexual abuse." But it also includes "verbal
and emotional abuse," including "insults, ridicule, humiliation, name calling."
This definition explicitly includes abuse that targets relations as well as the self,
such as verbal and emotional abuse "with regard to not having a child or male
child," as well as "threats to cause pain to any person with whom the aggrieved
person is interested." Finally, the law includes "economic abuse" as a form of
domestic violence, marked by "deprivation of all or any economic or financial
resources to which the aggrieved person is entitled under law or custom . . .
or requires out of necessity," "disposal" of property to which the plaintiff is
entitled (such as wedding jewelry, real estate property, etc.), and "prohibition
or restriction to continued access to resources or facilities which the aggrieved
person is entitled to use or enjoy by virtue of the domestic relationship

including access to the shared household" (Jaising and Sakhrani 2007, 387–88). This definition emphasizes not only physical harm but relational failures as causes of violence—lack of material sustenance typically expected in family relations, insults about reproductive capacity, violations of shared rights in property, and threats not only to the plaintiff's person but to her relations.[3]

The PWDVA is carefully framed to recognize that ties of kinship—both harmful and supportive—exceed the terms through which they are framed in other laws, offering a definition of rights that arises from practices of relatedness, rather than roles dictated by legal recognition (Mukhopadhyay 2019). For example, one major dilemma that faces women who seek legal support to address household violence is the question of where they themselves will live and how they will support themselves (Roychowdhury 2021). Previous laws did not address women's rights to residence, which precedent saw as arising from ownership of family property—only if one's name was on the deed did one have a legal right to reside in the home. "In fact," writes Indira Jaising, one of the lawyers who drafted the law, "married women have less protection against being thrown out of the house than tenants have against being evicted. While tenants and trespassers can only be evicted by 'due process of law,' women could simply be pushed out of the house" (2009, 53). The PWDVA articulated a right to residence in a "shared household," which arose from history of residence rather than direct ownership of property or legally recognized kin ties.[4] Such a framing not only protected women from having to weigh anti-violence support against the prospect of becoming homeless, but also extended the law's reach to live-in relationships, families oriented around ties of natal relationships, and women who could not readily "prove" their status as wives. Similar logics shaped access to protection, residence, monetary relief, and compensation. The PWDVA builds on beliefs about care, support, and dependence in household life that are familiar to counselors and families in Jaipur, and is designed to be sensitive to the ways that Indian family law and so-called custom marginalize women seeking support in the face of violence. The law also builds on women's rights activism directed at domestic violence legislation within India and transnationally by centering the recognition of the individual rights of the woman seeking support.

Language around gender sensitivity and sensitization was central to the drafting of the PWDVA, which was part of what distinguished it from earlier laws addressing household abuse and violence in India and marked its participation in a global effort to address violence against women as a human rights violation. Lawyers Collective, the group that drafted the original draft of the bill, explicitly discusses their use of United Nations materials on domestic violence legislation (Lawyers Collective 2012). Such materials, in turn, rely upon rights language deriving from the Convention on the Elimination of Discrimination Against Women and the Beijing Declaration and Platform for Action (Keck and Sikkink 1998; Merry 2006). Such documents marked a major turn in the global women's rights movement, by framing violence targeting women as distinctive violations of women's human rights.

Concerns about whether courts, laws, NGOs, and governments are "gender-sensitive" are the product of this turn in transnational women's rights activism, arising from the logics through which human rights law frames violence against women as a human rights violation. Foundational documents produced by the UN, such as the Declaration on the Elimination of Violence Against Women, passed in 1993, note that violence against women violates:

(a) The right to life;
(b) The right to equality;
(c) The right to liberty and security of person;
(d) The right to equal protection under the law;
(e) The right to be free from all forms of discrimination;
(f) The right to the highest standard attainable of physical and mental health;
(g) The right to just and favourable conditions of work; [and]
(h) The right not to be subjected to torture, or other cruel, inhuman or degrading treatment or punishment. (United Nations General Assembly 1994)

However, in practice, gendered violence becomes a human rights violation, rather than a crime or violation of civil rights, when states fail to recognize and appropriately prosecute harm in terms patterned by the gender of victims. To make the legal case that domestic violence represents a human rights violation, it is necessary to demonstrate a patterned lack of response among government institutions (S. Goldfarb 2011; Thomas and Beasley 1993). If the problem of domestic violence is framed as a patterned failure of state actors to respond to violence against women, then the solution becomes sensitizing state actors in order to reverse such discriminatory patterns. The UN's most recent edition of its Handbook for Legislation on Violence Against Women, for example, includes an entire section on "gender-sensitive legislation" that "recognizes the inequalities between women and men, as well as the specific needs of women and men" (United Nations 2010, 15). Such recognition requires "regular and institutionalized . . . training and capacity-building on violence against women for public officials" (2010, 18). Throughout the manual, the list of targets to be sensitized include not only public officials, but the police, educational curricula, legislation, the media, and the public.

In Jaipur, advocates of gender sensitization, informed by these transnational logics as well as by longstanding debates about the capacity of the Indian state to support women, framed sensitization as a problem of narrative inequality (Blommaert 2001; see also Briggs 1997). In theory, Indian laws from the constitution downwards treated men and women as equal citizens. In practice, women face well-documented challenges in lodging criminal reports, in having testimony properly collected in court, and in garnering support from lawyers and police. At each site, state actors from police constables to court magistrates often encouraged women to solve issues privately, at home. In this context, women's ability to narrate their experiences of harm in terms that were credible and effective for their intended audience were frequently called into question. As advocates drafted and defended a draft domestic violence law, they thought carefully about how such legal mechanisms might respond to women's unequal capacity to make claims from both kin and from the state. Such concerns had long been a part of grassroots movements in Rajasthan and across India, which sought to make women's demands more legible to the state, regardless of women's caste, class, or religious backgrounds.[5]

Counseling under the PWDVA: Facilitating or Blocking Justice?

Efforts to sensitize laws, state institutions, and individual actors to gender both center interactive practices and raise questions about their dynamics. Due to its complexity, as well as its wide-ranging definition of violence, the PWDVA creates several supporting roles meant to help plaintiffs navigate the law. These included "protection officers," "service providers," and counseling. As the UN Handbook on Domestic Violence Legislation points out, legal definitions of violence that include economic or psychological elements often require extra levels of sensitized support to both help women recognize that the legal system addresses such violence and to help document such violence. "It is therefore essential that any definition of domestic violence that includes psychological and/or economic violence is enforced in a gender-sensitive and appropriate manner. The expertise of relevant professionals, including psychologists and counsellors, advocates and service providers for complainants/survivors of violence, and academics should be utilized to determine whether behaviour constitutes violence" (2010, 25). Legislative efforts, like the PWDVA, both rely on interactive practices to facilitate gender sensitization and, at the same time, read those interactive practices as indexes of existing gender sensitivity (or its absence). On one hand, in order to fully recognize women's rights, the law requires supporting institutional actors who are already sensitive to women's needs; on the other, such actors risk becoming additional gatekeepers who prioritize family reconciliation. This transnational emphasis on gender sensitivity thus charged interactive activities like counseling with new force.

Counseling receives its own subsection under the PWDVA, under Chapter IV, "Proceedings for Obtaining Orders of Reliefs":

> The magistrate may, at any stage of the proceedings under this
> Act, direct the respondent or the aggrieved person, either singly or
> jointly, to undergo counseling with any member of a service provider
> who possess such qualifications and experience in counseling as may
> be prescribed. (PWDVA, IV.14)

The central role of counseling in the PWDVA provoked considerable concern for the women's groups that advocated for the law. Ironically, the PWDVA had been framed to confront the institutional dynamics that prevented women from accessing legal protection; yet the very tools through which it confronted those dynamics threatened to create additional gatekeeping between women and their legal rights. From the perspective of advocates for the law, if done in gender-sensitive terms, counseling could help women learn to identify their experiences as violence, intervene to put a stop to that violence, and provide legal and socio-emotional support. Done without sensitivity, counseling could be a tool to discourage women from seeking legal aid and condemning the violence they experienced.

In her review of the law's drafting and passage, Jaising discusses concerns that counseling might easily turn into coercive reconciliation. Advocates for the draft bill strenuously objected to the government's efforts to make counseling a mandatory step in filing a case under the act, out of concern that such mandatory counseling would be used to discourage women from pursuing further legal support (Jaising 2009). In *Law of Domestic Violence: A User's Manual for Women,* edited by Jaising and Sakhrani on behalf of Lawyers Collective, a substantial amount of space is devoted to carefully demarcating the scope of counseling given the PWDVA's "problematic" provision for it, perhaps to correct for the law's thin description of what precisely it might mean to "undergo counseling." The manual warns:

> Experience has shown that while litigation in domestic violence is rare, counseling, filing a complaint with the police, and recovering articles is what women generally want. . . . *The process of counseling is often confused with the process of reconciliation* . . . [but the PWDVA] lays down in detail that the chief objective of counseling is to ensure that the domestic violence faced by the victim is immediately stopped. (Jaising and Sakhrani 2007, 13; italics in original)

Here Jaising and Sakhrani seek to distinguish "counseling" from "reconciliation" by suggesting that the anticipatory structure of counseling (as opposed to reconciliation) is ending violence. When I attended a state-wide PWDVA implementation meeting in 2010, organizers hotly debated who was ratified to counsel, what counseling should look like, and the extent to which it should focus on the family as well as on the needs of the plaintiff. Such debates seemed to be the central terrain on which different women's groups defended their areas of expertise. Counseling interactions, interactions over which both the law and activists had little direct oversight, could make or break the implementation of the law.

At stake in these debates about counseling and service provision are questions of what the anticipatory structure of counseling should be: Should the end goal be, as Jaising writes, restabilizing the family, or recognizing rights to end violence? Following the binary of reconciliation and recognition that structured discussions of violence in women's rights organizations, these two potential outcomes appeared contradictory: to reconcile the family came at the cost of recognizing a woman's right to live free from violence. However, in practice, the differences between counseling and PWDVA casework hinged not on reconciliation versus recognition but instead on two different models of how to elicit and deploy speech in the service of reordering households.

Domestic Incident Reports: Thinking
Emotionally, Documenting Bureaucratically

PWDVA casework made strict documentary demands on counselors and other staff at Source of Strength, who divided their days between PWDVA cases and counseling cases. Beneath their shared focus on supporting women through interactive expertise, counseling and PWDVA casework drew on different anticipatory structures surrounding speech, family, and violence. These differences emerged most clearly as counselors worked to compile Domestic Incident Reports (DIRs), the task that dominated their exchanges with PWDVA plaintiffs.

Although the PWDVA and supporting documents like the *User's Manual* cited above carefully delimit the role of counseling and what counseling interactions should look like, at Source of Strength, counselors were not asked to counsel PWDVA plaintiffs. Instead, counselors, authorized by their counseling expertise, offered additional documentary and narrative support to plaintiffs by producing DIRs on their behalf. This is an important distinction: the work that Source of Strength counselors did for PWDVA plaintiffs was *not* counseling, but rather documentary supplementation that they were qualified to do because they were also counselors.

Over a single page, Domestic Incident Reports documented the incidents of domestic violence a plaintiff had experienced and the forms of relief she was requesting under the law; these DIRs are meant to then have copies filed at the local police station and with the magistrate overseeing the PWDVA case (figure 2). With a name that riffs on the familiar "first incident report," or FIR, produced at police stations to initiate a criminal case, the DIR underscores the legal gravity of PWDVA cases while emphasizing their difference from criminal law—beginning with their conditions of production by service providers who are gender sensitive.

Female plaintiffs were sent to Source of Strength by their lawyers or by the court magistrate. They typically came only once, although they might return if they were lacking a key piece of documentation or signature. They arrived at the counseling office with paperwork documenting "events of domestic violence" (*gharelu himsa ki ghatnaen*) collected by their lawyer: typed statements, medical files, and even receipts from wedding gifts and dowry items, often tidily stacked and wrapped in plastic bags from local clothing stores. These documents articulated which of the rights guaranteed under the PWDVA a woman was seeking. Counselors carefully read these materials and briefly spoke with the plaintiff

```
[Source of Strength's parent organization name]    [phone number]
                    [address of Source of Strength]

Honorable Upper Civil Judge_____ Order_____ Jaipur
Mrs_____vs. Mr._____ Mu. Numb. 08 Case No.  in _____ / In
regards to the case of the domestic incident report

Greetings/Sir,
        On the date of _____, an inquiry was performed on the case of
Mrs._____and Mr._____ (family matters).  Within which the testimony of plaintiff
Mrs. _____, jaati _____, age_____, residence_____, was
taken.  Having provided a photo copy of her complaint letter, the plaintiff said in her brief
statement that_____
_____
_____
_____
_____
_____
_____
_____
_____
_____
_____
_____
_____
_____
_____
_____
_____

In addition to us, on this occasion were available Mr./Mrs._____
_____ 2. Mr./Mrs. _____ also support the statements
of the plaintiff

[Space for signature]                        [Space for signature]

(Signature of plaintiff)                  (Counselor, Source of Strength)
The aforesaid report is presented by Source of Strength to the Honorable Court
                              [Space for signature]
                              (Service provider)
        Director/secretary/convener (legal cell), [Source of Strength's parent organization]
```

Figure 2. Translation and reproduction of Domestic Incident Report. Translation by author, with formatting of original form reproduced.

before filling out a DIR. They neither offered counseling to plaintiffs nor contacted family members who were not present. Information about plaintiffs, the date of their visit to Source of Strength, and several other identifying details had to be carefully entered in a ledger and then typed into a spreadsheet so that the organization could send documentation of service provision to the government when they re-applied for service provider status. In practice, scarce resources both from the state (which provided no direct financial compensation to service providers) and at Source of Strength meant that in their role as service providers, counselors could only provide documentation, without offering any of the additional support measures encouraged by the law.[6]

When I first asked Source of Strength counselors why the DIR was necessary, given the fact that they tended to repeat information, and even directly copy language, from the longer court documentation women brought to their meetings at the center, Hema explained that the court expected a plaintiff to feel more comfortable talking at Source of Strength. "We are women," she told me. "We think emotionally about her problems." Indu added that in contrast to the legalistic Hindi used in other documentation, they had been trained to write the descriptions of "incidents of domestic violence" in the DIR in simple spoken Hindi, in the first-person voice of the plaintiff. The first-person voice combined with "simple" Hindi was meant to index the authentic voice of the plaintiff herself. In order to be recognized by state institutions—here, the court—women's demands must be mediated: they must be made visible by someone who is aware of the constraints on women's ability to narrate the conditions of their family life, someone with the interactive skills counselors demonstrate when they discuss strategies like *samjhaana* and neutrality. As activists spoke about "sensitizing" various institutions and actors at meetings and outreach programs, they stressed the necessity of allowing women to speak for themselves, of listening to them, rather than their family members—even if those family members were on the woman's side. Counselors served as the hinge point for such sensitivity, mediating between household and court via a bureaucratic form. DIRs ratified plaintiff's rights to support by pointing to the conditions of rationalized yet sensitive production under which they are produced, marked by the formality of the DIR form, the single, first-person narrative of the plaintiff, and the past tense of the narrative. The audience projected by the DIR was not other family members, counselors, or activists, but a court magistrate. Counselors like Hema and Indu were neither participants in nor the audience for the document; they were merely expected to use their "sensitivity" to amplify the plaintiff's voice.

"We've Only Written What Your Daughter Says": The Anticipatory Structure of the DIR

Family counseling was premised on the basic assumption that, as Indu told me over and over when I pressed her for her opinions about the "real story" of a case, "we can't really know what is going on." PWDVA casework, on the other hand, asked them to verify exactly that, signing a document commenting on a household situation they felt they could not fully understand and then leaving them in the dark about the outcome. The practical tensions between these two modes of interaction emerge clearly in the case of Simran, a PWDVA plaintiff whose engagement with Source of Strength revealed tensions between interventions that conceptualized family as a multiply voiced phenomenon and interventions that excavated single voices that narrated past harms. Simran was particularly difficult to work with, exposing some of the challenges that PWDVA casework presented to counselors, and the different anticipatory structures that such challenges reveal.

Simran, along with her mother, father, and brother, squeezed into chairs around Hema's desk to obtain a DIR for Simran's case, having been sent to Source of Strength by their lawyer. Family counseling cases began with clients offering complex narratives about household disorder, with counselors encouraging clients to articulate what they wanted and inviting numerous other voices into the conversation. But plaintiffs like Simran arrived with such questions already answered: a lawyer already had filed the case, articulating what remedies Simran was requesting under the law, and capturing a narrative of the "incidents of domestic violence" that had led her to the counseling center. Counselors were tasked with helping plaintiffs further articulate these incidents and adding a more sensitive perspective to the case. However, in Simran's case, as in most others I observed, the practice of producing the DIR undermined counselors' abilities to offer such perspectives.

After Simran and her family settled in for a discussion with Hema and Indu, Simran's father pulled a large ream of paperwork from a zippered plastic bag. These were the documents that the PWDVA case had already generated, as the family met with their lawyer and prepared documentation for the court. Simran's father and brother explained that Simran was in the midst of a divorce, and that at first they had pursued a case for legal maintenance in family court, but were now trying their luck at a PWDVA case instead.

Already, Hema and Indu were prepared to intervene, moving away from a conversation about Simran with her male kin to a conversation with Simran herself. Turning from Simran's father, who had done nearly all of the talking so far, Indu asked for details about Simran's marriage. Speaking for the first time, Simran gave the place and date. Her father stepped in, adding that this had been her second marriage, that the first wasn't a fit (*fit nahi*).[7] Hema asked why, and Simran's father replied that there had been disagreements about dowry, no children, and a mutual divorce. Indu directed a question, quietly, to Simran, about why she didn't have children. Her mother began to answer, but Indu stopped her with a gesture, looking at Simran intently and waiting for her reply. Simran was silent as Hema shooed her parents and brother out of the room. Indu asked her again: Why were their no children from Simran's first or second marriage? Simran, in her mid-thirties, murmured something inaudible, and a confused exchange followed, in which Hema asked gently several times, "When did you begin relations?" Simran evaded her questions.

Although this work was premised on encouraging Simran to speak of her experience in her own words, such interactions were not, according to counselors, counseling. Instead, they asked only enough questions to make sure they understood the case before committing details to paper for the court. This work made both Hema and Indu deeply uncomfortable, even as it took up a growing number of hours of their workdays. As a result, they focused on the process of producing DIR paperwork itself, making sure that their brief report did not contradict any other existing documentation, in order to ensure efficacy in court. In most cases that I observed, they had an easier time with plaintiffs. Simran was unusual: most plaintiffs arrived at Source of Strength having already produced narratives of abuse with their lawyers and family members, and were able to efficiently work with counselors to narrate their experiences. They were familiar, in other words, with the genre of narrative that the DIR required. Simran's reticence at this stage of her court case was unusual, and Hema and Indu both responded with concern. Later, Indu would tell me that her reticence made them suspect something else was going on, perhaps in her natal household or perhaps with her mental health. Yet these concerns were outside the ambit of the official PWDVA case Simran sought to lodge. Indu, skimming the paperwork that Simran's father had passed her, murmured to Hema that there was no mention of Simran's previous marriage. She turned back to Simran and said, "Tell us the story of your marriage from the beginning, about your *sasural* [in-laws' home], any abuse [*marpit*]." These questions were designed to elicit a narrative about abuse that counselors could capture in the domestic incident report. All of this was in service of ensuring that she could complete the DIR such that Simran's court case would proceed smoothly, when she got her day in court. Indu wanted to capture what the DIR form described as "incidents of domestic violence."

Simran mumbled a few words. Indu reassured her, "We're all friends here" (*ham friends hain, apas men*).

Finally, Simran said, regarding her marital home, "It was fine."

This was not an answer that Indu could put on the official DIR. "So what happened?" she asked.

"I had to sleep alone," Simran explained. She went on to describe her struggles to fit in to her husband's joint household. They wouldn't let her in the kitchen to help cook but then criticized her for being lazy. They wouldn't give her new clothes when she requested them. Isolated, dependent, yet not able to be a part of reciprocal relationships of support and care: her story resembled those that many married counseling clients told. But "sleeping alone" and "not incorporated into housework" were not legible, legally, as abuse. It was at this point that Indu explicitly asked if her husband drank—he did—and if he ever hit her (*marpit*). Her goal was to confirm that "events of domestic violence" had transpired between Simran and her in-laws. While counseling cases, such as the case between Prema and Gopal described in Chapter 2, enabled counselors to contextualize drinking and *marpit* within a larger constellation of struggles, relations, and desires, the structure of the DIR merely required counselors to confirm abuse.

To do so with integrity and sensitivity, however, they had to hear it from Simran herself. Yet Simran would not give a clear yes or no answer to their questions about her experience. Instead, she suggested that Hema and Indu speak with her father about what had taken place.

Hema, betraying a hint of frustration, told her, "You are grown, decide [the answer] yourself" (*bari ho, khud ko decide karo*).

Indu turned to Hema and said, in English, "Hemaji, I feel she is not in herself."

Something was wrong. Indu and Hema were interpreting Simran's behavior on several levels, beyond merely confirming that she had experienced events of domestic violence. First, they were trying to learn about her experience in her marriage. At the same time, they were trying to understand why Simran was so reticent to speak about her experience—how to make sense of her silences. Finally, they were trying to make sense of the differences between Simran and other plaintiffs they had worked with. As they continued to speak with her, it became clear that they were worried Simran appeared confused when on her own with them because she herself was not the driving impulse behind the court case—that she was perhaps a pawn of her parents or brother in some other conflict with her in-laws. This violated the goals of Source of Strength, which was to elicit, amplify, and support women's own goals. It also violated the goals of the PWDVA, which was designed to amplify the needs and demands of female plaintiffs. Yet they were also tasked with supporting

Simran with the DIR she needed for her case. In treating Simran as a PWDVA plaintiff, they had to put aside some of their impulses as counselors.

Hema asked Simran, again, if there was any *marpit* at home. Simran said no. "Fine," Hema said, "just the mental kind [of abuse]" (*mansik taraph*).

Indu tried to get Simran talking more about the marriage, perhaps as a means of learning more information to capture in the report, perhaps as a means to offer supportive advice. "Do you ever go out [with your husband]?" she asked. Simran described attending several relatives' weddings. Indu explained that she meant things like trips together to the movies, to the park—like dates, time spent together as a couple.

"No," Simran replied, and then sat quietly.

"Why are you saying so little?" Indu asked. Hema added, "You have to tell us what happened in your home so we can make a report."

Simran remained silent. PWDVA casework often generated these impasses, where other family dynamics beyond protecting the rights of plaintiffs seemed to be in play, and yet the goal of providing a report prevented counselors from fully exploring those dynamics—such details were not necessary to ratify Simran's entitlement to remedies under the law.

Hema yielded and called Simran's mother back into the office. "Sit," she said. "She's not talking. Tell us what happened after she got married." In a counseling case, they might have worked harder to hear Simran's side of the story, eliciting as much speech as they could from her, even if it did not take them toward "incidents of abuse." Here, however, the task was to produce the report, which nominally supported Simran's "rights," even though they realized that a PWDVA case may not be the form of support Simran most needed.

Throughout, Hema and Indu tried to balance their job as service providers, capturing a convincing narrative, with their role as counselors, trying to help Simran's parents see her more clearly. Indeed, language familiar from counseling often appeared in interactions with counselors. For example, Simran's mother explained that Simran didn't "adjust" to her in-laws. Indu and Hema began to press her on Simran's own state. These included questions focusing on patterns that seemed to emerge from Simran's experience as a wife: Indu asked her about why her daughter had no children, in spite of being married twice, and Simran's mother insisted that it was the fault of both husbands. They also asked about Simran's behavior in the counseling center: Hema asked why Simran herself wouldn't answer them. Her mother replied that she was scared (*dar*).

"Why should she be scared of us?" asked Indu. "We're not the police and we aren't the court." Echoing the language counselors used to articulate their expertise in neutrality, here Indu refashioned this distinction as an affective stance. Counselors were a non-threatening audience; the narrative inequality that might shape Simran's experience at court should be lessened within the walls of Source of Strength.

However, rather than addressing Hema and Indu's questions about Simran herself, Simran's mother explained that Simran's husband was seeking a divorce. Several activist-organizers explained to me that lawyers often incorporated PWDVA cases, as well as criminal dowry crime cases, into divorce cases in order to support claims of harm as well as to request monetary support. Simran's court documents included a request for 200,000 rupees of maintenance (about 4,400 USD in 2010) under the PWDVA. Simran's mother followed this with a long story about a new potential marriage partner for Simran. Indu, in a frustrated tone, interrupted her. "What, so a third marriage? Then what? After a third marriage a third divorce and a fourth marriage?" What about Simran herself? Simran's mother turned the topic back to the problems in Simran's current marital home, her cruel mother-in-law. Throughout, Simran remained silent. In order to make sure the DIR confirmed, rather than contradicted, other evidence in the case, Hema read the court documents Simran's family brought, while Indu began to fill a blank page with notes, trying to pin down an explicit narrative about what went wrong, and when, for the purposes of the DIR. Some of the details Simran's mother provided, like the date when she moved back to her parents' house, differed from the court papers, and Indu asked for clarification, explaining that for the DIR to effectively support the court case, they needed key information to match.

Hema and Indu would provide the DIR for this family, as they always did for plaintiffs. However, they saw a deeper set of problems than the "incidents of domestic violence" they would narrate in the report. They shifted between an official register of information collection and informal diagnoses, advice giving, and scolding; counseling seeped into their paperwork practices.

"She has tension," Hema told Simran's mother, "she's *sust*," a Hindi term that means sluggish, rundown, lethargic. "Take her to the doctor and get her medicine." Whatever Simran had experienced with her husband and in-laws, her parents were also neglecting her needs. Hema and Indu were concerned by Simran's parents' focus on marriage (ending one, arranging another) as a solution to her problems. Later, they would tell me that the fact that Simran herself had so little to say also made them suspicious that her parents, not Simran herself, were motivated to pursue the case for their own monetary benefit. But as service providers, it was not their job to intervene in the relationship between Simran and her parents, nor to advise her parents on how to better support Simran, who was clearly suffering.

We all sat for a while in silence, Hema making notes; Indu filling out the form for the DIR; me, taking fieldnotes; Simran and her mother waiting across the desk from Hema; and Simran's father sitting just out of view in the courtyard, with Prema and *her* father. Prema's case was also unfolding at this time, and she was at Source of Strength for a joint session with Gopal, who did not turn up. Hema took a break from Simran's paperwork to call Gopal. Meanwhile, Indu was struggling to complete the DIR.

"The form isn't full," she said when Hema got off the phone, holding up the form to demonstrate that her description of the case only filled about two thirds of the allotted space to describe "incidents of domestic violence." She didn't want to damn Simran with a thin narrative of abuse. "But I don't know what else to write." She read it out loud. Simran's mother suggested adding length and substance by giving more specific dates. Indu told her that wasn't a good idea, because it might create conflicts with paperwork already on file. This, she explained, risked giving the impression of "manipulation" in court.[8] To avoid this, she told her, they used round dates, "like January 2010." Hema suggested that Indu add a final formulaic sentence about how Simran's husband's family had left her at her parents and never returned to collect her—a common sentence that appeared in both PWDVA and counseling paperwork to capture the neglectful nature of a client's/plaintiff's in-laws.

So here Hema and Indu were. They were not being asked to intervene in the familial dynamics before them, in which Simran's own parents seemed indifferent to the needs of Simran herself, even as they were supporting "her" PWDVA case. Yet Hema and Indu still took advantage of the opportunity to make Simran's parents understand.

At this point, both Simran's father and Prema's father returned to the counseling office. Prema's father angrily threatened to leave, since Gopal still had not turned up for the scheduled counseling session.

"He'll definitely come," Hema told him reassuringly, sending him back out.

Simran's father explained, in prim English, that his daughter had been silent in their conversations because she was "an introvert, not an extrovert."

Indu replied, shortly: "We've only written what your daughter says, not what you say." This was not, in fact, entirely accurate. Hema and Indu had in fact written a combination of information given by the nearly silent Simran, her mother, and the pre-existing court paperwork, with some stock narrative sentences to avoid having the DIR appear too short. Nonetheless, Indu was making a point, that this process was about capturing women's own narratives, drawing on the promise of the DIR and Source of Strength's potential as a service provider. Even if what Simran actually said was not adequate to support her court case, Hema and Indu could still structure their interaction with her around "what she says."

As if in response to this larger point about capturing plaintiff's voices, Simran's father replied, "She's a reserved type."

Indu asked again about what the plan was—what would happen after a third marriage? Another divorce? She then turned to Simran, veering off the script of a typical PWDVA interaction to give her advice about how to proceed in the wake of this second failed marriage, urging Simran to become a more active participant in crafting her own life in order to overcome her malaise.

"Don't think that you are unlucky [badkismat]," said Indu. "Don't behave like an Indian girl [ek indian larki jaisi]. Find a job. Stand on your own feet [apne pairon pe khare ho]. You're feeling a lot of tension, you are in a depression [tension bahut kar rahi hai, depression men hai]." As she spoke, Simran and her parents signed on the designated lines at the bottom of the DIR. "You read it!" Indu insisted before Simran signed, taking one last opportunity try and elicit Simran's full participation in the process. This was the last time Simran's family would visit the center; as with other PWDVA cases, Indu and Hema would never learn the outcome of Simran's court case.

After Simran left, I asked both of them what they thought of Simran and her family. Indu said that there was mental "torture": that Simran hadn't been allowed to cook in the kitchen, but was scolded for being lazy; her sister-in-law would turn off the water supply in the bathroom, humiliating Simran by making it impossible for her to bathe or clean herself after using the toilet; they wouldn't let her keep her wedding jewelry in her own possession. Indu added her own impression: that Simran was in a "deep depression." I asked obliquely about sexual issues, asking why there weren't any children. The family blamed the men, Indu told me. Returning to her role as counselor, she added, "but we don't know the whole story."

As Simran's case demonstrates, the individual voice captured in the DIR is in fact produced via a dialogic process that draws together a variety of voices across different modalities: court paperwork, mothers, fathers, plaintiffs.

Counselors used the same skills they drew on in helping counseling clients understand and adjust. For PWDVA casework, however, counselors had to frame the process of producing that voice as individual in nature in order to meet the anticipatory structure of a court case, where documentation narrated harms in the past. Such framing took the form of a sort of pedagogy of voicing. When Indu tells Simran's father "We've only written what your daughter has said," she's not so much describing the reality of producing the DIR as describing what the structure of the DIR is meant to suggest about the PWDVA—that it is a law that is sensitive to women's needs and voices. When Indu insists that Simran read the DIR before signing, she again underscores this goal.

Conclusion

The PWDVA was drafted in terms designed to both support women's rights to state protection and to recognize their dependence on specific forms of familial support, seeking to draw state and familial support into mutual reinforcement through a language of legal rights. Yet implementing the act required finding institutional spaces that could listen to plaintiffs with sensitivity. Family counseling practices and PWDVA service provision both recognize that women's ability to gain support by describing their experiences of harm are profoundly constrained by larger structures of gendered inequality at home and in public institutions. Both the PWDVA and counseling seek to simultaneously sustain and transform the family as a source of support for women. Both rely on the expertise of specific institutional actors, such as counselors, protection officers, or service providers, to articulate women's experiences in terms that are both sensitive to women's vulnerabilities as well as to the narrative inequality they face in official state venues. Both acknowledge that women's experiences of both violence and support are informed by their dependence on kin. They both acknowledge, and seek to act on, the narrative inequality that women face when seeking support in the face of household conflict and harm.

These similarities resulted in Source of Strength acting as a service provider under the PWDVA. Yet the interactions at the heart of each process are oriented around differing anticipatory structures: the court case, on one hand, and the household, on the other. Interactions between counselors and PWDVA plaintiffs are structured by the anticipation of a PWDVA court case, seeking to produce a textual narrative to serve as evidence of past household violence, which is then used to claim relief, support, and protection. Very little about the interactions that produce this narrative officially mattered for the anticipated outcome of PWDVA casework. Interactions between counselors and counseling clients, on the other hand, are structured around the anticipation of improved household relations in the future. In that context, interactions between clients and counselors, and between clients and kin, are a central site for addressing household harm.

As Simran's case shows, these differing anticipatory structures cast counseling and the PWDVA into an uneasy relationship, despite their similarities. Hema and Indu's impulses to explore the wider relational context of Simran's problems bled into their interactions with her family and shaped their efforts to elicit "only" what Simran said for the DIR as they interacted with her and her parents. From their perspective, PWDVA casework produced a dilemma: ostensibly, plaintiffs like Simran had already made up their mind about what kind of support to seek (in this case, legal intervention). As counselors, their job was to support clients and plaintiffs in their choices, providing a DIR. In Simran's case, however, they saw multiple signs that the PWDVA case was not a product of Simran's desires, but further evidence of attitudes on the part of her parents that were poised to expose her to further harm. Yet these insights were neither captured nor facilitated by the documentary process of the DIR. "Listening emotionally," as Hema put it, merely deepened these dilemmas for counselors.

While counselors navigated dilemmas between capturing "past events" of domestic violence and engaging the complexities of familial dynamics in the present in order to create a DIR, legal experts in India saw a different dilemma around counseling and the PWDVA. Done with sensitivity, they argued, counseling enabled the state to support women without further harming them—the sensitivity of counselors would, in turn, sensitize the state, overcoming discriminatory practices at police stations and courts. Here, gender sensitivity was a tool to lessen the narrative inequality that women faced in legal institutions in India, by amplifying women's narratives while reducing their exposure to institutional gatekeepers likely to encourage reconciliation with abusive kin. From this perspective, counseling was the interactive glue that held together interactions with women and their families, interactions with state-based institutions, and transnational frameworks of gender violence as a human rights violation. Done without sensitivity, however, counseling could be a tool to discourage women from seeking support, encouraging them to reconcile with their families, and coming to serve as yet one more mediating institutional space that turned women away from the rights they could access via the law. From this perspective, counseling held possibility, but also peril.

As this chapter has demonstrated, however, counselors' interactive strategies were not the product of individual commitments toward either reconciliation or toward supporting women's access to rights. Instead, their interactions with plaintiffs and clients alike took shape within anticipatory structures that oriented those interactions toward differing audiences, endpoints, and temporalities. For example, counselors were not eager to reconcile Simran to her family, either marital or natal. Indeed, Indu harshly criticized Simran's parents for using a PWDVA case to facilitate a divorce in order to marry Simran off once more. They weren't ambivalent about protecting Simran's rights. Instead, they were ambivalent about how their interactive expertise was pressed into a set of institutional processes that they could not fully track, institutional processes that furthermore did not in fact fully support the women they sought to help. In Simran's case, they repeatedly expressed concern that Simran was not getting support that she urgently needed beyond the legal case her family had launched on her behalf. While the DIR they wrote was oriented toward Simran's possible day in court, they also anticipated that Simran's future would be lived out in a household—either her parents' or with a husband and in-laws selected by her parents. Cases like Simran's suggested deeper dilemmas of interdependence that did not easily fit within the scope of the PWDVA. The ever-shifting, precarious nature of kin relations—and their generative possibilities—evaded the disciplining efforts of the law. But counselors' role as PWDVA service providers kept their eyes trained on past "events" of domestic violence. In providing sensitive support for PWDVA cases, counselors could not effectively counsel, because of how their interactions were shaped by the anticipatory structure of the court case. At the same time, they could not fulfill their goals of "listening emotionally," because of how the anticipatory structure of a future court case disciplined their interactions with plaintiffs.

While legal experts worry that the anticipatory structure of counseling is at odds with that of PWDVA and other legal casework, in much of everyday institutional life, these two structures coexisted, just as Prema and her father brushed elbows with Simran's parents in Source of Strength's courtyard. Indeed, clients often moved between them, exhausting efforts at counseling before counselors suggested (or clients requested) shifting venues to the legal aid clinic also run by Source of Strength's parent organization—or, conversely, counseling clients learned of the possibility of counseling through an initial encounter with police or a lawyer. The ma'ams viewed such movements with ambivalence. Some saw these movements between counseling and court cases as precisely what counseling centers were meant to facilitate. Others, however, saw legal interventions as a sign of "failed" counseling interventions, and disciplined counselors accordingly (see Kowalski 2018 for further discussion of this workplace hierarchy). These were debates over which anticipatory structures ought to dominate counseling interactions, reflecting what Srimati Basu has called the "problem of plenitude" in family interventions in India (2015, 208).

From the perspective of plaintiffs, counseling clients, and counselors, however, both the anticipatory structure of the court case *and* the anticipatory structure of the family rely on uncertain, unpredictable outcomes that remain largely outside of the control of participants. In one case, this uncertainty arises from the precarity of kin relations; in the other, it arises from the sexism and incapacity of the state. The mutually supportive, sustaining household and the smooth, effective court case were both points on a distant horizon, brought into being by their effects on interactions in the present. In an important sense, both the ideal, violence-free household and the successful PWDVA court case live most fully through these anticipatory structures and their effects on interactions at sites like counseling centers.

The presence of multiple anticipatory structures meant counselors could move between multiple possible futures, familial and legal, that are often portrayed in women's rights activism as mutually exclusive. Rather than treating counseling as reconciliation, a deviation from approaches that recognize women's rights to be free from violence, a focus on anticipatory structures suggests that counselors and organizers together generate a productive misunderstanding about the relationship between family, violence, and spoken interaction. While organizers support institutional projects that orient interactions toward labeling and diagnosing violence, counselors draw on local language ideologies that orient interaction toward sustaining relations, with the goal of diminishing future conflict and harm. Counselors approached household life as a shared set of efforts to manage interdependence through on-going conversations about reciprocity, obligation, and support rooted in shared beliefs about kinship. In families, people depended on others, but were also depended upon, in relationships whose terms were likely to change over time. Such interdependent relations generated forms of material and sentimental support that had the potential to transform as family members had children, grew old or ill, faced declining fortunes or prosperity, or grew closer or more distant. However, people do not always act according to the norms of kinship.

Because both of these approaches use interaction to address violence, counseling centers are able to sustain contradictory institutional aims of both sustaining families and liberating women from kinship. Chapters 4 and 5 turn from asking how counselors engage anti–domestic violence legal interventions to asking what their interactive strategies reveal about their models of family, speech, and violence. Chapter 4 examines how counseling cases drew upon the family as an anticipatory structure to shape interactions with clients in counseling casework. If the PWDVA assumed the primary goal of interactions with plaintiffs was to diagnose, label, and recognize violence, counselors approached the role of interaction through a framework of careful speech, attending to how clients' interactive strategies both called forth and communicated care in the context of interdependent family life.

CHAPTER 4

Careful Speech:
Generating Change through *Seva*

Counseling casework operated within an anticipatory structure where it was the family, not the law, that structured interventions and interactions. Counselors saw families as continually regenerated through ongoing practices of relatedness. As a result, counselors could act through those practices of relatedness to transform household life. Kinship values offered an open-ended interpretive framework to domesticate household changes, to manage differences between family members, and to smooth household conflicts. In drawing on kinship, clients could manage the dilemmas of interdependence that brought them to the center, acting via generative agency to act on and within their households.

With this focus on interpretation, counselors often discussed key household decisions in terms that initially struck me as contradictory. For example, a few months after I arrived in the field, junior counselor Indu announced that she was expecting her first child. In breaks between casework, she talked frequently about returning to her natal home, or *pihar*, to recover after giving birth. Indu was anticipating a break from housework and from performing *ghunghat*. She described the medically and ritually appropriate foods she would eat during the month-long period of postpartum rest observed by many communities in Jaipur, happily speculating that she would grow bored and fat.

By that point, I had noticed that many clients narrated this same period of recovery at their parents' homes not in terms of care but in terms of abandonment, being "left" by their in-laws (*chorna*). Such narratives were provided as evidence that in-laws and husbands were unloving, backward, and neglectful, especially in cases where women had given birth to a daughter. One day, as I looked over a case file for a client named Karuna, I asked Indu about this discrepancy. In the notes, Karuna described harassment from her husband and in-laws, and as an example she described being left at her parents' house to give birth and recover, one item in a list of complaints including dowry pressure, beating, and harassment. Yet according to the notes, Karuna's husband Virbhad asserted that she had asked (*mangna*) to go to her *pihar*. In counseling sessions that I observed, kin had similar debates about these visits. I asked Indu about the difference between her desire to go home, and Karuna's description of being abandoned.

Indu thought for a moment. "It's not compulsory" to go to your *pihar* after birth, she told me. "But in Marwari families like mine, going to your *pihar* is more comfortable. But it's not compulsory," she repeated, gaining momentum. "Your parents should invite you. Your in-laws shouldn't assume." Later in our conversation, she reflected on Karuna's well-connected family members, speculating that those social connections may have helped her access higher quality medical care. "Of course," she said, "we can't know if she really wanted to go or if she was pressurized."

Recovering from the birth of a first child is a situation that prompts new dilemmas of interdependence. New mothers shift from laboring to care for and support other family members to requiring significant care themselves, often in households where they still feel a bit like strangers. In sending their wives and daughters-in-law back home to their parents for this period, marital kin could appear to be many things: greedy in-laws who make inappropriate demands on a wife's kin; patriarchal conservatives demonstrating a preference for sons over daughters; caring and understanding relatives who recognized a daughter-in-law's emotional and bodily needs and nostalgia for home; or members of a community that shared valued rituals and customs.

Recovering at home was both a material and an interpretive act: an opportunity for invitation, assumption, request, abandonment. Indu, in turn, sought to teach me to evaluate cases for what interpretive frames like invitation or abandonment meant to clients and their kin. Although she herself thought a postpartum visit home could be positive, she did not think her job was to correct Karuna's interpretation of her own experience. Indeed, she denied the presence of strict norms ("it's not compulsory") as well as our ability to fully know Karuna's inner motivation. Instead, the debate in the case notes hinged on the interpretive dynamics of exchanges between kin—dynamics shaped by community background, but also by family connections, by desires and coercion—a complex web that we couldn't, sitting together in the counseling office, hope to fully untangle. Our task was to read Karuna's narrative in terms of what it suggested about the relations between her and her family members moving forward in time. By framing her time at her *pihar* as the result of abandonment, Karuna was telling counselors that her in-laws were neglectful. Virbhad contested this representation of his family by suggesting they had not withheld support from Karuna but given her permission to go.

As the subtle differences between labeling past violence under the domestic violence act and inviting kin to imagine familial futures in counseling casework make clear, counselors worked in a context informed by multiple models of how speech and spoken interactions ought to address household violence. Counselors spoke frequently about the powers of spoken interaction to remake (or break) households. Counselors and clients were highly alert to how spoken interactions reflected wider patterns of support, care, and reciprocity in families. They paid particular attention to how spoken interaction reflected exchanges of asking and giving between family members. Counseling interactions were oriented around spoken dynamics of asking and giving. Such interactions consisted of asking (for support, as clients; for information, as counselors) and giving (support and counsel, as counselors; information, as clients). Counselors used these parallels to intervene in patterns of asking-and-giving among family members, directing their speech so that it both represented appropriate patterns of asking-and-giving, and enabled the appropriate exchange of sentiments and materials within the household, focusing on local language ideologies about asking with affection (*pyar se*) and controlling behavior through questions (*rok-tok*).

By focusing on the generative potential of such interactive dynamics, counselors turned from questions of what family members should do to discussions of what those actions might mean, emphasizing the multiple interpretive frameworks that such actions might invoke and the multiple meanings they might entail. Taken together, this approach represents a strategy for addressing household conflict and violence that I call careful speech. By careful, I refer to speech that is cautious, alive to the risks that talk might reshape or disrupt relations. At the same time, precisely because it is careful in this sense, careful speech also suggests that the speaker is both involved in and working to sustain supportive relations with others, oriented toward a shared, morally valued future: that speakers care for others in morally appropriate terms. These ideas about speech reflect and reproduce ideas about *seva*, a complex term used in both domestic and political arenas in northern India. Often translated as "service," *seva* refers to exchanges of care, support, and service, reciprocated over time, that order relations between people who depend on each other at the scale of family and society alike. When people speak of *seva*, they acknowledge that making a home, *ghar banana* in Hindi, is an ongoing process made up of daily practices and actions that together call a shared future into being. Through strategies of careful speech, counselors draw on kinship values related to *seva* to remake household life.

This chapter explores how this model of speech, support, and family informed counselors' approaches to household conflict and violence. By attending to careful speech as a strategy for addressing household violence, I seek to reframe how we interpret the role of kinship in addressing violence and gender inequality. Counselors use careful speech, I argue, to help clients act with generative agency, transforming their relations with kin without appearing to abandon their own roles within relational hierarchies in the family. Through careful speech, counselors offer models for how people might continue to engage each other as relations, but in transformed terms. In drawing on careful speech, counselors help their clients model themselves as caring kin while also acting as if they are embedded in reciprocally supportive relations—potentially calling such relations into existence and generating a more supportive familial future. Counseling thus focused not on getting to the interpersonal or psychological roots of conflict, nor on imposing overt norms of how to be a female family member. Instead, counselors drew clients' attention to the interactive processes that both reproduce and transform families over time. In so doing, counseling practices echo the work of anthropologists of kinship, who have long underscored that kinship is processual, regenerative, and interpretive in nature.

Chapter 4 contextualizes counselors' strategies of careful speech within the ideologies surrounding family, social reproduction, and speech that give those strategies meaning. Beginning with a discussion of *seva*'s role in both intimate and institutional life, the chapter turns to how people in Jaipur discussed how daily practices of care and service ordered household relations, focusing particularly on interactive dynamics of asking and giving, control and affection. The chapter concludes by exploring the politics of careful speech in generating social transformation within and beyond the home.

Seva: Service toward the Future

Careful speech built on the open-ended, interpretive nature of *seva*, a central value of northern Indian family life. *Seva* can translate to "service to and respect for" (Cohen 1998, 117), as well as "service to humanity" (Watt 2006,

48).[1] As used in the context of family life, *seva* referred to the reciprocal practices of obligation, responsibility, and support that regenerated relatedness in the context of ever shifting household hierarchies—to activities that we might roughly translate as "care." Counselors referenced *seva* to help clients experiment with drawing on kinship to source support and engage dilemmas of interdependence. With clients, they debated whether specific actions counted as *seva*, according to whom, and why. Counselors and clients used *seva* as a framework for evaluating how kin should reciprocate and sustain interdependent relations, whether during a single interaction, such as preparing a meal, or over a lifetime. People described these actions in terms like *dhyan rakhna,* to attend to or take care of; *dekhbal karna*, to care for or look after; *care karna,* to care (using the English loan word); and *palna,* to nurture or nourish. They also both described and performed interactive activities, like *samajhna/samjhaana,* to understand and explain; *sikhna/sikhaana,* to teach and learn; and *adjust karna,* to adjust. These terms constituted a connected set of practices for discussing how people should look after one another in a social world shot through with interdependence.

These practices of *seva* contextualize interdependence within the hierarchies that are fundamental to intergenerational relationships across northern India (Cohen 1998; Lamb 2000, 2013; U. Menon 2013; Vatuk 1990). Sarah Lamb argues that *seva* expresses the "long term, deferred reciprocity" that orders the relationships between generations (2000, 51–52). Junior family members—particularly daughters-in-law—are expected to serve elders through material practices such as bodily care, while elders reciprocate with "hierarchical gifts ... blessings ... affection ... but also curses and complaints" (62). Such transactions "enforced hierarchical relations" because "what juniors gave to seniors ... and what seniors gave to juniors were necessarily different ... because of each party's different statuses and capacities within the hierarchy" (66).

Yet precisely because *seva* is a vector through which hierarchy exerts its grip, particularly on women, it is also a potential source of generative agency. Writing of her research in Odiya households, Usha Menon suggests that "while doing *seva* is an indication of a junior wife's subordinate position within the family, it is also the ladder she climbs to achieve success and, ultimately, influence and centrality ... through every act of cooking, serving, and feeding, she is giving of herself to others within the family and making herself a vital channel of the family body" (2013, 186). Similar logics shaped descriptions of household life in Jaipur, particularly in the multi-generational households where many counseling clients lived. When people suggest they are performing *seva*, they suggest that their actions contribute to the interlinked production of ordered selves, ordered homes, and an ordered society through embodied dispositions that weave everyday actions of care into a larger story about coordinating toward a mutual and morally valued future (Dickey 2000; Lamb 2013; Vatuk 1990).

Kin accused clients who did not adequately perform *seva* of disrupting household flows of support, care, and respect in the present as well as across generational time. Clients described mothers- and sisters-in-law who blocked them from using the shared kitchen (as, for example, Simran did in Chapter 3), or insulted their cooking or household chores; such issues were especially devastating because they prevented clients from participated in household *seva* and, in turn, from becoming kin. Older women frequently insisted that the care provided by their daughters-in-law did not rise to the standards of the *seva* they had provided for their own elders. These assertions are critiques of individual daughters-in-law, but they are also commentary on the social order of the present, of broken ties of reciprocity.

Just as *seva* offered a framework for linking present practices to valued futures, it also offered a framework for drawing together various scales of social experience. *Seva*'s semantic range encompasses actions that are both private and public: caring and serving kin; working for an employer, worshiping a deity, and, importantly, participating in social charity and welfare activities. People described performing *seva* for the less fortunate, for the nation, and for society at large. In such contexts, *seva* served as a "node of political discourse and practice" that ties intimate actions to large scale social orders and distant time horizons (Srivatsan 2006, 427), an element of "techno-moral politics" (Bornstein and Sharma 2016; see also Bornstein 2012; Chidambaram 2012; Ciotti 2011; Srivatsan 2006; Watt 2006). Counselors saw themselves as performing *seva* through their work, as did their bosses, the organizer ma'ams. Counseling centers were themselves "social service organizations," or *samajik seva sansthans*. Through helping their clients make sense of *seva* in their kin relations, counselors and ma'ams performed *seva* for society as a whole.

Seva was thus at the heart of the vision of social transformation that animated counseling centers. *Seva* envisions both reproduction and transformation arising within always-hierarchical relations that orient people toward a morally valued, shared future that requires constant care and attention to call into being. As such, *seva* could both generate and domesticate change—whether that change took place through the regenerative labor of reproducing families and selves over time or through social transformation, such as working to shift women's status at home and in society at large. Such labor required "the *seva* of those capable of mastering the ever more technical politics of keeping bodies and voices lip-syncing to the future," to borrow a phrase from Lawrence Cohen (1998, 150).

Yet whether the everyday labors of household care constituted *seva* or not relied on further interpretation—and debate—amongst kin. For example, a case at Center for Advice and Protection pivoted, in part, on the amount of sugar that the client, Lalita, had been stirring into the tea for her parents-in-law. Lalita's husband worked abroad, managing stores that his family owned in East Africa, while Lalita lived with her parents-in-law. She wanted to negotiate with her in-laws, who she felt were too controlling; she was leaning toward taking her child and, importantly, her wedding jewelry (essentially a savings account) back to her natal home until her husband returned. Gita, the counselor at Center for Advice and Protection, spoke both to Lalita and, separately, to her parents-in-law. Who was responsible for the escalation of household tensions? Was Lalita a flawed daughter-in-law, or were her in-laws overly controlling? Debates surrounding these questions took place on the stage of household minutiae. Lalita's in-laws hotly contested her standing as a good daughter-in-law. They argued that Lalita deliberately neglected them, failing to perform the *seva*, the caring service, that was their right from her as a junior relative. As a central illustrative example, her father-in-law told counselor Gita that she regularly served him *phika chai*, tasteless (that is, sugarless) tea.

In the home, making tea was one way junior female kin might perform *seva*, by transforming the resources of the household into material sustenance that recognized the needs and desires of kin. In reality, households might be strained by intergenerational, gendered, and interpersonal differences between kin, as well as financial constraints that render the relatively expensive milk and sugar used in tea especially dear. Yet served at home—or even at the workplace—tea offered a ritual that demonstrated such differences were ordered by caring actions. Made with milk, sugar, and spices, the specificities of a cup of tea can vary dramatically, so that making tea to a person's specifications can be an act of recognition and respect. The sequence of heating water and milk, without overboiling or scalding, requires time and attention. In serving her in-laws sugarless tea, Lalita appeared to be enacting a minor rebellion, withholding household resources and denying her father-in-law a simple daily pleasure. Day after day, the tasteless tea appeared to both highlight and deepen the other conflicts between Lalita and her in-laws. From their perspective, the tasteless tea suggested a disrespectful stance toward elders or a potential mismanagement of household money or an inappropriate grudge. The sugarless tea suggested that something was wrong and whatever that was, it was Lalita's caring labor that should put it right again.

When asked about the tasteless tea in her session with Gita, Lalita did not dispute her father-in-law's accusation. But she contested her in-laws' interpretation of her tea-making as uncaring and neglectful. Her father-in-law had been diagnosed with diabetes, she told Gita. In contravening his desires, she cared for his aging body. Her *phika chai* represented an effort to sustain her aging in-laws' bodies and health through an intimate recognition of their corporeal needs—an act of *seva*. To quietly meet the needs of ones' elders without being asked, one eye always on the many complex needs of kin: this was ideal caring daughter-in-law behavior. Wasn't it? Was it *seva* to contravene an elder's wishes by conforming to what you believed best for his health and ultimately the material health of the household? Or by acting authoritatively, by dictating access to minor daily pleasures, was Lalita upending the very relations of interdependence that *seva* is meant to mark and reproduce? As they told the story of tasteless tea in a fractured home, Lalita and her in-laws were making arguments about how best to sustain each other in the face of transnational kin ties, aging bodies, and other changing family dynamics. The fact that Lalita's parents-in-law saw the *phika chai* not as care but as inappropriate control, and the fact that Lalita, at other moments in counseling sessions, expressed frustration with how controlling *they* had become of *her* behavior, together suggested that Lalita's tea-making may in fact have been as much defiance as it was care. As in many cases, *seva* suggested a continuum that faded into neglect at one end and tightened into control and coercion at the other. Counselors set the stage for family members to debate where, on that continuum, their behavior fell, to nudge behavior away from those threatening borders between *seva*, neglect, and coercion.

This was the generative potential of *seva* in action: acting to sustain relations in the present, you also transformed them. In transforming those relations, you worked to sustain them. *Seva* both emphasizes and organizes differences between people, whether those differences arise between senior and junior kin, or between activists and those they wish to serve.

Contestations over *seva* grounded household conflicts within a larger set of concerns about how behavior in the present calls a particular future into being, whether at the scale of a specific household or the scale of society as a whole. In counseling sessions, *seva* anticipates a future that is familial, but does not foretell what kind of family that future contains, the qualities embedded in those future relations, nor the larger order such relations participate in. In framing actions as *seva*, as respectful care and service not only of bodies and relations in the present but of a valued future yet to be called into being, kin and counselors alike could act to transform that future, domesticating the changes it might offer as sources of order, rather than disorder.

Ordering Interdependence: Gender and Signs of Conflict in the Joint Family

In Jaipur, people often described healthy households as households where *seva* ordered ties of interdependence across generations. While not all households were multi-generational, the joint family offered a template for assessing whether practices of relatedness sustained these ties or broke them. This was the template through which many client families interpreted conflict, whether that conflict was present or perceived to be lurking, on the horizon. One reason the sugarless tea carried such significance for Lalita's parents-in-law was that it was a potential sign of a deeper reluctance, on Lalita's part, to provide the *seva* necessary to sustain the family forward in time. Seemingly minor, the sugarless tea suggested that the long-term reciprocities of household life might be at risk. Such long-term reciprocities were put at risk in sending a son to work abroad, as with Lalita's husband. Yet the gendered logics of social reproduction in Jaipur meant that Lalita's husband's behavior was hazily presented, from afar, as sustaining the family via material support. Lalita's daily practices, however, were scrutinized as if through a loupe: at various points, her in-laws questioned how the chemicals in the sugar-free sweetener she provided them affected them, provided a detailed accounting of the specific hours she spent using the computer, and noted the precise times she put her children to bed, with what effects for their school performance the next day. As a *bahu*, a daughter-in-law, these intimate activities served as signs of a family oriented toward a shared future—or a family that wasn't.

Both counselors and clients believed that good families resulted when family members ceded a bit of their own autonomy to create a family out of the many potentially divisive differences separating family members, by providing *seva* across differences between kin. Such differences resulted from the patterns and transformations of the life-course, as people entered households through birth and marriage, and left through death, divorce, or separation, moving across multiple axes of interdependent relations with others. For example, at least ideally, daughters-in-law depend upon their parents-in-law and husbands for material support. Children depend on their elders for care and education. Yet over the years, as familial elders age, they come to depend upon their adult sons and daughters-in-law. While daughters-in-law depend upon their marital families for support, those families also depend upon the reproductive labor of their daughters-in-law. Jaipuris spoke frequently about the dilemmas that arose in these cross-cutting relationships of interdependence, when fulfilling obligations in one relationship might prevent fulfilling other reciprocal obligations. Recall Gopal, the husband in Chapter 2, who worried that cooperating with his wife's desires and needs might mean abandoning the grandparents who raised him; or recall counselors' concerns about Simran, in Chapter 3, whose parents were so focused on their parental obligation to get her married that they were failing to appropriately care for Simran. Such dilemmas risked irresolvable conflicts that disrupted the connections of service and care, of *seva,* meant to sustain families into the future.

At the same time, such dilemmas around interdependence were also informed by cohort-based shifts in how people grew up and what they expected from their families and their futures. Family members also differ in terms of personality, taste, and temperament. The Sharma family, whose case I discuss in Chapter 5, offers a typical example. Within the Sharma household, family members were divided by generation, by gender, and by their differing ties to the household. Anju, the client, had recently married into the family; her husband was the youngest son. She shared the household with her husband's elder brother and that brother's wife, Pratima, as well as her mother- and father-in-law. Beyond these kin-based differences, the Sharma household also managed other meaningful differences. Family members came from different parts of the country (Anju, for example, grew up in another state). They had different levels of education (Anju's husband, for

example, was twice as educated as his parents, and Anju was more educated than Pratima, even though she was younger).

These many differences provide, in turn, opportunities for kin to perform *seva*, and to interpret the presence of care, sustaining support, and shared orientation toward the future—or, as in Lalita's case, to debate what practices meant about that shared orientation. Widespread representations of good families presented such families as tidy, organized, interpersonally harmonious, and oriented to social development and progress, connecting familial dynamics in the present to social, as well as familial, futures. Such representations emerged starkly on an educational "Family Chart" poster that was sold widely at stationery stores in Jaipur. This chart was produced alongside other educational posters that ranged from presenting the names for animals to historical figures to illustrating the "good habits" of ideal boys and girls ("brush teeth; salute parents"). In addition to an illustration of a multi-generational family, posed for a portrait, with each family member labeled, it featured a contrastive pair of images, a "small family" and a "large family." Similar contrastive images are widespread in pedagogical materials focused on education, family planning, and development in India.[2] In the drawing of the "small" family, the family appears posed for a studio portrait, the two parents with their arms around a tidily dressed son and daughter; the son holds a ball. The large family—here, "large" means too many children—appears in candid action. In the foreground, two boys tussle, one with his hand around the throat of the other, hand lifted to strike. The father, in kurta-pajama rather than the Western clothes of the small family's father, points at the children while raising a cane in their direction, mouth open. An unattended toddler crawls at his feet, near a book and slate carelessly tossed on the floor. In the background, the family's mother rolls rotis on a *chakla*, a round wooden board, set on the floor. With her other hand, she pushes her disheveled hair away from her eyes; a pot bubbles on a burner set on the floor. Behind her, a daughter is putting dishes away on a shelf, looking over her shoulder, perhaps at her fighting brothers. The home depicted, with a mother cooking on the floor, multiple activities like play, food preparation, discipline, and studying in a single room, suggests economic precarity. Quarreling brothers and a father raising a cane suggests a violent atmosphere. An open book splayed on the floor near a daughter engaged in housework suggests educations deferred or ignored.

The "small" family appears better off than the big family, at least by superficial markers such as leisure time (marked by sports equipment carried by the children), tidy hair, and clothes. The causal connections, however, are left to

the viewer. Is the larger family experiencing conflict because too many children have strained household resources? Or is the lack of family planning a sign of other problems elsewhere? Perhaps this household needed stronger guidance from elders. Or perhaps they needed to better cooperate with a developmentalist state counseling them to have fewer children. The tidy, ordered, "small" family requires no attempt at interpretation from viewers, while familial disorder depicted with the large family raises questions about individual, familial, and community failures. In this way, people throughout Jaipur treated the surface order of family life as a primary site to read developmental status, class, and caste difference. Such order is read across everything from public spaces in the home to the bodies of kin, particularly female kin, whose bodily comportment, household management, and interpersonal behavior are read as reflections on the family as a whole. Trupti, the middle-aged social work student visiting Source of Strength as a trainee, told us a story about how in the early days of her marriage, her mother-in-law forbade her from riding a motor scooter because there was no way to do so without arriving at her destination with a disheveled sari and hair. Laughing at the memory, she mimed how taking off a helmet inevitably mussed a carefully tied back hairstyle. Who knew what people would think about that, what they might say?

To those I knew outside the counseling network, the very notion of seeking outside help for family conflict was potentially a marker of class and status. My upper-class landlady during fieldwork in 2010 repeatedly explained my research to household visitors by describing counseling centers that served "*nichle wale log*," lower-class people. She had drawn this conclusion based on assumptions about higher-status families being better able to avoid conflict without needing intervention—or having too much to lose in exposing their conflicts to outsiders. When she shared stories of family conflict in her own household, she asked: How could such well-educated people struggle to resolve their disagreements over property?

Even counselors, at both Source of Strength and Center for Advice and Protection, would sometimes voice surprise when female clients appeared especially affluent. In front of one client, Indu burst out, "It's amazing that you are being harassed [by your family] even though you seem so nice," referring to the quality of her clothes and self-presentation. Outside of clients' hearing, counselors gossiped about fancy jewelry and other accessories in light of revelations about neglect and harm. Counselors knew, and frequently explained to others, that relative wealth did not guarantee a household life ordered by care, respect, and service. Indeed, from my own observations, it was

middle-class clients who were best able to engage with the counseling process, because they had resources like literacy, control over their working hours, interpersonal skills, and the ability to respond effectively to the demands of the institutional site. Anecdotally, my impression was that the economically marginal clients who came through the centers were often rerouted to other institutional sites, ranging from police stations to other NGOs or temporary shelters. In part, this is because their problems had more explicitly material bases, and those material stakes were often higher—not how to inhabit the house but rather having a house to inhabit at all. Nevertheless, the notion that higher-status households were more likely to be ordered by conflict-free relations marked by *seva* was still present at counseling centers. As people drew connections between households ordered by *seva*, status, and develop-ment, they drew connections between the household and society as a whole. Sugarless tea, disheveled hair, quarreling siblings: these are all potential signs of how one's behavior, the quality and tenor of relations with others, reflects on the order of the home, community, society as a whole.

Signs of disorder underscored the precarity of kin relations, as family members constantly worked to domesticate ongoing changes, seeking to frame differences between kin as generative, rather than disruptive, of family life. A household that succumbed to this precarity was a "spoiled home" (*bigre hue ghar*). Counselors would occasionally make asides to each other, or me, about spoiled homes as homes permanently broken by conflict, over-come by irreconcilable differences. They were particularly alert to the ways that outside interventions, including counseling, had the potential to deepen conflict beyond the possibility of repair. Sometimes clients would tell coun-selors that a family member had told them not to seek outside help because it would spoil their home, or that their kin had accused them of spoiling the house. At other times, counselors used the threat of a spoiled home as leverage over family members. At other moments, counselors distinguished between counseling and legal interventions in terms of which interventions might spoil the home and which might repair relations strained by conflict. The verb "spoil" (*bigarna*) emphasizes the active nature of this destruction: it is the same verb used for cooking mishaps, when the dal is too soggy or when someone ignores a pot of milk boiling for tea and it scalds. The word suggests not passive decay but rather an active process of creation gone awry due to a lack of care and attention.[3]

The spoiled home was made viscerally available for client reflection as they approached the Center for Advice and Protection, one of the counseling centers where I conducted research. After passing the small police station building next door, clients passed piles of household goods as they proceeded to the small outbuilding that contained the center. Dining chairs were upended onto couches whose cushions were torn and moldy; side tables stood with weeds growing in the gaps between wood that had shrunk and re-expanded in the monsoons; rusting refrigerators leaned against air coolers with case numbers painted sloppily on their sides. These stacks of furniture were the result of disputes over dowry being adjudicated by the neighboring police station, but they served as a powerful reminder of the destructive potential of household conflict. As family members fought over these goods, and the relations that they represented, the goods themselves had lost all value. The wrong kind of intervention into household conflict might literally spill your family's guts, leaving them uselessly exposed to sun and weather, rather than within the household, where they might become unremarked upon supports of everyday life.

The labor of ordering households via practices of *seva* was thus high stakes, and highly gendered. The male relatives of clients often suggested that it was the women of their household who were responsible for ordering differences through *seva*—and building on these assumptions, they represented clients as inadequate kin and women. Anju Sharma's husband and father-in-law, for example, both blamed Anju for the household conflict that brought the family to Source of Strength. Her husband described her emotional fragility and physical weakness as the cause of the conflict, telling counselors, "The whole system [*vyavastha*] in our house, the whole situation, will break down [*kharab ho jaegi*] now because of her." The household "system," Anju's husband implied, was one in which other family members may have to carry an unfair burden of household labor, resulting in quarrels and tension.

His father underscored how this, in turn, reflected Anju's failure to adjust to his family's norms, using a common idiom: "For *us*," he said, "*seva* is worship" (*seva puja hai, hamare*) (see Chapter 5). In blocking appropriate gendered flows of care and service, Anju was not participating in moral flows of respect.

Lalita's father-in-law, when not complaining about tasteless tea, engaged in long narrative monologues in which he framed his control of household resources as evidence of his role as a giving, permissive patriarch, while portraying Lalita as failing to reciprocate with the care appropriate to her familial role, instead sitting at the computer, squandering expensive electricity and bandwidth, talking to "who knows" online, and letting the children stay up too late on school nights. "What kind of a woman is this?" he asked rhetorically throughout his descriptions of Lalita.

Counselors also valued *seva* as a tool to order households and address conflict. But they frequently undermined these representations of *seva* as the province of laboring women, instead underscoring the reciprocal nature of interdependence and the requirement that elders and male kin care for those who depended upon them. They did so by emphasizing how spoken interaction could both reflect and perform *seva*, attending to how *seva* was reflected in spoken patterns of asking-and-giving and guiding clients toward strategies of careful speech.

Asking and Giving: Control and Affection in Speech

Even though *seva* is often described in terms of material exchanges of support, *seva* is also interactive, instantiated and contested through speech. Careful speech enacts *seva* in spoken interaction, both generating and indexing—pointing to—existing supportive relations. Through strategies of careful speech, *seva* became a tool to help women build incrementally more livable lives in complex joint households and at the same time a method to orient kin to interactive practices through which everyone in society's various hierarchies could act on the future. Clients and counselors debated *seva* by discussing inappropriate forms of asking, and various means of giving in response to requests. In this way, the vast, multi-scalar implications of *seva* became accessible at the scale of everyday conversations, open to intervention from counselors and family members. Counselors attended to client's speaking styles as a diagnostic of household dynamics and clients offered kin's speaking styles as evidence of their neglect or harm, often directly voicing what kin had said to them to perform the harmful nature of their speech. For example, many clients described insults they faced by performing their mothers-in-law chiding them in curt tones—"*you* do this, *you* do that"—using the most intimate and potentially derogatory version of the second person imperative in Hindi. Such voicing demonstrated that for their mothers-in-law, even requests took the form of insults, addressing daughters-in-law like servants rather than kin.

Counselors thus intervened in the speech of clients and their kin by addressing how family members should ask and what they should give, as well as modeling forms of careful speech within counseling contexts. As the example that opened this chapter shows, actions like dropping your wife off at her parents after birth could represent neglect, abandonment, or appropriate permission in response to a request, depending on both how family members negotiated the decision in the moment and on how they narrated it going forward. Clients and counselors thus discussed how to ask appropriately, as well as how, what, and why to give.

In analyzing counseling interactions, I use the labels "asking" and "giving" to draw together a range of verbs that counselors and clients used to describe spoken exchanges, requests, and demands. These include requesting material goods and permission, such as the request to return home for childbirth (*mangna*, to request), as well as for information (*puchna*, to ask [a question]). They also include the verbal pairs that emphasize paired, reciprocal action central to intergenerational family life: good kin taught junior kin how to participate in the family and, in turn, good kin learned the wants and needs of others (*sikhaana*, to teach, and *sikhna*, to learn). Good kin worked to understand others (*samajhna*). In turn, they sought to resolve differences by making others understand (*samjhaana*).

These interactive actions of asking and giving could, people suggested, offer the space to act independently without fomenting conflict. By making other family members understand your wants, needs, and frustrations, family members could both obey and respect elders while following their own desires. In a conversation about joint family life, a middle-class resident of Jaipur in her mid-twenties, not affiliated with a counseling center, told me, "If your grandparents are saying, 'don't wear jeans,' then maybe you don't wear them. [Or] maybe you make them understand [*samjhaana*], you make the communication gap less, then it's OK. It's not that kids have to obey everything. But they shouldn't disrespect them. They should try to make them understand things clearly."

Echoing others, as well as popular representations, she framed a generational divide explicitly as a communicative problem, a "communication gap" that could be solved by interactive strategies (as opposed to a problem of inequality only to be solved by erasing the hierarchical differences between grandparents and grandchildren). By making familial elders understand, junior family members can engage in potentially disruptive activities (such as wearing jeans, which some family elders believe are inappropriate clothing for young women) without disrupting household hierarchies.[4] Explaining, as well as teaching (*sikhaana*), were key ways that daughters-in-law could be appropriately incorporated into families without coercion or abuse.

As the example of grandparents suggests, careful speech was never only about words. Instead, spoken actions interwove with, and changed the effects of, material practices. Closing the "communication gap" could transform a young woman's outfits from disruptive, disrespectful behavior to something "okay." In some cases, such spoken actions were themselves material. Just as *seva* could shade into neglect or coercive control, so too could the interactive dynamics of careful speech. Counselors and clients suggested that asking was never just a request for things or information, but could be exerted as a potential form of control. Such control may come from other speakers, or it may come from the words themselves, reflecting northern Indian language ideologies about the potential effects of speech itself to act on social contexts beyond a speaker's intentions. "*Bura mat bolo,*" people often remind each other in Jaipur: speak no evil, because you may bring that evil forth into the world by uttering it. One counselor shared a saying with me that someone had sent her in a text message chain: "Words are under your control until you speak them. Once you speak them, you are under their control."

Both in counseling centers and beyond, people described the coercive edge of asking-and-giving in terms of *rok-tok*, the construction of verbal impediments to the actions, movements, and requests of others—particularly family members that are younger and female. The power of *rok-tok* to confine and arrest the movement of young women was graphically illustrated by a commercial for a lightweight scooter aimed at women, the Hero Honda Pleasure, that aired during my period in the field. Beginning with a shot of a son breezing out of a house, helmet in hand, as his mother bids him farewell with a simple, "Bye, son," the commercial quickly cuts to the daughter of the house (played by Bollywood actress Priyanka Chopra). Keys in hand, she moves to leave as her brother did, and her mother immediately asks her, "Where are you going?" A giant animated question-mark appears before the daughter, blocking her way (as in figure 3). As she navigates her way outside of the house, more family members, as well as a pair of disapproving-looking neighbor aunties, pepper her with questions, which also appear as animated question marks. She does battle on this interactive terrain, batting away each question with a clever comeback. In the final scene, she climbs onto her Hero Honda scooter, which blasts through the remaining question marks. As she peels one last question mark from her scooter and tosses it in a garbage can, she turns to the camera and says, "The questions will increase, but so will the fun!" and zips away.[5]

This commercial literally animates the arresting power of *rok-tok*, showing how family members and neighbors can deploy questions to impede action (as well as constructing freedom from such questions as "fun" and

Figure 3. Blocked by questions, still from Hero Honda Pleasure "Questions" commercial, 2010. Screenshot from YouTube.

pleasurable, an object of desire for the young modern woman, who requires expensive consumer objects to help her overcome these impediments). People I spoke with in Jaipur, including counselors, explained *rok-tok* as a series of questions meant to impede one's actions, and clients occasionally performed the *rok-tok* they faced at home: Indu voiced it as "Where are you going? Why should you go there now? With whom?" Such questions are not meant to elicit information, but rather to voice disapproval of the addressee's plan of action in order to potentially alter it.

Lalita's mother-in-law explicitly articulated the contrast between *rok-tok* and speech that reflects appropriate asking and giving. When counselor Gita asked why they had restricted Lalita's access to the family's internet-connected computer, her mother-in-law first denied that she had done so, and then explicitly contrasted *rok-tok* with asking and giving: "There's no *rok-tok* in our house, no *rok-tok* at all. Whatever she asks [*mangna*], we give [*dena*]." Far from controlling Lalitha, she argued, they supported her through asking-and-giving. (The pairing of the verbs *mangna* and *dena* can also have the sense of, "Whatever she asks [to do], we allow.")

If *rok-tok* represented coercive asking that interrupted exchanges of asking and giving, the ideal way to ask was with affection, "*pyar se*."[6] Counselors often told women to speak with affection as they articulated their needs and desires to family members. In doing so, they drew on common uses of *pyar se* in colloquial Hindi. When I explicitly asked Hema about what it meant to ask or explain with affection, she gave me the same example that I saw her give clients. Grabbing a box of paperclips on her desk, she told me that if a client wants her husband to have better behavior (*vyavahar*), she should ask with affection. She held up a lone paper clip. "Say you're asking for one paper clip," she said. "If you ask with affection [*pyar se mangte*], I'll give it to you. I'll give you all of the paperclips." She held up the box to demonstrate. "But if you ask insultingly [*gali se*] then I won't give you even one. *That's* what I explain [to clients]." In Hema's example, the content of the request is immaterial—a point she underscores by using paperclips, relatively mundane objects. In counseling sessions, I saw her use potato chips and pens for the same example. Hema's example suggests that by speaking with affection, clients had the potential to remake dynamics of support in their home, precisely by asking in terms that acknowledged their position in household hierarchies. In asking with affection, women could negotiate the coercive demands of hierarchy even as they seem to acknowledge its demands.

This could mean different things depending on the relationship in question. From a young wife, for example, acknowledging the authority of her in-laws might mean acknowledging that the elder might find the request inconvenient or inappropriate (as in the example regarding jeans and understanding above). For senior kin making a demand of junior kin—a mother-in-law asking a daughter-in-law to complete a task, for example—asking with affection might mean realizing the various competing demands the daughter-in-law faced, and making it clear that she recognized those constraints. It is striking that when I asked Hema to explain "speaking with affection" to me, she focused less on the mechanics of how one might speak with love—what to say, in what tone of voice—than on the end results of such speech: being given what you asked for, whether paperclips, or money, or proper behavior.

Strategies of careful speech not only took the form of using asking and giving to, for example, obtain permission to wear jeans, or to justify withholding sugar from tea. Careful speech could also interrupt harmful exchanges of words and affect. Counselors exhorted clients not to allow "petty matters" (*choti-moti baten*) to spiral into large-scale conflict by reframing exchanges of hurtful speech. At Center for Advice and Protection, organizer Prithvi ma'am advised a client, "If you get insulted in your house, don't return it. . . . If someone calls you a spoiled woman [*bigri hui aurat*], don't get sulky, do you understand? Don't add fuel to the fire [*ag mat jalao*], don't fight about petty matters." Here, the client is urged to reduce the energy of household disputes by disrupting exchanges of insult—by controlling both her speech ("don't return [the insult]") and her response ("don't get sulky [taish]"). This is not a trivial task: calling someone a "spoiled woman" is a nasty insult with implications about morals and sexual reputation; such insults were often the first thing clients described when explaining why they were seeking outside help. Yet by reframing such insults as a "petty matter," counselors framed these problems as something that their clients could control by managing exchanges of speech.

How could merely speaking with affection, with care, generate household change? It is easy to hear this advice as a suggestion that clients shift their own inner responses, rather than holding other family members responsible for their harmful behavior. But to do so is to misunderstand how advocates of careful speech understand the relationship between speech and the inner feelings of speakers. When a family member speaks with affection, their speech need not reflect genuine feelings of affection, nor do they need to cultivate such feelings for such speech to be effective. Instead, requests, demands, and explanations offered via careful speech point toward the obligations and connections generated by the speaker's relationship with their addressee.

For example, Hema and Indu drew upon speaking with affection as a mode of asking and giving when speaking with a client, Smitha, who was seeking help with her husband's inappropriate behavior. Disappearing for days at a time without warning, he would return home drunk on *daru*, local moonshine. He refused to hand over part of his earnings to her to run the household in his absence, which both Smitha and counselors agreed represented a failure to support his spouse and family. Yet Hema and Indu framed one potential solution as speaking and acting affectionately. Such an approach did not require Smitha to abandon her position that her husband's behavior was disruptive and wrong. "You don't have to agree," Hema suggested, using the verb *manna*, which can mean not only "agree" but also "accept" and "obey."[7] "You just have to do things affectionately [*pyar se*]. Don't fight." She continued, "Explain yourself with affection [*apne ap samjhaao, pyar se*]." While Smitha's requests were legitimate—for money to run the household, for information about her husband's whereabouts—she needed coaching in how to represent them.

Indu voiced an example of how the client seemed to be communicating with her husband, speaking in a loud, bossy voice: "'*I* want this, *this* is how it should be' [main *chahti*, yah *hona chaiye*]. Don't be like this—instead, try to make compromises [*samjhaish*]." Hema and Indu were suggesting Smitha reorient cycles of asking-and-giving in her spoken interactions. Rather than responding with anger or fighting to her husband's absences from home and refusal to give appropriately when asked, she should, instead, offer an explanation—make her husband understand her and her needs. By speaking with affection, Smitha could "give" (recall that "explaining" is a central way that giving is enacted in speech) before asking. All of this could be properly managed if done with affection—but not in the manner that Indu offered, where "asking" is replaced by declarative statements. Speaking with affection, Smitha might receive understanding and compromise. Hema emphasized the importance of hewing to household hierarchy when speaking with affection, adding, "don't use 'tu' [the second person singular] when you talk."[8] In Hindi, the second person singular plays a complex role, and its uses walk a tightrope between command, insult, and intimacy, depending on context.

Such advice sits in tension with what transnational women's rights movements understand to be the goals of such mediation activities. At first glance, Indu's advice seems to amount to making Smitha responsible for her husband's failures—failures over which she has little control—by suggesting she be more pleasant. This interpretation is not inaccurate. But at the same time, it was precisely because Smitha had so little control over these wider material problems that Hema and Indu focused on how she might remake the quality of her relations via spoken interaction; from their perspective, such spoken interactions were key moments of building and sustaining relatedness, and thus elements of family life that Smitha could act on in the present. At the same time, they carefully focused on Smitha's behavior to ensure that what she said she wanted aligned with what she seemed to truly want and need.

Hema and Indu immediately turned to the project of eliciting Smitha's desires. Hema went on to ask her what she wanted—a standard question in counseling sessions—in a cheerily bossy tone, marking a turn in the session: "So, right now, what do you want? Tell [*bol*]!" Hema's imperative "tell" is, here, in the very second person singular form that she just advised the client against using; deliberate or not, this shift suggests a move to an easy, backstage intimacy, underscoring the flexibility of these interactive strategies across different contexts and modeling, to the client, the role of different modes of asking, explaining, and compromising across different audiences. In asking the client this question, Hema and Indu gave her the opportunity to practice the correct way to make requests. Smitha eventually suggested that she wanted to invite her husband in for joint counseling. As they collected details such as names and numbers in order to call her husband, Smitha's body language visibly relaxed.

At one moment, as Hema took down her husband's name and address, her face edged toward a shy smile. "Look," Hema said, smiling and turning to Indu, "she's become happy at [hearing] the name of her husband." Such strategies, which counselors often deployed, seemed designed to draw clients' awareness to the potential reordering effects, the material outcomes, of spoken interaction. Indeed, this response to "her husband's name," the positive effects of the client's reaction, had implications for how Hema and Indu proceeded.[9] Later, Hema told me that she believed this client did indeed see a future with her husband, as she had suggested, and that response was part of how she knew.

Careful speech helped counselors, whose primary mode of intervention was interactive, connect spoken interaction to larger dynamics of *seva* in the home. Through strategies of careful speech, in turn, the nature of what constituted *seva* itself could be contested and redefined. In appearing to point toward the *seva* that orders homes, careful speech had the potential to call those relations of care and respect into existence, serving as a creative index, a sign that produces what it seems to gesture toward (see Gal 2013; Silverstein 2003). Strategies of careful speech allowed women to speak as good daughters-in-law and wives while gently expanding the edges of what, precisely, "good" daughters-in-law and wives did, said, and desired—an iterative, tinkering approach to changing families. In invoking the obligations of household hierarchies, even as speakers sought ways to act on their own terms, careful speech enabled female kin to act to transform household relations while continuing to remain legible within them.

In drawing on *seva* and its performance through careful speech, counselors highlight and take advantage of kinship as a process to create change, acting not to diagnose fixed features of household life (abusive husband, neglectful mother-in-law) but to reorient its ongoing interactive creation. Neither individual families, nor the larger concept of what makes a good family, are permanently set. Kinship—the relations between people, what they mean, how they are practiced, referenced, and fulfilled—is processual, shifting over time as families shift and contexts change. Strategies of careful speech acknowledge and build upon this, taking advantage of the open-ended nature of familial futures. All of the cases referenced in this chapter reflect substantial violations of expectations around family and support, violations that counselors believe harm women and violate their honor and dignity. No one should call anyone a spoiled woman. Husbands should not drink excessively, hurt their wives, or withhold financial support. Parents-in-law should not criticize, humiliate, or coercively control daughters-in-law for attempting to care for them. Careful speech, and the relations ordered by *seva* that such speech appears to index, play on the ever-emergent, ever-renewing nature of social hierarchies. Careful speech offered counselors and their clients a tool to act on these relations without engaging in adversarial debates about what they meant about fixed qualities of family members or the household, looking away from harmful pasts toward the potential of a more sustaining future. This future took shape in individual households, where daughters-in-law might, through careful speech, remake exchanges of insults and withheld resources into sustaining exchanges of support. This future took shape at the scale of society; counselors and organizers referred to the work they did to support women and families as *seva* as well.[10]

Conclusion

Careful speech reflects care in the sense of both cautious respect and awareness of where a speaker stands in relation with others. At the same time, in reflecting care in this first sense, it reflects and reproduces shared ideas about *seva*, the exchanges of care, support, and service that good family members reciprocate over time to sustain the differences that regenerate but also threaten to divide households and the larger kin networks within which they operate. In directing attention away from the referential nature of speech and toward its performative, generative elements, counselors helped their clients become more explicitly aware of how spoken interactions reflected and created a household ordered by *seva*. In doing so, they simultaneously pursued tempests in literal teacups while encouraging clients to see such matters as "petty," unworthy of being elaborated into involved quarrels and disputes. By intervening in how family members authorized their narratives about intimate life and their claims on one another, counselors worked toward transforming the effects of the hierarchies that structured household life, cultivating a generative agency that manifests in the ability to sustain kin relations moving into a more supportive familial future.

Careful speech relied upon the fact that behaviors, relations, and actions could be interpreted and reinterpreted as evidence of conflict, coercion, or care. As a result, even as counselors drew on ideas about what it meant to be a good family member, they weren't necessarily enforcing explicit rules about kinship. To return to the example of going to one's natal home, or *pihar*, to recover after childbirth, counselors were not focused on the "shoulds" of household behavior so much as on the "hows" and the "whys." When Indu evaluated client Karuna's narrative of being abandoned, and compared it to what Virbhad, Karuna's husband, said about granting Karuna permission to go, she was not trying to catch either speaker in a lie—in fact, as she told me, such clarity was impossible. Nor was she trying to convince Karuna or Virbhad that there was a correct model of kin-based exchange surrounding childbirth and recovery. Instead, she was evaluating Karuna's narrative and Virbhad's counterpoint for evidence about how their household was ordered. This story emerged through how Karuna, Virbhad, and their kin performed such narratives within the center itself, allowing counselors to explore how *seva* ordered relations in their household.

Counselors and clients did not necessarily associate specific practices, actions, or sentiments with *seva*. A household decision, like where a daughter-in-law recovered from giving birth, could signify many things—and those meanings might shift over time. Indeed, as time passed and Indu's own pregnancy progressed, her narrative about returning home shifted as well, and she began to sound more like clients, talking not about the care she anticipated at her *pihar* but the neglect she was experiencing in her marital home. This shift was the result of her mother-in-law's refusal to grant her permission to go to her *pihar*. Indu was visibly upset by the decision, and the story came to feature prominently in her veiled complaints about her mother-in-law. In disregarding Indu's own desires at this important moment, her mother-in-law showed that she was not treating Indu with the kind of empathy and care she would show her own daughter. In other words, in insisting on caring for Indu herself, she failed to treat Indu as lovingly as she would treat a "real" blood relative like a daughter. At the same time, Indu seemed to bristle at a whiff of insult in this refusal—a suggestion that Indu's *pihar* might not be able to adequately care for Indu and her new baby. While clients like Karuna narrated their visits to their *pihar* in terms of neglectful abandonment (*chorna*) rather than request and permission (*mangna*), Indu saw neglect in the refusal to let her stay at her *pihar*.

Because careful speech played on and through the multiple possibilities of kin relations, it made kinship into a potential tool for agency, rather than a set of constraints that prevented female family members from acting to create a valued future. Counselors' approach to sustaining families through careful speech connects to ideas about how to generate agency through speaking in relation with others, ideas that appear not only in debates about household life but in efforts to create social transformation at broad scales in India. "Family" structured the future that counselors imagined, a future in which clients were sustained by interdependent relations and equipped to manage the dilemmas that such relations provoked. From this perspective, family was not a container, a place that women were sent back to or constrained within. In other words, it would be a mistake to interpret counselor discussions of *seva* and careful speech as efforts to push women "back" into some vision of a traditional family life. Instead, the practices of relatedness that sustain families are highlighted as tools to act on and participate in the future.

Such an analysis requires treating "family" and "kinship" as intersecting but distinct categories. Women's rights activists, as well as anti-violence scholars, often frame the "family" or the "home" as a fixed domain within which women experience harm (see Kowalski 2021). Such representations of the home destabilize romanticized representations of the family as a "haven in a heartless world," highlighting the violent gender dynamics that underwrite expectations about family life (Bumiller 2008; Price 2002). However, even as such representations denaturalize idealized notions of the family, they also oversimplify the complexities of kinship systems that structure families and reproduce them. Arguments about relatedness, care, and sustenance can be deployed to argue for transforming models of the family, as well as for reproducing those models. In the context of household life in Jaipur, where kin move across generational distinctions over the course of time, as vulnerable daughters-in-law become powerful mothers-in-law, as sons grow into heads of households, as children are born, educated, and grow, agency involves holding open the possibility of improved relations in the future, often by demonstrating the care and support one can provide (or is entitled to) today.

Strategies of careful speech shaped how counselors engaged the categories associated with legal interventions that addressed violence. Building on counseling's role as an intervention that could both support women seeking legal help as well as helping them avoid the often inadequate and even harmful experience of actual legal cases, counselors saw counseling's value arising precisely from the fact that they helped women *avoid* the kind of labeling language that might precipitate legal intervention (or even suggest such intervention). Overt diagnostic labels, whether deployed by counselors or family members, risked permanently entrenching conflicts. "So how can there be peace in the house now?" Hema, a counselor at Source of Strength, would sometimes ask, rhetorically, after discussing a case in which some form of apparently irrevocable break had occurred, often mediated by legal or police intervention. Such interventions had the potential to reify differences and disagreements in ways that were nearly impossible to overcome, and not always in terms that clients themselves might desire. Careful speech reordered household relations without risking deepening conflict with labels whose effects may exceed the desires of clients.

Such strategies, however, place counselors at odds with the goals of the women's rights network within which they work. Women's rights movements imagine that speech targets violence primarily through labeling and condemning violence. Seen from this perspective, strategies of careful speech are at best a failure to support women and at worst represent a conservative retrenchment of patriarchal values. When, under the umbrella of addressing domestic violence, counselors rely on strategies of careful speech, they appear to women's rights activists to be rejecting the label of "violence," and thus the condemnation of violence that such labels are presumed to entail. Chapter 5 turns to the differences between labeling and careful speech, which reflect differing approaches to how interaction acts on and resolves gendered violence.

CHAPTER 5

═══════

Labeling Violence versus
Ordering Interdependence

Strategies of careful speech informed how counselors approached cases of overt violence, as well as how they mediated between their clients and potential legal interventions. In the context of organizations that were oriented toward women's rights, such strategies of careful speech led to jarring exchanges.

"I'm taking my rights!" (*apne haq lene wali hun!*), one longtime client, Rani, shouted, concluding a breathless narration of the latest twist in the ongoing struggle to secure support from her husband's family.

Hema and Indu sucked in their breath. "Don't say that," they told her.

The two counselors knew Rani well, as she had been coming to Source of Strength for over a year. They were in the midst of trying to negotiate with her in-laws for support, money, and a sewing machine she could use to generate income and a modicum of financial independence. Rani was very clearly the wronged party. Her husband had had an affair with another woman and had children with her. Complicating matters further, Rani had only daughters, while the other woman had given birth to sons, prompting jealousy and competition for the support of her parents-in-law and other kin. Rani was paranoid that her girls weren't being given the support they deserved, particularly given one daughter's chronic medical condition. Rani's family was somewhat conservative; Rani herself had only an elementary school education and had never expected to work outside of the home. Her husband's family was lower-middle-class; they had enough resources that Rani's humble requests should not have been burdensome. Yet Rani's husband had a habit of coming to counseling sessions, agreeing to offer support, and then never following through. Rani thus returned to Source of Strength again and again, often on

unscheduled visits, regaling anyone who would listen with passionate monologues about how she had been wronged.

"I'm taking my rights!" "Don't say that." In this exchange, Hema and Indu
appear to counsel Rani away from the exact labels that, according to transnational women's rights activists, she should be using. Rather than inciting
her to speak, counselors are instead telling her what not to say. Yet analyzed
through the prism of careful speech, where speech both reflects and generates supportive interdependent relations, this exchange begins to make sense.
Hema and Indu were skeptical that any legal challenge would be successful,
given Rani's meagre means. More likely, she'd wind up embroiling both her
in-laws and her natal family in a legal fight that would only drain the family
resources further, starving her further of support, impoverishing her children,
and making it even harder for her husband to support both her and his second
family. Moving the case to court would end the fluid negotiations, multiple
possible outcomes, and diverse forms of social pressure counselors engaged
in with her husband and his kin, imperfect though all of these options were.
Unlike the counselors, a court magistrate would not patiently listen to long,
winding narratives that intertwined descriptions of legally actionable problems, like denying a wife maintenance money or hitting her, with descriptions
of acute jealousy, paranoia about what one's in-laws might be plotting, rage
that an interloper's sons receive better gifts than one's own daughters, and
heartbreak at being abandoned—all frequent themes in Rani's conversations
with counselors.

"What can we do?" Hema said to me at one point while reflecting on this
particularly long and frustrating case, the thick case file on the desk in front
of her. "If we tell Rani's husband to leave the other woman, then *she'll* be in
here asking for our help." If counselors resolved the root causes of Rani's vulnerability, they would only provoke new vulnerabilities elsewhere—another
destitute woman with mouths to feed. Hema saw herself as responsible not
just for Rani but for sustaining this whole network of materially and interpersonally precarious relations.

From the perspective of transnational discourses on gender violence,
counselors appear to be throwing yet one more impediment in Rani's path
to becoming an autonomous, rights-bearing subject, rather than helping her
access the rights she is claiming. In transnational women's rights discourse,
in order to address gender violence, such violence must first be labeled. From
this perspective, labels like "violence," "rights," and even "gender" serve as

signs that an institution or individual condemns violence and believes in gender equality. One interpretation, from this perspective, might be that counselors do not fully understand the definition of "domestic violence" or do not see such violence as a violation of a woman's rights. A more generous reading might suggest that something was lost as these terms were "translated" from cosmopolitan, English-language contexts to the counseling centers, perhaps reflecting some cultural incompatibility between the "global" arena of women's rights discourse and the "local" setting of counseling (Merry 2006; Englund 2006). Taken together, these analyses focus on whether counselors understand and appreciate the meaning of specific labels.

Counselors took diverse forms of not only physical but mental and material violence extremely seriously. It was the labels themselves that they sought to avoid.[1] From counselors' perspectives, labels like "rights" or "violence" risked perpetuating, rather than resolving, harm. By narrowing the potential interpretations of a situation, labels narrowed the range of potential outcomes. As a result, the act of labeling violence could deny women the generative agency that arose from sustaining and being sustained by kin relations. When counselors and clients avoid language that evaluates the quality of the relation itself, the relation remains, in some way, recoverable. Harm, conflict, and neglect are made (potentially) temporary, enabling the possibility that the family as a whole can one day conform to ideals of intergenerational support and reciprocity. Confronted with a sexist and broken court system, such strategies seemed no less naïve or precarious than Rani's announcement about claiming her rights.

Counselors approach labels with caution not because they do not appreciate the meaning of the labels themselves, but because of the language ideology that informs how they approach the intersections between spoken interaction, household violence, and interdependent kin relations. In other words, they did not disagree about the meaning or the value of rights and violence as key political categories. Instead, they had a differing vision of how spoken interaction acts to sustain relations and create change. Language ideologies connect systemic patterns in language use to systemic representations of types of person, interaction, context, and relation, in both overt and covert terms (Irvine and Gal 2000; Irvine 1989; Woolard 1998). Such ideologies structure how people understand the role of spoken interaction in reproducing or transforming social worlds, illuminating the "political as well as cultural dimensions of therapeutic talk" such as counseling (Carr 2010b, 5; see also Bauman and Briggs 2000; Keane 1997).

Both counseling strategies and women's rights discourse rely upon language ideologies that, in turn, reflect differing problematizations of gender violence—differing understandings of what kind of a problem gender violence is and how, in turn, to solve that problem (see Bacchi 2012 and Hodžić 2016 for further discussion of problematization in women's rights discourses). Women's rights activists have long argued that naming gender violence as violence is a foundational moment, both at the scale of social movements as well as in the trajectory of individual women who face violence at home. Activists and scholars highlight the act of labeling harmful relations as violent because, the argument goes, doing so denaturalizes such relations and, in turn, emphasizes that unequal relations between men and women is socially contingent, and thus open to transformation. From this perspective, by labeling these experiences of harm, discrimination, and exclusion as "violence," institutions, laws, and individuals can reframe phenomena formerly seen as private as public in order to demand a response from politically powerful institutions such as the state, creating social change by recognizing women's rights as citizens and humans.

By unpacking the language ideologies that inform labeling violence strategies, we can better see how these language ideologies might obscure our ability to make sense of anti-violence interventions that use interactive strategies other than labeling, such as careful speech. Counselors approached household violence as a symptom indicating that *seva,* the care and respect kin owe one another, had tipped into coercive control or frayed away into neglect and abandonment. As a result, counselors worked to fix the limits between neglect, harm, and *seva* via careful speech. In using the verb "fix," I draw upon the word's multiple meanings, not only in terms of correcting or setting right something that is broken, but also in the sense of making firm or stable something that is tentative or shifting, as when a photograph is fixed in a darkroom, bringing a particular image into focus on the page. In seeking to fix the limits of *seva,* counselors worked with clients to discuss and catalog their expectations about how best to depend on others, offering clients and counselors alike new opportunities to make kin understand, offering new visions of what household life could and should look like. Their strategies of careful speech focused on the capacity of speech to regenerate, rather than label, relationships.

Such capacities were informed by the richly multilingual context in which counselors worked, which underscored the ways that linguistic choices might frame a speaker's claims. When Rani spoke of taking her rights, for example, she spoke of taking her *haq*. Much of the official language around women's rights in Jaipur, however, used the word *adhikar* for rights; for example, Rani's exchange with counselors took place beside a tattered poster in Hindi that exhorted female readers to *Wake up! Know Your Rights!* (*jago! adhikar apne jano!*). The word *adhikar* is what is typically used in discussions of women's rights (*mahila adhikar*) or human rights (*manav adhikar*); the PWDVA provides women *adhikar* to maintenance and protection. *Haq*, in contrast, has a less official feel to it, resonating with traditions of collectively held entitlements where an individual claim can be disruptive (Madhok 2009; 2015).[2] The word choice itself indexes something about the person claiming the rights. Srimati Basu, for example, shows how representations of the *haq lene wali*, the one who takes her rights, are used to discourage women in Delhi from pursuing the inheritance claims to which they are legally entitled from their natal families. The *haq lene wali* is greedy, selfish, a bad sister who causes family discord (1999). Given the linguistically plural environment of counseling, where multiple registers of Hindi flowed across conversations and documentation, counselors were likely responding in part to this framing. Indeed, another possible reading of their response, "Don't say that," *aise mat kaho*, is "Don't speak that way"—an invitation to reframe the demand, rather than abandon its contents. Labels like *haq* could narrow Rani's range of future options by framing her as a particular kind of speaker, acting in a particular kind of context. Better to remain careful in one's speech.

This chapter analyzes how counselors' strategies, on one hand, and women's rights activism, on the other, are shaped by representations of how spoken interaction acts on selves, relations, and social worlds. Drawing on foundational texts in women's rights activism, I illustrate the taken-for-granted ideologies about speech, self, and relation that inform how activists and scholars evaluate anti-violence interventions, a set of strategies that I call *labeling violence*, for heuristic purposes. In putting careful speech and labeling violence side by side, this chapter facilitates an "estranging comparison" that makes visible the covert language ideologies that animate both strategies (Elman and Pollock 2018). In doing so, I argue that counselors depart from global expectations surrounding anti-violence interventions because they draw on a language ideology that problematizes violence within a different model of how speech acts on the world. Beginning with a discussion of how counselors respond to evidence of direct physical violence, the chapter reviews the language ideologies that animate labeling violence strategies in transnational women's rights activism. Finally, the chapter explores the case of Anju Sharma, a client whose kin were overtly violent within the counseling session itself, demonstrating how counselors drew on careful speech strategies to help Anju cultivate generative agency.

Labeling Violence: An Origin Story and a Language Ideology

Women's rights activists around the world rely on the act of labeling violence in order to de-normalize and thus "take seriously" the problem of gender violence (Bumiller 2008, 3). In northern India, naming violence has long been central to women's movements—indeed, pre-dating the rise of transnational violence against women discourse.[3] Both in India as well as globally, the act of labeling harmful interpersonal behaviors as violence is framed, by women's rights activists and scholars, as a foundational moment that enables both activists and victims to work toward gender equality. The label "violence" allows victims of violence to connect with others and reimagine themselves on local and global scales. It enables activists to lobby governments for support and track the effects of their interventions (Merry 2016). Social movements and organizations obviously do far more than label violence in their work to address gender violence. Yet "labeling" encapsulates a deeper set of assumptions about how language use reflects and acts upon both self and society. In this chapter, I use "labeling violence" as a shorthand for these representations of language use, which inform how scholars and activists evaluate sociolinguistic activities that address gender violence. While labeling is by no means the only interactive activity that activists and scholars engaging violence value, women's rights movements have long centered labeling in evaluations and interpretations of anti-violence activities.

The label "violence" is at the heart of the foundational story of global gender violence campaigns. Charlotte Bunch's classic piece "Women's Rights as Human Rights," published in *Human Rights Quarterly* in 1990, places the labeling of violence at the heart of efforts to frame women's rights as human rights, reflecting the approach to language and violence that shapes labeling violence strategies. Bunch's article was part of a wave of organizing efforts that culminated in a number of anti-violence laws and United Nations declarations that placed women's rights on the agenda of human rights in the early 1990s, with gender violence a central platform issue (Keck and Sik-kink 1998; Hemment 2007; Merry 2006). After establishing the moral force of human rights—"one of the few moral visions ascribed to internationally" (1990, 486)—Bunch goes on to argue that women's rights are indeed human rights issues because they are issues of life and death. Here, she provides a list of examples from around the world of moments across the life course when women are exposed to differential harm, beginning in the womb and lasting through adulthood. Bunch's list of gendered harms (a list of "staggering" statistics of death and battery across countries, for example [489]) leads her into an analysis of what, taken together, such statistics represent.

Bunch then spells out the logic of how labeling gendered harms as violence produces political change:

> Contrary to the argument that such violence is only personal or cultural, it is profoundly political. It results from the structural relationships of power, domination, and privilege between men and women in society. Violence against women is central to maintaining those political relations at home, at work, and in all public spheres. Failure to see the oppression of women as political also results in the exclusion of sex discrimination and violence against women from the human rights agenda. Female subordination runs so deep that it is still viewed as inevitable or natural, rather than seen as a politically constructed reality maintained by patriarchal interests, ideology, and institutions. . . . If violence and domination are understood as a politically constructed reality, it is possible to imagine deconstructing that system and building more just interactions between the sexes. (1990, 491)

I quote Bunch at length here, because this passage illustrates the ideology that links the interactive act of labeling violence to a broader political vision. By grouping the diverse phenomena of harm and violation that she lists under a single category, "violence," a clearly gendered pattern emerges, allowing Bunch to translate the larger import: "The message is domination," she writes (491). In decoding this message as one about power relations, rather than innate qualities of men or women, Bunch is able to problematize these phenomena as political, rather than "personal," "natural," or "inevitable." By labeling violence as a piece of a political system, women's rights activists can offer an alternate politics of gender and power. Bunch suggests that labeling violence as violence brings this alternate politics into being by provoking a change in vision. "Failure[s] to see" and subordination "that is viewed as inevitable" give way to new visions and understandings that in turn generate the capability to "imagine" new "interactions between the sexes." The passage reflects an assumption that the act of labeling transparently reflects what people "see" and "understand."

The label of violence offered a powerful lobbying and organizing tool. Organizations could source funding to pursue the task of educating various stakeholders about the meaning of gender violence via outreach activities such as training sessions or gender sensitivity workshops, while waiting for wider legal or social change.[4] While Bunch's article describes institutions, women's rights discourse also came to view labeling activities as a sign that individuals see, understand, and condemn gender violence. In a review of anti-violence initiatives in Rajasthan, for example, scholar-activist Kanchan Mathur describes how "violence"—from within and beyond the household—emerged as a central issue for women who participated in solidarity building activities in rural Rajasthan. Mathur suggests that naming violence is connected to a host of other interpretive activities. Such new interpretations include understanding oneself as an individual, rather than a member of a family; seeing oneself in the context of new relations with other women in a context of social solidarity; and being able to "deconstruct" binaries of "good and bad" women, of honor, and of shame (2004, 220). She writes:

The first step in checking violence against women is the "naming" of the violence . . . women have learnt to identify it as an assault on their beings, which is not to be suffered in silence. Naming is a process of creating a category that helps in the classification of experiences. (336)

Here, the labeling of violence shifts from a feature of institutions, as in Bunch's piece, to a feature of individual understanding, an activity that marks a changing inner subjectivity. Women who resist using the label violence—whether practitioners or victims—she suggests, "did not clearly perceive this as an injustice" (336).[5] In response to this spontaneous naming of violence, Mathur shows how various projects arose to organize complex training and sensitization workshops, to help women learn to reevaluate their self-image by connecting with other women over a shared experience of violence, a reevaluation that women then carry "within themselves to their villages and areas of work . . . to counter violence both within the family and the community" (323).[6]

In centering the act of labeling violence as foundational for both social movements and individual victims, these authors draw upon a globally powerful language ideology: referentialism. Referentialism refers to the belief that the primary, perhaps only, function of language is to label things with words—and that expert and lay evaluations of language use ought to primarily assess whether labels are used accurately, drawing on assumptions that the meanings of words are stable across time and have "true" meanings that can be traced to some clear origin point (Hill 2009; Silverstein 1976). While reference is one among the many functions of sociolinguistic interaction, referentialist language ideologies make these other functions difficult to articulate and analyze (Jakobson 1960). A referentialist understanding of language leads, in turn, to beliefs that what people say reflects (or should reflect) what is inside of them—an ideology that links language use to understandings of personhood as well as morality, shaping how audiences evaluate not only words but actions. In this case, your words are labeling things inside of you as the speaker and making them—and thus your interior truth—apparent to your interlocuters. From this perspective, "speakers do not reshape the meanings of words, they choose them in order to correctly represent the world. Thus a word reveals the speaker's state of beliefs about the world, and also reveals the speaker's communicative intentions to assert some truth" (Hill 2009, 64; see also Carr 2010b; Duranti 1993; Keane 1997; Rosaldo 1982). For example, folk ideology about racism held by white people in the United States encourages people to evaluate things like word choice to determine whether or not a speaker "is" racist (Hill 2009). In addiction treatment in the United States, practitioners expect addicts to learn to realign their speech with their inner truths to recover from their addictions via an "ideology of inner reference" (Carr 2010b). Yet alternate models of language and personhood are always present. In the United States, for example, addicts occasionally "flip the script," reappropriating the semiotic tools of inner reference to other ends; as they do so, they cultivate a sophisticated awareness of the precarity of seemingly stable processes of reference (Carr 2010b, 18–19).

As an interactive strategy, labeling violence is animated by referentialist language ideology, which speakers and observers use to interpret the use of the term "violence" and related key words. Activists treat the meaning of "gender violence" as stable, with an origin point (perhaps a legal or UN document); speakers then choose this label to match their inner beliefs and fulfill their intentions.[7] When individuals use the label, in turn, listeners assume that this use reflects inner beliefs about the political origins of gender violence and the necessity of acting to change that violence. Referentialist language ideology also shapes how people interpret the absence of "violence" as a label. When people and institutions do not use the label violence—or related categories, like "rights" and "gender"—cosmopolitan observers worry that this represents a labeling choice reflecting an inner belief that violence is not a serious problem, or is not something that can and should be changed.

Referentialist language ideologies are so deeply ingrained in the models of personhood, speech, and social relations that inform global anti-violence movements that they even inform the interpretations of scholars who are highly attuned to cultural difference and the frictions of translation in anti-violence work. For example, even Sally Engle Merry, whose work carefully demonstrates how culture mediates anti-violence interventions around the world, reads interactive engagements primarily in terms of labeling. Observing several cases at a counseling center attached to a police unit in Delhi, she writes,

> Money, rather than violence, was the focus of concern. . . . I found the lack of attention to the violence quite striking. Cases were interpreted in terms of dowry and debt despite horrific stories. Reconciliation focused on the exchange of goods. The women clearly had no good alternative to returning to their violent husbands. (2006, 142)

Here, Merry reads the absence of a direct interactive engagement with violence—marked, presumably, by the use of the label to condemn harmful conflict—as a sign that practitioners are not attending to or interpreting cases in terms of violence. Discussions of money, dowry, debt, and goods are taking place "rather than" discussions of violence (rather than alongside, or as a form of, discussing violence). In turn, reconciliation is interpreted as a "return" to violence. Read against a referentialist ideology of labeling violence, any interactive work that does *not* involve directly labeling violence is often interpreted as happening *instead of* engaging issues of violence.

Taken together, these passages demonstrate a set of assumptions about how language enables speakers to act on the world and on themselves. Labels, here, are a form of control and agency, providing speakers—ranging from women suffering in violent households to transnational women's rights advocates—with the ability to connect phenomena together or distinguish between them, to source resources and political capital, and to stake a claim for intervention. Such labels are meant to make the unsayable sayable, to bring silent suffering into speech, and to pathologize what would otherwise be seen as normal behavior—all interactive activities that are central to women's rights movements around the world. To deny or downplay the importance of labeling violence, in turn, appears to deny speakers the agency to label their experiences, and to suggest that the violence they experience is not a problem.

The word "violence" is enormously powerful. By making gender violence nameable, activists around the world fought to transform it into a problem that could be solved, rather than an inevitable feature of intimate life. The transnational women's rights movement has seen incredible success in getting gender violence on the table, from the United Nations to nation-states' legal systems to a wide range of development projects, precisely because it harnessed the shared, unspoken preoccupations over referentiality that define modern subjectivity and directed them toward making the personal political (Hodgson 2011). Governments and transnational and civil society organizations are arenas that run on referentialism and ideals of inner reference and transparency reflected in language use. By externalizing the language ideology that animates labeling violence strategies, however, we can better explore the assumptions about how spoken interaction reflects and acts upon selves and relations at play in how mainstream women's rights activism problematizes gender violence. This, in turn, raises comparative questions about the language ideologies that animate careful speech.

Pareshani (Harassment) vs. Violence: The Limits of Careful Speech

Far from suggesting that counselors did not see violence as a serious problem in women's lives, careful speech reflected how seriously they took it. Yet rather than seeing the violence as a problem, primarily, of unequal gender relations in the abstract, they took violence to be a result of a breakdown of *seva*—of care, respect, support, and reciprocity in family relations. When counselors did engage in labeling practices, it was often to point out how harmful behavior had spilled over the edges of appropriate care, service, and respect. In disordered homes, *seva* could break down in two ways. On the one hand, family members might care too much, verging into harmful coercion or abuse. On the other hand, they might not care enough, leading to neglect. Often, counselors pointed to both these issues in a single case. Because they believed that harm arises when households are disordered, and because they, like clients, believed *seva* orders the home, counselors traced the operations of *seva* as they explored sources of household harm.

Counselors and clients almost never spontaneously used the word "violence" in Hindi (*himsa*) or English when they described what was happening at home. At counseling centers, as throughout India, multiple languages and registers overlapped—Hindi that ranged from legalistic state language to Marwari- or Punjabi-inflected slang, and English loan words and phrases that, depending on context, served as slang, official technical or legal terms, and euphemisms (such as *relations* to reference sexual intercourse or *wife* to refer to a spouse while respecting naming taboos). For outside audiences, center organizers used high-register Hindi words to describe the issues clients faced as *pira*, suffering, or *krurta*, cruelty. Clients described specific instantiations of what could be labeled violence: beating or slaps; verbal insults and quarrels; withheld financial and material support. When clients described such experiences in the abstract, they used a common Hindi word, *pareshani*—trouble, suffering, or confusion—describing themselves using the adjective *pareshan*. Counselors, in turn, used this as an umbrella category in their case notes.

Pareshani does not translate straightforwardly to "violence." Counselors themselves translated it as "harassment"; in English language materials that they produced, such as the chart of settled cases they kept behind their desk, they grouped cases by categories like "harassment by in-laws" and "harassment by husband."[8] *Pareshan* describes the interior state of the victim; it leaves unstated the relational sources of that interior state. It also lacks the moral-ethical valences of the English violence or Hindi *himsa*. In everyday speech, people used *pareshan* to describe everyday annoyances, such as biting mosquitos, as well as more serious issues. "Don't bother me," *mujhe pareshan mat karo*, I often heard clients distractedly say if their children demanded their attention too frequently during sessions. The English word *violence*, by comparison, from its earliest etymologies, captures a sense of being violated by another. The word draws our attention to the source of the harm and the fact that it crosses some boundary of what is acceptable.[9]

If labeling harmful actions as violent is a central interactive goal, this widespread use of labels like *pareshan* seems to demand intervention, precisely because it could be read as normalizing women's experiences of violence as not particularly significant. From a labeling violence perspective, people exert control on the world—and enact their political goals—by correctly diagnosing and labeling phenomena. Precise labels like violence give women the ability to connect phenomena together or distinguish between them, to source resources and political capital, and to stake a claim for their rights. From this perspective, a label like *pareshan* seems like a euphemism that disempowers women by diminishing the severity of the violence they experience, suggesting that being harmed by one's kin is more like a passing inconvenience rather than an injustice—a swarm of mosquitos that can be batted away.

From the perspective of careful speech, however, *pareshan*'s euphemistic qualities are powerful. Rather than focusing on how language labels context and the interior truths of speakers, careful speech focuses on how language constitutes context, regardless of the interior truths of speakers. Recall the idiom that Indu shared with me from her group texts: "Words are under your control until you speak them. Once you speak them, you are under their control." These ideas about speech and institutional interaction led counselors to avoid directly labeling behaviors and relations with diagnostic or evaluative language. Such language risks narrowing the anticipatory structures available to clients. For counselors, who work in legally, medically, and familially plural spaces, labels held the potential to narrow the possible horizons of a case, driving it into a legal setting, for example, and taking away the possibility of diverse forms of familial care—or, conversely, returning a case to the family that might benefit from legal intervention. The counseling process shaped these anticipatory structures, as well as being shaped by them. Maintaining these multiple anticipatory structures took enormous care. Through strategies of careful speech, counselors sustained these anticipatory structures so that clients could move across them as needed, sustaining their generative agency to act on and through their kin relations. For example, counselors simultaneously promise clients protection from disruptive legal interventions while using the threat of legal intervention to discipline unruly family members to cooperate with the process.

Maybe the issues will eventually provoke a divorce, but maybe they can be brushed away like a nagging child. Perhaps these issues will cause a rupture, but perhaps they can be remembered as a petty matter (*choti-moti bat*), something that, in Veena Das's language, can "be folded into ongoing relationships" (2007, 8), raising questions of how those relationships, in turn, can bear the weight of memories and experiences of harm. Counselors suggested that counseling transforms women's lives because, done well, it can lead female clients who have not often been asked for their opinions to draw their own conclusions about what paths to follow. Because this process takes time and conversation, both counselors and clients took care not to foreclose any potential outcomes with careless language, with labels that might come to control them.

Because *seva* manifests on a wide variety of material grounds, counselors had wide-ranging conversations about household life with clients. Far from limiting their understanding of what constituted harm and neglect, their perspective called a wider range of household behaviors into question. Most often, counselors pursued these questions by exploring how resources were allocated in the household, and clients discussed their household problems in those terms: "He does not give me money for expenses [*kharch*]," clients explained to counselors. "He sold my jewelry." "They ask for more dowry." Defensive in-laws often countered women's claims of abuse by listing the many concrete ways they had cared for their daughters-in-law, listing foods they had fed her, trips they had taken as a family, instances of illness when they looked after her. For counselors and clients alike, signs of broken relations were legible not only in bruises but also in empty pockets and hungry bellies.

For example, middle-aged Shruti was brought to Source of Strength by her sister, who was concerned about her health. Like a small but significant minority of cases at Source of Strength, Shruti was experiencing problems not with her in-laws but with her grown son and daughter-in-law, with whom she lived. She was dressed unlike any woman of her age and social class that I had seen in Jaipur, wearing loose men's cargo shorts that ended mid-calf, revealing swollen shins covered by brown-purple blotches. I thought they were bruises, but Shruti's sister went on to explain that they were a complication of Shruti's diabetes, a situation her sister blamed on her grown son and daughter-in-law, who weren't looking after Shruti properly.

Shruti's son and daughter-in-law had brought her to Jaipur to stay with them. Unfamiliar with the city, Shruti was trapped at home, dependent on her children—her daughter-in-law in particular—for everything. But her daughter-in-law was not supportive; in fact, Shruti said, she even threatened that if Shruti kept requesting her support, she'd lodge a court case against her, using one of the laws designed to protect women from abuse within the household. Shruti's sister was upset not only because of her sister's poor health, but also because of what she perceived to be a breakdown in the chain of *seva* meant to bind kin across generations. In visceral detail, she described the caring labor (*seva*) that Shruti had performed for *her* mother-in-law, how she took care of her when she was sick and she couldn't feed herself anymore, how she washed her without complaining. "Nowadays," she asked rhetorically, "what do our daughters-in-law do for us?" (*ajkal, hamari bahu hamare sath kya karen?*). For Shruti and her sister, as for the counselors at Source of Strength, those purple sores might as well have been bruises. In addition to being a diagnostic sign of uncontrolled diabetes, they indicated neglect of the needs of Shruti's aging body. Such neglect was a failure to reciprocate the care to which Shruti was entitled, given the care she had provided to others.

On the other hand, counselors often turned women facing what appeared to be life-threatening violence to other institutional sites. For example, Preeti, a working-class woman in her early thirties, was sent to Source of Strength by her lawyer. Her hand was loosely bandaged. She explained to Hema, the senior staff counselor, that her husband cut her palm with a knife and broke her wrist in the course of a struggle, miming her husband holding a blade to her throat while she attempted to protect her neck with her hand. He had been trying, she explained, to pimp her out to his friends. Hema looked at her hand and breathed in sharply, a gasp of sympathy. Preeti told her all she wanted was a divorce. Hema told her that she needed to go directly to the police and lodge a criminal case and begin divorce proceedings, a service that Source of Strength did not provide. "We *connect* families here," she said multiple times, "we try to join them together" (*jorne ki koshish karte hai*). Restored relations, however, were not an appropriate solution to Preeti's conflict. Preeti was frustrated, asking Hema angrily what exactly Source of Strength did if they didn't help people like her. Hema did not merely send Preeti away, however. Instead, she coached her on what to say at the police station, feeding her terms like *marpit*, beating, a label that Preeti herself hadn't used when she described what her husband did to her, as a way to cue the police to begin a First Incident Report. She also strategized with Preeti about which station to visit, based on what Hema knew about where sympathetic officers were posted. She would later call the station to let them know Preeti was on her way. As Preeti left, Hema half-heartedly offered to register a counseling case for her, if she was interested in reconciling with her husband, but Preeti shook her head and said that she was only interested in a divorce.

Hema was moved by Preeti's story; although I witnessed their exchange, she explained it to me again once Preeti left. Preeti needed the direct help of the police, she told me—she needed a criminal case report, and a restraining order against her husband. Hema told the story two more times that day— first to a member of the office staff, and then again to Indu, both of whom also responded with shock and dismay. As Hema's reaction makes clear, the staff at Source of Strength were under no illusions about the fact of violence in Preeti's home: in fact, they were outraged. But her needs extended beyond Source of Strength's main institutional goals, which centered on working to reconcile families, or, in cases where such reconciliation was impossible, to help family members separate without involving the state in the form of courts and police. In Hema's eyes, Preeti's needs demanded an immediate state institutional response, not the careful, minute, repetitive framing and reframing of claims of care and neglect that took place over the course of a typical counseling case. The violence in Preeti's home exceeded the limits of care that counseling was designed to fix.

Fixing Kinship by Reordering Interdependence

As Preeti's case suggests, counselors saw their job not as labeling violence but locating it within a larger constellation of care, coercion, and neglect in households, in order to fix kinship. Counselors encouraged clients to draw on strategies of careful speech to both correct and stabilize their interdependent relations with kin. This meant, in some cases, deepening relations of interdependence. But at the same time, counselors also used careful speech to condemn behavior that was violent or harmful. By drawing out various family members' actions toward one another, both in narrative form as well as in the counseling office itself, counselors attempted to fix those limits by educating family members about why their efforts to order the home through caring practices might be experienced as harmful, or, alternately, why what they thought was disorder might in fact be *seva*.

These dynamics emerged clearly as Hema and Indu worked with Anju Sharma and her sister-in-law, Pratima. Anju's parents had approached Source of Strength. Anju's phone calls home had become brief and she seemed unwell; they worried someone in her husband's household was hurting her. Indeed, Anju's case involved clear evidence that she was experiencing what activists around the globe would label as physical violence. Her mental distress was legible not only to her parents but to counselors and to her husband and his family. She had bruises on her forearms; she was too thin; when she came to the center to meet with counselors, she appeared terrified. Yet Hema and Indu did not seek to label Anju's experience as violence. Rather, they sought to expand the terms through which Anju and her kin understood their dependence on each other. Anju's case illustrates how counselors understood careful speech to act on relations disordered by harm and neglect.

After Anju's parents contacted Source of Strength to evaluate what was taking place in the Sharma household, Hema contacted Anju's in-laws, the Sharmas, to assess what (and who) was harming Anju, and how Anju herself fit within the broader constellation of relationships in the joint family. Yet even in the opening meetings of Anju's case, counselors debated not violence but appropriate forms of household care, as they convinced Anju's in-laws that counseling was a worthwhile intervention into their household life, using the promise of a restored balance of *seva* as a way to convince the Sharmas to return with Anju for counseling.

From the start of the case, counselors worked toward exploring the limits of care and harm in the household. Yet while this work was diagnostic, seeking different sources of disorder, counselors pushed the Sharmas to focus on sources that they could act upon and transform, highlighting their duties and responsibilities rather than labels for what was taking place at home. The mere fact that the Sharmas cooperated with Source of Strength suggested that they, too, perceived their household life to be disordered. Hema and Indu initially met with Anju's father-in-law; her husband, the Sharma's youngest son; and her husband's brother's wife, her *jethani*, Pratima. Hema told them that Anju's parents had visited the center from their home in a neighboring state because they felt "uneasy" about how Anju was being treated in her marital household. While neither counselor had met Anju yet, they explained to the Sharmas that, based on their conversation with her parents and their attempts to speak with Anju on the phone, they believed her to be experiencing a great deal of fear because of how the Sharmas treated her.

All three Sharmas reacted defensively to Hema's suggestion that any disorder was rooted in their relationships with Anju, insisting that they adequately cared for her. Anju was weak and frightful by nature, they suggested, and her personality was disordering relations in the household. Neither Hema nor Indu argued with this assessment. Instead, Hema suggested they take advantage of Source of Strength to help allay Anju's parents' concerns. Skirting the question of what had taken place, she added, "At home, there should be a healthy atmosphere" (*healthy atmosphere hona chahiye*). Bringing Anju to Source of Strength would "improve the atmosphere" (*mahaul accha banega*) and help reorder family life. But in order to do so, Hema went on, she needed to talk to Anju herself.

Ultimately, the Sharmas agreed to return with Anju. As they began to leave, Hema addressed one of the explanations the Sharmas had offered for Anju's struggles: that Anju and her family were from another northern Indian state, and she was unfamiliar with local norms of interaction. Yet as she did so, she was careful to avoid labeling behaviors or personalities, gently using the Sharma's sense of identity to underscore their obligations to care for Anju rather than to assign blame. "I understand that you think this is about 'culture,' that you think, '*we* people are Rajasthani.'"

Anju's *sasur* (father-in-law) nodded and added, "*seva puja hai, hamari*"— for *us, seva* is worship.

Neither Hema nor Indu contradicted him. But Indu added, in a firm voice, "The responsibility for every member of your family is on *your* shoulders" (*ghar ke har sadasya ki zimmedari hai apke upar*). Rather than diagnosing disorder as a result of irreconcilable regional differences or fixed personality features, Indu and Hema elicited Anju's *sasur*'s ideas about what he valued and folded those values back toward supporting his kin. Rather than affirming Anju's *sasur*'s suggestion that Anju was failing to play her role, she reminded him of *his* responsibility to care for *her*, and to all the household's members, as the head of the family. Anju filled multiple roles in the household. As a junior family member, she was expected to care for and respect her elders. Yet as someone who was hierarchically junior, she was also entitled to protection and support. Indu reframed Anju's role within the household, suggesting Anju was deserving of *seva* as one of a collection of dependents within the family. In so doing, she set the stage to potentially locate the problem of violence in Anju's household as a problem of neglect, of unbalanced *seva*.

This process of locating violence in relations of disordered interdependence continued when Anju returned with her husband and sister-in-law, several days later. Anju's husband had suggested that one obvious source of tension in the household was the conflict-ridden relationship between Anju and Pratima who, as Anju's elder sister-in-law, was also an affine in the Sharma household but hierarchically senior to Anju, as well as older than her.

The men of the family lounged on their two-wheelers in the lane while Anju and Pratima sat in the counseling office. When they disembarked from the family's motor scooters, both had the ends of their saris pulled down over their faces; in the Sharma family, we were to understand, women practiced *ghunghat*, or veiling, before senior male kin as a sign of respect. As soon as Anju, Pratima, Hema, Indu, and I were alone in the office, however, Pratima relaxed forward in her chair, propping her elbows on Hema's desk and pushing her sari back as she began chatting about their family life. Like most clients, she kept her sari draped casually over her shoulders. Anju, on the other hand, kept her sari pulled almost exaggeratedly low over her face as she sat, ramrod straight on the edge of her chair, shrinking into herself, eyes straight ahead. She was extremely thin. She was distressed about being called in for counseling, and Hema reassured her by emphasizing the lack of labeling in the counseling process: "We're a family counseling center, we didn't call you here to tell you that you're wrong [*galat*]."

Throughout their conversation with Anju and Pratima, Hema and Indu were carefully nonconfrontational. They used the counseling process to simultaneously explore how Pratima failed to be someone on whom Anju could depend, and to coach the two women in how to better act on and through household hierarchies. In particular, they attempted to soften the sharp hierarchical distinctions that Pratima drew between herself and Anju. By engaging Pratima and Anju in extended conversations about everyday household life, Hema and Indu created an interactional space where they could observe Pratima's attempts to care for Anju, and Anju's responses, in real time. Yet in labeling the harm they observed, they would draw not on "violence" as an abstract category, but on embodied kin relations, and the potential they held for Anju and Pratima to change their relations with each other and with other kin.

According to Pratima, Anju was causing disorder. She was weak and unable to fully participate in household labor, making her seem lazy. Pratima worked hard to get counselors to ratify her version of what was going wrong by claiming her own actions as *seva*. Anju, on the other hand, remained mostly silent during the counseling session with Pratima, nervously twisting a handkerchief in her lap. Pratima tried to explain to Hema and Indu that she was not the source of the household disorder that had harmed Anju, framing her interactions with Anju in terms of *seva*. "We have taken such good care of her" (*iska itna dhyan rakha*), she asserted. She gave the counselors examples of how she had cared for Anju by teaching her. "She [Anju] puts safety pins in her sari [to hold it up] here and here," she said, pointing at the pleated folds of synthetic fabric at Anju's shoulders and waist. "I also put pins in my sari. I *showed* her where to put those pins." Pratima had tried to help Anju learn to better wear wifeliness as she went from donning the simple tunic and pants of a *salwar* suit as an unmarried girl to the complicated draping involved in wearing a sari, as married women do in many Jaipuri families.

In so doing, Pratima suggested, as did many family members of clients at Source of Strength, she had worked hard to incorporate Anju into the household in an orderly and caring manner. In fact, Pratima went on to suggest, it was Anju who disordered the household by emphasizing her difference from the rest of the family. Pratima accused Anju of lying to her parents about the jewelry her in-laws had given her at her wedding. Appallingly, according to Pratima, Anju had speculated to her parents that her mangal sutra, a necklace symbolizing a woman's marriage, was fake instead of real gold. Given the material and symbolic importance of gold in marriage exchanges, such a claim—an insult, really—would suggest that the Sharmas could not appropriately or honorably support Anju, or that they did not think her or her family to be worthy of real care.

"But of course it's gold!" Pratima said, reaching down into Anju's sari, pulling out the long chain of Anju's necklace and vigorously shaking it at the counselors. As she did so, she yanked Anju forward by the neck, seemingly without noticing. Pratima had moved seamlessly from defending her interactions with Anju as *seva*, demonstrating her caring actions by pointing to folds in Anju's sari, to directly and roughly handling Anju. Her movements were abrupt, harsh. Both Hema and Indu registered a split second of dismay, but in the moment, neither counselor responded.

Instead, Hema redirected Pratima, reminding her how challenging it was to assimilate to one's marital family (*sasural*). She reminded Pratima not to react to Anju's efforts to adjust with so much anger, emphasizing the limits of appropriate emotional expression. "It's a matter of getting angry," she said. "There should be a limit to anger" (*gusse karne vali bat hai. gusse ka maryada hona chahiye*). Pratima repeated Hema's words in agreement, chatting on about details of household economy and chores.

Anju, on the other hand, remained silent for a long time. When she did finally speak, none of us could hear her as she bent forward, mumbling into her sari. Taking a moment to re-emphasize the appropriate limits of caring hierarchy, Hema reframed Pratima as a caring model for behavior:

> Sit up straight—there ought to be confidence in your heart [*man me confidence hona chahiye*]. Pull your chair closer, like *didi* [elder sister]. *Jethani* and *devrani* [elder sister-in-law and younger sister-in-law] should be like sisters to one another. [*jethani devrani bahan jaisi honi chahiye*]

Hema was coaching Anju in how to engage with the counseling process and with female intimates as a junior wife. At the same time, she used her instructions to model how Pratima might effectively instruct Anju by example. As she did so, she reframed the nature of their relationship by addressing Pratima with the term *didi* rather than the affinal label *jethani*. *Jethani* and *devrani* are terms for the wives of younger and elder brothers. They are hierarchical labels, encoding both differences in seniority between brothers as well as affinal relationship (the kinship terms for a brother's wife [*bhabhi*] and for a husband's sister [*nanad*], which, along with husband's brothers' wives, are all "sister-in-law" in English, are distinct in Hindi). *Didi* is still hierarchical—it refers to an elder sister—but is an intimate, respectful form of address suggesting that Anju and Pratima are "like sisters"; people use the term to respectfully yet intimately address non family members. Hema underscores her point by explicitly refiguring the women as sisters (*bahan*). In doing so, she also reframes Pratima's behavior as a model for Anju to emulate.

As they displaced the tensions between Anju and Pratima away from the hierarchical differences between *jethani* and *devrani*, Indu and Hema were able to introduce the question of how "cultural" difference could be bridged through careful speech. Hema listed some differences between family practices in Rajasthan and family practices in the part of the country that Anju had grown up in—differences in how people show respect to family members, and differences in the timing and materials of gift exchanges between families, particularly in terms of jewelry. But, importantly, many of these differences were encoded in speaking styles.

"Rajasthani people are straightforward," Hema said. "Their language is like that. . . . The problem is that Anju's ways of being in the world [*sanskar*] are from [her home state] and your ways of being in the world are from Rajasthan. It's a way of speaking [*bolna*] that's different. Maybe that's part of the problem." Hema was suggesting that what appeared to be normal interactional patterns to Pratima—what she might conceive of as marking *seva*—might be experienced by Anju as neglectful or coercive. But unlike the hierarchical difference inherent in a *jethani-devrani* relationship, this form of difference could be properly managed. Because this was a problem of communication, it could be managed via careful speech as Anju adjusted to her new household. Hema and Indu suggested that this responsibility, to care for Anju by helping her cope with her new Rajasthani life, was on Pratima's shoulders.

Indu drew on asking-and-giving to make her point, with the paired verbs learn and teach, *sikhna/sikhaana*. "You've learned well [how to be a member of the Sharma household]," Indu told Pratima. "Now teach her."

Pratima was clearly upset by the implied accusation of neglect. She shot back, "I have taught her. I've done so much teaching."

Hema responded by reminding her of Anju's mysterious bruises, suggesting that some of Pratima's "teaching" might constitute harmful, disorderly control.

Pratima replied, "I don't know about the marks [*nishan*]."

Hema turned and asked Anju where her bruises had come from, but none of us could hear her reply. Indu scolded her, telling her to straighten her sari away from her face "so we can talk properly." Anju did so, but Pratima talked over her, grabbing one of Anju's arms. She gave it a hard shake.

"Like this," she said. "Maybe someone made a mark like this."

"But who made those bruises?" Hema asked again.

"People get bruises like that all the time," Pratima replied.

Anju silently raised her arms to show Hema and Indu the bruises.

Pratima continued to insist on the caring nature of her interactions with Anju: "We have cared for her in all ways," she said, adding, "We give her food and clothes!" As she listed some specific items Anju had been given, Anju began to cry silently.

"Why are you crying?" Indu asked.

Anju sobbed harder, shaking, and Hema reassured her: "Don't be afraid. . . . This is your sister, you have to say to her, 'I don't like this thing.'"

As Anju continued to cry, Pratima delivered a series of retorts about Anju's fear and congenital weakness. She grabbed Anju's head, forcing it backward to expose her neck to the counselors, illustrating some point in her argument that Anju was weak.

Indu snapped, "Even in front of us you do this? It doesn't seem good [*acchi nahi lagti*]." Indu indicated a gap with her hands, palms flat and facing upward, one at chin level and one below her chest. "You think, 'I am the *jethani*,'" she said, raising the upper hand farther up, "'and you are the *devrani*,'" moving the lower hand farther down. "This isn't good."

By asking, "Even in front of us you do this?" Indu suggested that Pratima's overt aggression in a formal institutional space spoke volumes about what her behavior toward dependents must be like in the household, when no one was watching. Indu was making explicit what she and Hema had been hinting at as they spoke about Anju and Pratima as "sisters" and as they emphasized Pratima's responsibility to teach Anju. Through her attempts to care for Anju as a dependent, Pratima harmed Anju with her exaggerated sense of seniority. But the problem, for Hema and Indu, was not that such hierarchical difference was present. They did not work to separate Anju and Pratima, nor did they suggest creating a model of household life in which all family members were treated as independent, autonomous equals. They did not dispute the idea that Pratima's responsibilities included disciplining Anju into the family, nor that part of that process involved teaching her how to appropriately occupy household hierarchies. They did not rely on a labeling violence approach to diagnose Pratima's actions as violent. Instead, at this critical moment, Indu focused on how to evaluate and reframe the relationship between the two women via careful speech. What they labeled—in creative, dynamic turns—were kin relations. "This is your sister," Hema had said in order to prompt Anju to speak. "You think, I am the *jethani*," Indu had said, adding gestures that underscored the fact that the meaning of *jethani* was itself fluid, shifting, and dependent on Pratima's behavior. The key diagnostic action here was not to label the presence of violence, but to locate that violence by fixing kin relations.

On the surface, Indu's verbalization of what Pratima might be thinking about her relationship with Anju—"I am the *jethani* and you are the *devrani*"—was accurate. Anju and Pratima could no more change this feature of their relationship than Anju's husband could change his place in the birth order of his brothers. But to better order the household, *jethani* and *devrani* alike had to see the hierarchical difference between them as something that connected rather than divided—as something that made them "sisters." Yet this version of siblingship, borrowing from sisterhood to make sense of marital ties, offered Anju the space to make claims on her family members, to "have confidence in her heart."

Careful speech enabled counselors to brainstorm ways for Anju to exert generative agency while condemning Pratima's behavior as a failure of kinship. By framing her requests for support as efforts to order household difference, Anju could act on the household and transform her position within it. To do so, she would need to learn the tools of careful speech most appropriate to her Rajasthani in-laws.

The topic of household interaction arose again when Anju returned once more with her husband for a follow-up session. Taking up a theme from their session with Anju and Pratima, Hema and Indu discussed the importance of direct, or "straight," speech (*sidhe bolna*). "Speaking straight" has a sense of clear communication, speaking to the point without detours or obfuscations.[10]

Straight speech would help Anju better incorporate herself into the circula-
tions of asking-and-giving in the household.[11] Hema and Indu told her that
because she was so withdrawn and so shy, she might not always fully understand what was happening in household interactions. They encouraged her
to use the ideology of asking-and-giving to help integrate herself into the
household—the more she interacted, the more comfortable she would feel.

Hema drew on ideas of how careful speech ordered the home to model
some straight speech for Anju. "If you have free time, ask, What do you want
to eat today? Or ask, Why are you angry [if someone seems angry]?" She then
turned to Anju's husband and told him, "Counseling is absolutely necessary
for Anju," to help her learn these techniques.

Indu addressed the receiving end of asking-and-giving, suggesting that
Anju look at people as she interacted with them in order to fully understand
what was happening: "Maybe they are not angry [*naraz*] but are teasing you
instead [*mazak urate hai*]!" Without fully immersing herself in the interaction, Anju couldn't know for sure.

Indu and Hema used their own interactions with Anju as teachable
moments, instructing her in how to speak properly: they told her to pull her
pallu, the end of her sari kept draped over her face in public, away from her
face as she spoke to them; they told her to speak more loudly; they asked
her to give them eye contact and reacted with delight when she did so. Indu
told her several times, "If you learn to speak straight, all your problems will
be solved" (*sidhe bolna sikhe, sare problem solve ho jae*). By materializing
their requests to "speak straight," literally removing physical impediments to
communication, Hema and Indu lay the ground for a more open exchange
of asking-and-giving.

Pratima's overt physical handling of Anju was unusual; it was the only
time I saw a family member aggressively touch a client during a counseling
session, although verbal aggression was more common. However, the advice
Indu and Hema gave about care, and their efforts to reorder household interdependencies through careful speech, were consistent with what they did in
many other counseling cases. Hema and Indu took seriously Anju's bruises
and Pratima's yanks and shoves. But they understood those bruises to represent a larger disordered household "atmosphere" in which family members
were not fully supporting one another. By identifying how, precisely, different family members' efforts to engage interdependent relations exceeded
the limits of *seva*, they hoped to solve the problems that left Anju bruised,
weak, and frightened. They located Anju's bruises in a broader landscape

of unfulfilled relations of interdependence. They offered alternative models of interdependent kin relationships through which hierarchy might order rather than disorder, support rather than harm.

Conclusion

After conversing with various family members, the Source of Strength counselors persuaded the Sharmas to allow Anju to visit her parents and to keep a mobile phone her parents gifted her. A few weeks after this meeting, Anju returned with her husband. Hema and Indu were pleased to see her smile and speak audibly, although she still appeared thin and her body language remained hesitant. They took these changes as signs that Anju's household situation was slowly improving. Yet they also, offstage, vented to each other, to the organizers helping manage the case, and to me, about how much work had gone into just these few incremental changes for Anju. Strategies of careful speech were painstaking, frustrating, and carried uncertain outcomes.

Although Anju's case clearly featured what many outside observers would call domestic violence, counselors drew on careful speech rather than labeling violence as an interactive strategy. As they did so, they focused on exploring, and then fixing, the limits of appropriate *seva* and harmful neglect and coercive violence. As I have argued, these strategies did not reflect a refusal to take violence seriously. Nor did they reflect a different definition of violence. Instead, these strategies reflected differing ideas about the role of spoken interaction in addressing domestic violence. Women's rights movements around the world focus on the political importance of labeling violence, a project that mobilizes shared, unspoken language ideologies that define language's function as labeling items in the world and revealing interior truths. Careful speech, however, reflects an understanding of language's primary function as constituting, rather than merely labeling, the social world. As a result, speakers take care with labels, attentive to the possibility that such labels may foreclose, rather than open, pathways out of violent situations. For activists, the act of labeling empowers and creates better futures. For counselors, labeling disempowers and limits the possibility of positive change. For counselors, careful speech preserves the promise of a better family. For activists, such neutrality suggests a refusal to recognize injustice and gender inequality.

As strategies, labeling violence and careful speech frame agency as arising from speech, meaning, and relations in profoundly different, even contradictory, terms. Yet they continue to coexist at counseling centers, and the contradictions between them have not yet undermined the promise that many northern Indian women's rights organizers see in counseling and mediation as a practice to address violence. Why? One answer may be the difficulty of articulating the differences between these approaches *as language ideologies*, rather than differing definitions of violence or differing levels of sensitization to women's rights concepts. Many of the language ideologies that shape people's perspectives on their social worlds are difficult to externalize and articulate, or seem so obvious as to need no further elaboration. While concerns about meanings, definitions, and translation are at the heart of transnational women's rights activism, questions about language ideologies are rarely discussed and difficult to fit into existing models of education, sensitization, and training, all of which share with labeling violence a focus on language's labeling functions.

What do these differing language ideologies mean, for understanding counseling practices, for conceptualizing anti-violence efforts across scales of local and global, and for understanding how kinship and relationality intersect with concepts of rights? It is to these questions that the conclusion of this book turns.

Conclusion: Toward a
Politics of Interdependence

[Mother] had shown me a bird in the sky who was trying
so hard to fly in one place. . . . The whole sky was the
bird's. But what use was it? What use was an empty
endless sky?

       —Geetanjali Shree, *Mai* [trans. Nita Kumar]

Feminism is both caught and freeing.
       —Clare Hemmings, *Why Stories Matter*

Counselors help clients navigate dilemmas of interdependence that arise within the conflicting demands women face as they regenerate relations with kin. In doing so, they must confront the simultaneous pressures to both sustain and transform Indian families in the service of supporting women. Counselors theorize agency as generative, modeling for their clients a mode of social action that arises within, rather than against, the crosscutting ties of interdependence that constitute family life. Such an approach is compelling because it acknowledges and accommodates the significant commitment many people in Jaipur have to living out their futures within interdependent relations with kin, while at the same time opening such relations to the possibility of transformation. Counselors approach household violence as a form of harm that involves many components beyond husbands and wives, contextualizing harm and neglect alike within kin networks that involve crosscutting relationships of authority and interdependence. As they do so, they reinforce widespread expectations about joint families as patrilineal, and even patriarchal, structures. But at the same time, they underscore that, as

Ruha Benjamin writes, "all kinship, in the end, is imaginary. Not faux, false, or inferior, but . . . a creative process of fashioning care and reciprocity" (Benjamin 2018, 64).

This approach to agency, kinship, and relatedness shapes the interactive practices counselors deploy to support their clients. From afar, these practices appear to prioritize reconciling women to their families over helping women recognize and access their rights as individuals. However, in this book I show that what differs is not counselors' definition of household violence, nor their belief that violence represents a serious moral and material problem. Instead, what differs is their understanding of how spoken interaction acts on household violence and conflict—an understanding that, in turn, draws upon their approach to how interaction references and reproduces interdependent relations. While organizers and activists in Jaipur, as around the world, centered labeling violence as an interactive practice, counselors sought to order interdependent relations by focusing on careful speech. Careful speech simultaneously opens up kinship systems to generative agency while strategically reinforcing expectations of reciprocity, obligation, and submission that assume unequal gender relations. Such strategies suggest that the extraordinary resilience of patriarchal family norms in northern India—and indeed, elsewhere—may result not only from investments in tradition but, paradoxically, from efforts to open such norms to the possibility of change within a sociohistorical context that is profoundly ambivalent about acknowledging interdependence. At the same time, again paradoxically, these strategies show that such norms can offer tools to imagine more sustaining futures. As counselors and their clients grapple with dilemmas of interdependence, they reveal that we need multiple models of how to be in relation with others, not fewer.

These findings suggest that anthropologists and other social scientists investigating women's rights organizations must pay close attention to the politics and practices of talk that animate those organizations. Far from "mere" talk, these practices play a constitutive role in the activities of moral imagination at the heart of social change, connecting what happens within the institution to interpretive frameworks that extend far beyond the institution's walls. At the same time, these findings suggest that anthropologists of kinship and relatedness need to attend closely to how women's rights discourse, particularly around intimate violence, facilitates debates and contestations over the politics of interdependence. And finally, these findings indicate that scholars of women's rights more broadly ought to take kinship and relatedness seriously—not as sources of hallowed tradition, nor as dangerous spaces of harm, but as sources of generative possibility. Precisely because of its awkward relationship to these narratives of progress, kinship offers a novel analytic space from which to explore questions of violence and intimacy. It offers a different angle of engagement with the dilemmas of interdependence that continue to call the liberal subject upon which mainstream global feminism relies into acute question.

To understand how counselors conceptualize speech and violence, it is necessary to examine how family and politics intertwine in terms both distinct to the history of northern India and shared across what Elizabeth Povinelli has called the "liberal diaspora" (2006, 80). Counselors work within social, legal, and familial contexts informed by histories, moral-ethical commitments, and ideologies that differ from those of women's rights workers in Boston, Paris, or even Mumbai. But to reduce an analysis of counselors' mediating work to a project of cultural comparison misses the potential of counseling and other frontline practices. It ignores the potential for Jaipuri counselors to offer arguments about rights, kinship, and gender justice on equal footing with normative pronouncements about women's rights issued by bodies like the United Nations.

Productive Misunderstandings: Connecting Labels and Careful Speech

When I have written and presented about Anju's case in other venues (Kowalski 2016), readers and listeners often want to know what happened. What was the resolution of the case? Ultimately, the resolution was deeply unsatisfying. Multiple ma'ams made asides to me, after the family left, about how much work—hours of counseling with staff, arranging meetings, and then meeting with ma'ams to "settle" the case—had gone into negotiating a visit with Anju's parents and the ability to use a phone. It was both something and also maybe nothing. Months later, when I was dividing my time between Source of Strength and other field sites, I walked by the central conference room to see Anju's parents waiting again. Her father held a new mobile phone in a box, gingerly between his hands, perched on his lap. He asked Hema to call Anju's in-laws, to see if they would let her have a new phone. The old one broke. There was a studied silence around this statement—Hindi distinguishes between "the phone was broken [by a person]" and "broke" as in "the phone broke," and he used the latter term. Yet it seemed unlikely that Anju's parents would travel all the way to Jaipur from another state just to replace a phone that fell apart. Hema said she would try to reach Anju's in-laws. She seemed skeptical. Anju's father, sitting in the conference room, holding that phone like a precious gift, like a lifeline that needed to be delicately threaded through current and potential conflicts, to sustain his daughter in an unknown sea of difficult relations, captured both the hope and profound inadequacy of counseling. I don't know if Anju ever got the new phone; I left the field not long after this. I don't know if her parents gave up on counseling and sought other interventions. I don't know if things ever got better, if Anju "adjusted," if she and her husband established their own household, if her parents-in-law grew too old to frighten her, if Pratima's behavior changed. Counselors don't know these things either. Every counselor and ma'am I spoke with had anecdotes about running into former clients, or clients returning, full of praise for the changes they had experienced. But also, sometimes clients or their kin reappeared because the phone broke, the drinking started again, the in-laws didn't fulfill their side of the agreement, the baby was a girl, there really was another woman.

Counseling and mediation practices are unsatisfying. They do not always satisfy clients. They do not satisfy the activists and organizers who run counseling centers. They do not satisfy scholars who see reconciliation as a refusal of gender equality. They do not satisfy counselors themselves, who frequently express the limited nature of what they are able to accomplish. As many of the examples in this book show, they often frustrate narrative conventions. And yet, counseling practices have only increased in prominence. By 2017, pilot programs in counseling in Jaipur had been expanded across the state, connected to women's police stations. A Google Alert set to pull references to family counseling on Indian websites reveals near weekly Hindi-language newspaper pieces touting the success of various counseling centers across northern India. These articles use counseling centers as sources for anecdotal data on causes of family conflict. "Mobile phones are a big reason marriages break up, due to interference from the *sasural* side," one headline reads from Jhansi.[1] "Counseling centers will open in nine locations to save broken marriages," reads another headline from Patna.[2] If counseling is so unsatisfying, to so many stakeholders, why do institutions keep offering it?

One reason why it is urgently necessary to explore how frontline workers deploy interactive practices under the guise of counseling is that "counseling," however defined, constitutes so many of the interactions that women have around the edges of official legal interventions into their families' lives. In

2010, counseling—relatively cheap to offer, amorphous in content and form, flexible in terms of expert ratifications—served almost as the caulk, molded to plug the many gaps in India's legal approaches to gender violence. Counselors in Jaipur deployed strategies of careful speech as they mediated across a range of scales and services: between individual women and a faceless state bureaucracy, between the ambitious goals of women's rights activists and the daily details of making a life through compromise with others, between transnationally oriented metrics targeting gender equality and local desires for reciprocal, supportive relations. Counseling and other interactive practices held this rickety structure together, even as they helped women avoid being harmed by its more unstable parts. Whether we see this as a potential source of promise or as a problem to be solved, it is vitally necessary to contextualize the interactive strategies such frontline workers use as they talk women through conflict and change.

Counseling is an effective tool for this task precisely because the murky role of interaction in women's rights NGOs facilitated a productive misunderstanding about how talk might address violence. Productive misunderstandings emerge in contexts where multiple approaches to addressing social challenges come together, generating plural medical systems, legal systems, and family systems. In a study of Tswana medical concepts, for example, Julie Livingston demonstrates that efforts to translate biomedical concepts into Tswana systems generate productive misunderstandings where practitioners and patients are able to weave these systems together because they do not fully acknowledge the substantial gaps between them (2007). Similarly, Jennifer Cole shows how Malagasy wives and their rural French husbands, through a "working mis/understanding," are able to sustain two distinct schemas of who counts as kin, even as they collaborate to sustain those kin relations (2014). Cole points out that this misunderstanding is both generated by and in turn reproduces the unequal social world within which these couples live out their marriages, where marriage migration itself is a product of inequalities between France and Madagascar, inequalities between rural France and its urban centers, and unequal treatment of citizens by the French state. As both Livingston and Cole demonstrate, even as such productive misunderstandings allow diverse actors to work together, they also reify the distinctions between the different perspectives that they bridge.

Transnational social movements, such as women's rights activism, are key sites for such productive misunderstandings (Watkins and Swidler 2013). Gender violence projects, in particular, generate plural approaches, with violence being variously framed as a medical, psychological, legal, socio-structural, and familial problem—each framing suggesting, in turn, a strategy for intervention (counseling women, educating citizens, offering legal aid, lobbying the state, teaching medical personnel to interpret injured bodies, reforming family dynamics and gender norms). In turn, such strategies may be internally plural—for example, legal approaches to violence may incorporate criminal law, civil law, alternate forms of dispute resolution, and institutional forms of restorative justice. In India, legislation dealing with household violence, marriage, and divorce appears in criminal law, civil law, and personal codes, which vary by religious community. These plural approaches to gender violence offer actors at various levels multiple anticipatory structures with which to frame their work—multiple goals to work toward and futures to imagine. These structures do not always align, even as actors, such as organizers and counselors, work closely together.

Because careful speech and labeling violence are both interactive strategies that address violence through speech, they generate a productive misunderstanding that enables counseling centers to pursue two contradictory goals: sustaining the good Indian family, on one hand, and transforming the family by extending women's rights as individuals and citizens, on the other. Language ideologies often operate behind reflective awareness: "labeling violence" and "careful speech" are my analytic labels for interactive activities that struck practitioners as common sense and obvious. Precisely because these ideologies operate in the background, they generate a productive misunderstanding about addressing violence that is central in sustaining women's rights organizations in Jaipur. For much of the everyday work of counseling, the productive misunderstanding between counselors and organizers about how interaction addressed violence allowed this contradiction to disappear from view, allowing counseling centers to sustain both an idealized version of the patriarchal family as well as an orientation toward rights-based approaches to violence, beneath a veneer of talking to clients. This productive misunderstanding enabled counselors to move between dependence as a marker of individual difference to be overcome and interdependence as a feature of relationships that are continually being generated through interaction.

This productive misunderstanding was heightened by the class-based hierarchies that structured women's rights organizations. Because counselors spent the bulk of their time counseling clients and triaging cases, they frequently relied on strategies of careful speech to reform household life. The organizers of counseling centers, on the other hand, stepped into counseling cases but also ran citywide workshops, wrote grant proposals, evaluated programs, and otherwise networked with the broader network of women's rights institutions in Jaipur and beyond. This work meant that they more frequently emphasized the power of naming violence as a social project. However, the shared focus on interaction—counseling, training, sensitizing—allows counseling practices to move forward via a productive misunderstanding, with each set of participants seeing themselves in a shared endeavor of talking through household harms in order to support vulnerable women and create social transformation. When differences between counselors and organizers do rise to the surface, they are often addressed by suggesting additional training or sensitization programming for counselors, in line with the referentialist language ideologies that labeling violence entails (if counselors are not using "violence" correctly, they must better learn and internalize the meaning of the term). Associated with powerful global and domestic narratives about gender inequality, labeling violence was the strategy that won out when the contradictions between these strategies rose to the surface. But in the regular working life of counseling centers, such differences were submerged within the amorphous label of "counseling."

One response to a misunderstanding is to resolve it so that both sides believe the same thing. But as scholars who have discussed productive misunderstandings demonstrate, such misunderstandings can be tremendously generative, "zones of awkward engagement, where words mean something different across a divide even as people agree to speak" (Tsing 2005, xi). *Samjhaana*—the explaining that counselors and family members described as a central tool in ordering family relations—is itself an acknowledgement of the power of the productive misunderstanding, the value of making the communication gap smaller, but not insisting that it fully close, of dwelling within dilemmas prompted by the competing obligations to others that we carry, in the face of desires for differing futures and complex evaluations of the past.

Toward a Politics of Interdependence

By attending to the language ideologies and interactive practices that animate counseling, the politics of counseling practices become visible. I follow Summerson Carr in treating politics as "the interplay between acts that make what is contingent seem natural and just, thereby excluding other possibilities for how things could be, and acts that demonstrate the contingency of what has been accepted as natural and just, thereby introducing alternative possibilities for how things could be" (Carr 2010b, 218). "Labeling violence" and "careful speech"—interactive strategies that overlap in practice—are both connected to wider social projects that highlight the contingency of seemingly natural and fixed phenomena: social order, gendered and generational inequality, patterns of interdependence and care. Yet both are caught in the interplay that Carr describes, seeking to create change by calling on elements of social life that are meant to be stable but are too often precarious and contingent: legal processes, in the case of labeling violence, and relatedness, in the case of careful speech. Brought together, each strategy highlights the contingency of the other.

Rather than treating counselors' arguments and actions as practices that have not yet been fully disciplined by human rights discourse, I take seriously the political claims they generate around interdependence, kinship, and rights. What contingencies do these interactive strategies bring into view, and what forms of precarity do they naturalize and take for granted? The claims that emerge in counseling work point the way toward a politics of interdependence: an approach to inequality, power, entitlement, and obligation that focuses not on rights-bearing subjects, but on interdependent relations, a politics both generated and concealed by a productive misunderstanding between labeling violence and careful speech. What would it mean to incorporate such a politics, one rooted in kinship systems, into our scholarly approaches to intimate violence and gender equality?

In a discussion of what she calls "precarious kinship" in Indian psychiatric interventions, Sarah Pinto asks, "How and in whom does the vulnerability of relations accumulate?" (2011, 381). The politics of interdependence at the heart of counseling engages this question, exploring how the obligations and sustenance of interdependent relations can be distributed more fairly across kin, so that the elder sister-in-law is more like a sister; so that elder male kin know that they, too, are responsible for *seva*; so that the "vulnerability of relations" is not born only by those with the least power and authority. Such a politics engages the precarious nature of kin relations—the ever-present possibility that the other will walk away, fail to reciprocate, or find themselves in circumstances that make support impossible—as both a risk and a tool. Where the liberal politics of mainstream women's rights discourse sees dilemmas of interdependence as situations to be either resolved or abandoned, counselors sought, through generative agency, to dwell within and reshape those dilemmas.

In recognizing that dilemmas of interdependence cannot be fully resolved, counselors echo scholarship that questions the heavy focus on individual choice and agency in liberal emancipatory politics (Abu-Lughod 2010; Borovoy and Ghodsee 2012; Kittay 2013; Mahmood 2005; Mol 2008; Tronto 2014). The dilemmas of interdependence counselors face are in no way limited to Indian families, but sit at the heart of liberal efforts toward social change. Mainstream global feminism has not figured out how to engage these dilemmas, let alone resolve them, often portraying women as caught between inappropriate and oppressive dependence on others and liberating independence.

In the epigraph that begins this conclusion, the narrator of Geetanjali Shree's novel *Mai* captures such dilemmas in the form of a bird, at once free in an open sky and caught, flapping in place. Told through the eyes of a daughter and son of an elite rural family, growing up in a well-to-do household and then leaving the village for education, *Mai* orbits around the main characters' desire to liberate their mother, *mai*, from the silence and servitude in which they perceive her to live. Yet as the novel unfolds, the meaning of Mai's silence is called into radical question—calling into question, in turn, the reliability of the novel's first-person narrator, who longs to insert Mai into a narrative of liberation from the household and its relations, even as those relations are what bring the narrator's very voice into being. Is what the bird experiences freedom, or emptiness? The voice of Shree's narrator blends, throughout the novel, with the voices of other kin, and so the reader does not know if the question—"What use was an empty endless sky?"—is the narrator's or her mother's or both (Shree 2017, 64). In her postscript, the novel's translator, Nita Kumar, suggests that the central tension of the novel is the effort of the narrator and her brother to "free" their mother from what they see as the repressive norms of rural, elite life. "It is the saving (*bachana*) of her," Kumar writes, "the pulling her out (*nikalna*) of the house, the whole business of reform. . . . [T]he novel has two foci: the mother, *mai*; and the saving of her, or creating of the not-mai. . . . Mai is—in the early narrator's voice—hollow, absence, nothing. Not-mai, or the saving of her, stands for fullness, for choice and personhood" (Kumar 2017, 184–85). As the novel unfolds, the narrator's sense of absence is revealed to result from the limits on her own perception. Yet the world of "choice and personhood" offers no language for her mother's modes of presence and action (leading Shree herself to create this language via evocative metaphors of curtains, empty rooms, ladders and pits, and birds in the sky). Kumar points out that this apparent binary tension between "nothing" and "fullness" runs through reform and activism targeting women in India, an ambivalent tension where *nikaalna* (*nikalna* in Kumar's transliteration) can mean both "pulling out" but also, as frequently used by counseling clients, "cast out," abandoned by kin.

In her analysis of how feminism tells its stories, Clare Hemmings describes Western feminism itself in a very similar position to the bird, "both caught and freeing" (2011, 2). In her book on theory, Hemmings draws our attention to how feminist theories get "caught" in categories and histories that may undermine their radical promise. Mainstream liberal women's rights activism is caught on a particular vision of the individual, one that is unsustainable not just for women like Hema, Indu, Gita, and the clients they serve, but for all of us. The opposite of "mai" cannot be "not-mai," because at the end of the day, the interdependent labor of caring for others is vitally necessary. A politics that insists on replacing relations with not-relations is a politics that cannot help us answer the question of how to distribute interdependency's vulnerabilities in terms that are meaningful, sustaining, and just, rather than unthinking, unequal, and lethal. To move beyond these individualizing models, it is necessary to engage in careful listening, even if what scholars and activists hear does not always match their own normative goals. Such listening, crucially, must move beyond tracking referential content, to the models of speech, care, and social action that interactions bring into being.

While women's rights activism portrays kinship as a constraining grid, many scholars critical of development discourse have pointed out that the linear model of social progress away from relations, toward an independent individualism that shakes off social ties, is itself an equally constraining grid—a train track where one can either chug into the future, slide back into the past, or get derailed. This model, too, holds the potential for structural violence and harm. Global women's rights discourse projects normative categories of personhood, social relations, and agency. As with other transnational development projects, rights discourse assumes a great deal about the value of agency as expressed through autonomous action and choice, connected to longstanding liberal arguments about the nature of rational individualism. Yet scholars have long pointed out that the individual autonomy assumed by human rights is elusive, even in places most understood to operate under its terms. Ethnographic examinations of care work, dementia, disability, chronic illness, and frayed medical systems in the United States and Europe have shown that autonomous individuality is a heavy burden indeed, unequally and incompletely achieved even in places where it is already assumed, and produced through relational practices that are quickly hidden from view (see Buch 2015; Thelen 2015). Keeping these insights in mind allows us to consider the rich understandings of interdependence that counselors deploy not as evidence of cultural alterity, or social evolution ("they can't do individualism yet") but instead as an alternate response to contradictions embedded in the very project of liberal personhood, contradictions that people face everywhere where rights and recognition are pegged to individual action, in spite of the fact that individuals only ever act within deeply social worlds.

Acknowledging interdependence has serious implications for how we conceptualize gender equality, as well as how we understand the complex intersections between violence and kinship. As Judith Butler has suggested, "equality cannot be reduced to a calculus that accords each abstract person the same value, since the equality of persons has now to be thought precisely in terms of social interdependency" (2020). The reality is that gender inequality is tangled in the material and moral labor of social reproduction: wiping noses, managing school fees, maintaining a public face that reflects a family's social status. Such labor is undervalued, if it is explicitly valued at all. Under a mode of capitalism that has weaponized individualism, it is extraordinarily difficult and perhaps impossible to sustain the interdependent relations necessary to reproduce persons, families, and social structures over time without exploiting either the unpaid labor of female kin, or the poorly paid labor of other, more socially marginal women. In these conditions, the family is asked to serve as a social unit that both sustains and conceals these interdependencies, enabling us to burst into the public sphere wearing fictive robes of independent individualism. This is the central dilemma of interdependence that confronts liberatory projects that seek to work toward gender inequality. Without addressing interdependence, we cannot fully address the violence such inequality relies upon and reproduces.

Indian family counseling practices alone will not and cannot solve these problems. It is difficult to look at the global histories of either the nuclear family or the multi-generational joint family and find in either a particularly liberatory or equalizing narrative. Women around the world need both legal rights and transformations in the politics of intimate life. What counseling practices reveal are the dilemmas that rights and legal approaches leave unnamable and thus unresolved, offering new articulations of the question with which counselor Indu began this book: "What's the way forward?" We need many models of relationality to think our ways through various forms

of Indu's question, some of which will pull us, awkwardly, away from progress narratives into questions of kin-based obligations and regeneration. The
politics of interdependence at the heart of counseling practices reflect the
reality that we all, across the life course, depend on others in overt and subtle
ways, to sustain bodies, cultivate voice, and generate meaningful senses of
personhood and action.

NOTES

Introduction

1. All individual and organizational names have been changed. Throughout the book, I also have adapted potentially identifying details for counselors and for their bosses. While the organizers of counseling centers were eager for their organizations to be identified by name, I have decided to follow anthropological practice and anonymize site and individual names, in order to protect the identities of the counseling center staff who are the focus of this book.

2. This book focuses on how labels like "violence" are used. Throughout, I use "gender violence" to refer to the categorization of certain harmful phenomena within transnational women's rights discourse, including scholarship, as "violence whose meaning depends on the gendered identities of the parties . . . the meaning of the violence depends on the gendered relationship in which it is embedded" (Merry 2009, 3). I use "household violence" and "domestic violence" as largely etic categories—categories of practice, though the line between emic and etic frequently blurs when studying women's rights organizations—to describe harm, conflict, and neglect that counselors, clients, ma'ams, and laypeople saw as violations of norms for healthy relationships at home. I discuss the many categories counselors and clients used for these harms throughout the book. Throughout this book, I have avoided the label "intimate partner violence," or IPV, which is frequently used in international comparative research on violence in intimate relationships. That is because, as this work shows, few of the people engaged in counseling saw such violence as contained within conjugal partnerships, even if the husband was a primary perpetrator. It is important to emphasize that I use these labels as heuristic, not diagnostic, in nature. Throughout this book, I am interested in how people define and problematize (Bacchi 2012) various forms of harm and neglect, not in adjudicating whether or not what people described was violence. As Veena Das writes, "instead of policing the definition of the term violence I hope that by engaging the very instability of this definition, I can show what is at stake in naming something as violence" (2008, 284).

3. Such theories address the perennial question of how to both acknowledge that all social actors are structured by the social orders in which they live, while also pursuing and explaining sources of social transformation. Such theories treat the relations between structure and agency as dialectic and dynamic, ever open to change as people deploy familiar categories in new settings and confront internal contradictions (see Bourdieu 1977; Ortner 2006; 2005; Sahlins 1981; Sewell 2005 for foundational elements of this debate).

4. Tsing uses the concept of contaminated diversity to draw our attention to how best to attend to the interdependence of people, species, and objects as they encounter and transform one another over time. She writes, "The evolution of our 'selves' is already polluted by histories

of encounter . . . worse yet, we are mixed up in the projects that do us the most harm. The diversity that allows us to enter collaborations emerges from histories of extermination, imperialism, and all the rest. Contamination makes diversity. . . . If categories are unstable, we must watch them emerge within encounters" (2015, 29).

5. A return visit in 2017 underscored the importance of my role as a student in shaping access to counselors in 2010. In 2017, I was an assistant professor, and was accompanied by a research assistant, Indu, who had worked as a counselor in 2010. As a result of this status, I was treated with more respect by the ma'ams. At the same time, however, the organizations where I interviewed counselors, and the counselors themselves, were a bit more reticent to allow me to observe working life. My sense was that my presence was read as more evaluatory—rather than educational—because of my different professional status. This shift reflects the hierarchies that shaped counseling centers as workplaces. As an unconnected and often awkward foreign student, it wasn't clear where I fit in that hierarchy. As a professor, with slick business cards and a PhD from an American university, I was much more similar to the ma'ams—a status that opened some doors and closed others.

6. In this book, I use quotation marks to capture dialogue that I noted live in my jottings during cases. I typically jotted down dialogue in Hindi, with larger contextual information in English; where I think the Hindi language terms may be of interest to others, I include them in parentheses.

7. In telling the story of the cases I observed, I rely on Laura Ahearn's "practice-based theory of meaning constraint" (Ahearn 2010, 56). Ahearn argues that ethnographers focus not on nailing down a definitive interpretation of an interactive event, but instead the range of possible meanings—and constraints on possible meanings—within that event: "we must shift our focus away from searching for definitive interpretations and instead concentrate on looking for information that constrains the type and number of meanings that might emerge from an [interactive] event" (56). In many ways, counselors' own interpretive strategies were very much aligned with a practice-based theory of meaning constraint. In a context where most family members avoid deploying names and even terms of kin-based address, narratives quickly spiraled into a flurry of third person pronouns with unclear antecedents. Sometimes, counselors could clarify for me, based on their more sophisticated read of the context. But sometimes they were also hazarding an interpretive guess. Was the wedding loan for a sister, or a close female cousin? Who was the "he" of the anecdote—a husband or father-in-law? Hema, Gita, and Indu were all quick to acknowledge that they also didn't always fully grasp the details clients threw into their stories of distress.

8. This approach raises complex questions about consent as it is distributed across institutional actors—questions that the highly individualizing consent templates of American IRB processes do not fully capture. I did my best to follow the ethical norms around privacy and consent that shaped counseling centers. In some cases, this meant that people assumed they could consent on behalf of others, and in other cases that they couldn't consent on their own behalf (similar dynamics were often at play within counseling cases themselves). I obtained consent from site leaders to observe, and obtained consent from counselors to interview them and to observe their work. Counselors at other sites often requested I obtain consent from their bosses before they consented to being interviewed; I complied. These requests reflect the hierarchical nature of these institutions, and the sense of distributed agency that informed counselors' work (see Hull 2012 for a similar account of agency distributed across individuals). As I write above, I remained highly sensitive to cues from counselors that I absent myself from the counseling office. I also frequently reminded the counselors and staff I knew best that I was researching

counseling, particularly around personal disclosures. I also changed names, and, in some cases, identifying information, such as neighborhood of residence or workplace, about counseling clients. All the cases I describe here are quite typical of counseling casework, making it difficult to identify individuals based on the stories I share.

9. In a follow-up trip to Jaipur in 2017, I learned that these debates had continued; in visiting prominent scholars of counseling and social work at the Tata Institute of Social Sciences, a nationally prominent school of social work in Mumbai, I learned that such debates are widespread across India, as people debate whether counseling is psychological or social work. By 2017, counseling had indeed been institutionalized, with counseling centers in every police district. But this meant that oversight had been shifted to a government ministry, and as political parties in power shifted, leadership became a resource distributed in patronage networks, meaning that highly experienced organizers often lost control of centers that they had helped found. See Roychowdhury (2016) for a discussion of how funding, ideological approach, and strategies for social change came together at similar marriage mediation centers in West Bengal.

10. This binary framing is also an effective way to frame domestic violence as a sign of social backwardness and connects women's rights activities to powerful global narratives about social progress. Such narratives frame human rights as a triumphal recognition of the sovereign individual subject, liberating her from the oppressive social structures of the past. The reconciliation/recognition binary connects this longstanding narrative to behaviors easily observed by researchers on short site visits. Are practitioners using labels like "violence" to condemn what is happening in client homes? Are they encouraging clients to condemn violence and understand themselves as autonomous subjects with legal rights (see Kowalski 2021)?

11. Much as a research focus on a future cure in the context of degenerative, chronic illness erases the caregiving labor of people who sustain and support the ill person in the present, an emphasis on ending gender inequality and violence in the future risks erasing the generative power of "relational labor" in the present (see Seaman 2018, 63).

12. Many critiques of mainstream women's rights movements take aim at precisely this model of personhood, noting its role in the continued domination of the postcolonial world by the West and the neoliberalization of social activism by enabling the takeover of once-radical feminist projects by the depoliticizing processes of NGOization (Abu-Lughod 2013; Bernal and Grewal 2014b; Hodgson 2011; A. Sharma 2008).

13. The ongoing debates about the shape, temporal trajectory, and persistence of the joint family offer a number of different definitions of what, precisely, counts as a "joint family." I follow Patricia Uberoi's definition in treating the joint family not just as a household structure "but . . . an ideology and code of conduct whereby the relations of husband and wife and parent and child are expected to be subordinated to larger collective identity" (2005, 378). This "code of conduct" is also one that the Indian state has relied upon as a means to deliver welfare and care for the vulnerable since independence (Majumdar 2007; Newbigin 2010; Uberoi 1996). The history of the study of the family in India is itself marked by attempts by Indian sociologists to seek within the joint family a source of national cultural unity, efforts that intensified after Independence, as researchers sought evidence to support hypotheses about kinship and development, ranging from the subdivision of arable land to the management of fertility. See Chapter 2.

14. I thank one of the anonymous reviewers of this manuscript for the framing of "practical and ideological" impediments to single living in India.

15. Indeed, when I arrived on a festival day to visit a counselor who had separated from her husband and was living with her child in a rented flat, a neighbor leaned over a balcony and

asked her a series of highly invasive questions about when the child's father would come, if he would come, and where he was. The counselor—unafraid to say what she thought—snapped back. "Do you have some important business with him? Why do you care where he is?" But the exchange appeared to put a heavy damper on her mood, as we drank tea and set off fireworks on her roof; after her child left to play with a toy I brought, she shared her exhaustion with this neighbor's constant questioning. Later in the day, a group of cousins came to visit, but anyone older than their mid-thirties were conspicuously absent, and her visiting kin had a slight air of pity and condescension, even as everyone tried to cultivate a celebratory mood.

16. Mahmood writes in the tradition of Michel Foucault and Judith Butler, and, following their lead, traces processes of discipline and embodiment as situated within discursive fields that determine the bounds of what is sayable (see Butler 1997; Foucault 1980; 1991). Other anthropologists of agency, such as Ahearn, write in the tradition of linguistic anthropology, drawing on theories deriving from Mikhail Bakhtin and C. S. Peirce that focus on how meaning-making activities act upon and generate the social world (see Bakhtin 2010; Peirce 1956; Parmentier 1994). While these two approaches have substantially different philosophical foundations, they both focus on the discursive nature of agency and can be productively brought into dialogue. Both traditions emphasize that power shapes the social via determining the limits of what is sayable, thinkable, feel-able, and considered within the bounds of "normal" (see also Comaroff and Comaroff 1991). By focusing on how norms are put at risk each time they are deployed in interaction, an interactively-informed approach facilitates ethnographic analysis that can track the subtle ways people act on the world through describing it (see Abu-Lughod and Lutz 1990 for a discussion of these overlapping uses of "discourse").

17. This approach to agency strongly resonates with Sumi Madhok's arguments about "speech practices" as a modality of agency for *sathins* working with the Women's Development Program in Rajasthan. By speech practices, Madhok refers to the creative ways that *sathins* rework the "received scripts" offered by development discourse, as their encounters with such discourse encourage novel forms of moral self-reflection and awareness (2012, 63). Madhok's discussion of these speech practices, and what they reveal about the complex ways *sathins* make, and are remade by, encounters with development discourse, echoes linguistic anthropological accounts of "metapragmatic awareness" (Carr 2010b). I build on Madhok's key insight that speech is a central arena for working out what it means to act in relation with others. However, my analysis is informed by the careful attention to meaning and meaning making within US-based traditions of cultural and linguistic anthropology. Rather than speech, then, I attend to interaction. And, rather than drawing a stark line between "action" and "speech" (which is read as not action) (Madhok 2012, 62), I build on intellectual traditions that analyze interactive activity as the foundation of social action and self-making, rejecting analytic distinctions between "material" and "semiotic" (Agha 2007; Keane 2003). This approach, as Chapters 4 and 5 reveal, allow us to analyze the distinct language ideologies that circulate in anti-violence work in India, which draw differing connections between speech, self, and action.

18. See Basu 2015 for a vigorous critique of alternate dispute resolution (ADR) as a tool for gender equality and alternative to legal mechanisms (9–12). Basu argues that mediation practices risk substituting the "hegemonic regulation" of "community norms" in place of the hegemonic regulation of the state, thus reproducing gender norms. Essentially: both the law and the dynamics that undergird ADR are sexist. But, as Ellison shows, ADR techniques often get folded into other strategies, understandings of self, relations, and interactions. Basu quite accurately points out that mediation techniques often fail to deliver on the promise of extending

rights to individual liberal subjects, particularly for women. Here, I want to clarify that this book does not seek to celebrate counseling as "more authentic" or less constraining than the law or transnational women's rights discourse. However, building on the insights of anthropological theories of interaction and practice, I trace how iterative performances of seemingly fixed norms might generate forms of social transformation, and who is served by those transformations. This approach requires taking seriously language as social action (rather than "mere talk" in place of substantive legal or redistributive change) (see Keane 2003 on breaking down the distinction between material and semiotic). Again, in the spirit of awkward kinship, I try to move away from interpretive frameworks that insist that the only pathway to rights and equality runs through liberal legal traditions. At the same time, these analytic approaches offer even greater analytic purchase on how resilient seemingly patriarchal gender norms are, reproduced even as people seek to sustain one another as they work for change.

19. Scholars of NGOs have pointed out that "technologies of talk" emerge as central for NGO activities (Watkins, Swidler and Hannan 2012). On one hand, technologies of talk are flexible. The content and structure of interaction is malleable, allowing institutions to easily shift their focus to meet changing donor interests as needed. On the other hand, interactions seem easily measurable. This was certainly part of the work at counseling centers. Staff like Hema and Indu kept careful logs of the number of cases they worked with. Such data was packaged into reports sent to the federal government body that helped fund the center and prominently displayed in charts that hung on the counseling center walls. The number of women served and the number of cases resolved served as key metrics of the center's success.

20. In unpacking not just the content of counseling sessions but the language ideologies that inform them, I put anthropological research examining the translation of human rights concepts in dialogue with a longstanding debate in South Asian studies about the transformative potential of speech genres associated with women, such as ritual songs and laments. In this earlier body of scholarship, scholars debated the moments of seeming "resistance" in women's songs or ritual recitations. While scholarship has since questioned this emphasis on "resistance" (Abu-Lughod 1990), this research raised powerful questions about ritual, performance, and interaction: How do women's interactive activities reproduce or change larger structures? How do seemingly traditional roles contain seeds of change (for anthropological investigation see Ahearn 2010; Jeffery and Jeffery 1994; Raheja and Gold 1994; Raheja 1995; Wilce 1998; a large body of literary and cultural studies also pursue this question)?

21. Scholars who study domestic violence as a category thus confront an uneasy question about the relationship between labels and phenomena. Anthropologists and other scholars document the recent origins of the label "violence against women," demonstrating the extent to which this category is contingent on other social processes, such as the growing role of universalizing human rights rhetoric in transnational women's rights activism and the need to find a solidarity-building issue that seemed to transcend political differences (Hemment 2004; Keck and Sikkink 1998; Merry 2006; Wies and Haldane 2011). Such anti-violence activism relies heavily on the act of labeling violence in order to de-normalize and thus "take seriously" the problem of gender violence (Bumiller 2008, 3). To critically analyze the label can feel like suggesting that such phenomena are not, in fact, problems. Some scholars engage this dilemma by analytically distinguishing between interpretation and phenomenon. For example, Sally Engle Merry suggests that cultural meanings give violence power, thus requiring a holistic approach to gender violence in social, historical, and cultural context (2009, 5). She writes, "rape and violence within intimate relationships are of course ancient practices with a global distribution; what is new is

the creation of a global social movement which *names these phenomena*, links them to gender practices, and sees them as basic to gender subordination" (2009, 19; emphasis mine).

Chapter 1

1. The activists I knew in Jaipur told me they felt the *mahila thana* system was ineffective—in part because women police officers were often no more sympathetic than male officers, and in part because there was growing skepticism about the ability of the criminal justice system to adequately address domestic disorder and violence without causing greater harm. Rajasthan was at the forefront of the development of *mahila thane,* and Jaipur's two *mahila thane* had served as pilot sites for the program. Similar programs have been developed globally to varying success (see Hautzinger 2007).

2. Such organizations ranged from highly formal, with stand-alone buildings and organizational structures that ranged across the country as a whole, to more informal networks of individuals who had some standing in the community and helped families reconcile in times of trouble. These organizations might, initially, have helped arrange the marriage that was now under duress, and might also have participated in formalizing the marriage at the wedding.

3. The practice of strategically emphasizing different institutional qualities, or even strategically withholding details of institutional intervention, are qualities that scholars note throughout northern India at both NGO and clinical sites—what, in the context of mental health care, Amy Sousa calls "diagnostic neutrality." See Chapter 5 for further discussion (Sousa 2016; A. Sharma 2006).

4. Because "counseling" is often one item in a laundry list of social services that organizations offer, many political and religious groups list counseling as one of their services. Srimati Basu found evidence that some family counseling centers in West Bengal are closely tied to political parties (Basu 2006). Religious organizations—themselves sometimes connected to political organizations, such as the Hindu-right political organization the Sangh Parivar—also offer "counseling" as a part of their outreach efforts.

5. At the time of my return visits in 2013 and 2017, I found that Source of Strength had shifted locations to a site owned by the city government. The new site was in far better shape than the previous one had been; it was larger, airier, and brighter. Gone were the low corrugated metal ceilings and the extension cords looped from the main house to power the ceiling fans. The former site is now empty and awaiting demolition; a block of flats will likely be built in its place by the landlord. The shift to a rent-free government site did not, however, alleviate financial strains, as the organization was now financially responsible for the much larger building's upkeep and utilities.

6. As they distinguish between different expert and lay ways of speaking, counselors rely upon what linguistic anthropologists call "registers," "cultural models of action that link diverse behavioral [interactive] signs to enactable effects" (Agha 2007, 145). Registers invoke a context, a type (or types) of person, and a set of relationships through recognized patterns of interaction: semantic choices, stylistic patterns, accents, grammatical structures (see Carr 2010a; Gal 2018; Matoesian 1999 for examples of registers and the constitution of expert discourse). Importantly, registers never appear in isolation—they are only recognizable to a potential audience if they can be differentiated from other registers, and these differences frequently index differences in value as well (see Irvine 1990). Among the registers in circulation at Source of Strength: an informal register of complaint in which clients spoke, marked by colloquial Hindi, a specific set of vocal

cadences, and the repeated asking of rhetorical questions to implicate the listener. Other work on north Indian languages suggest that this register is widespread across northern India and its diasporas (Brenneis 1984; Wilce 1998). There was the register that counselors used in scolding or correcting clients. There was the register counselors used in soliciting information key to registering the case, identifying the problem in the home, and guiding clients through paperwork. Counseling always happened within and against a broader imagined world of other registers—the registers involved in household disputes, in court cases, at the police station.

7. Rao frames counseling within what he portrays as longstanding forms of advice-giving that are distinctive to India. He argues, for example, that continuity exists between the work of present-day counselors and the events of the *Bhagavad Gita* (a canonical text in Hinduism, dating back to the second century BCE, in which the god Krishna advises the protagonist Arjun on the battlefield as he faces enemies who are also his kin). Rao suggests that this long legacy of advising was snuffed out by colonialism, which substituted rigid norms and conventions for the sophisticated and wise advice of Krishna. Today, he argues, those rigid conventions are dying out, yet nothing has replaced them. "The very important forces of social change, namely, industrialization, urbanization, mass media of communication, and the like, have battered the traditional social connections and institutions and made several dents in them . . . contemporary Indian society . . . provides enormous opportunities for individual choice of action. The *zeit geist* [*sic*] of contemporary Indian society is quite hospitable to counseling; in fact it makes counseling essential" (2002, 285).

8. Elements of Rao's arguments directly cite key concepts from classic family systems therapy. Concepts based in family systems theory also appear in texts generated at elite research centers like the Tata Institute for Social Sciences in Mumbai and are then disseminated through networks of NGO workers and training programs throughout India. In Jaipur, I came across counseling training materials at field sites and at the Institute for Development Studies, where they were appended to reports concerning the role of counseling in women's rights activism; Source of Strength briefly hosted two MSW students as trainees over three weeks, and they shared their textbook with me. Family systems therapy has its roots in the mid-twentieth century United States, yet resonates with long-standing Indian conceptualizations of how individual pathology arises within disordered social relations. Family systems therapy emerged as a way to address individual mental health problems after World War II. Family systems theory resonated with a growing interest in psychoanalytic models of personhood among mental health professionals. The approach also resonated with social workers, who were concerned, at the time, about addressing "social problems" through individual interventions, while answering the question of why particular communities seemed to suffer the same social ills generation after generation. Family therapy—and family systems theory, which supported it—relied upon a psychoanalytic model of the person in order to explore the interactive roots of pathology. As a therapeutic approach, family therapy was meant to correct for what was perceived to be an overly individualizing bent in American culture and therapeutic interventions (Dore 2008; Weinstein 2004). Family systems theory was part of a larger set of efforts to theorize social function in mid-twentieth century social science, theories that in turn pinned both individual and societal development to the shifting role of kinship as a structuring force in social life (McKinnon and Cannell 2013; McKinnon 2013a; Trautmann 1987). Though a full exploration of how family systems theory came to India is beyond the scope of this book, the modes of transmission were likely quite direct; the Tata Institute for Social Sciences, one of the first sites that trained

professionalized social workers in India, was founded by Americans in the early twentieth century. Although family systems theory has progressive roots in the US, designed to track the individual in context and move away from pathologizing arguments about individuals, it feels conservative in India, precisely because it insists on locating the individual in the family. As a result, this perspective sits uncomfortably with the more explicitly feminist goals of organizers who coordinate family counseling programs.

9. See, for example, mid-century scholarship by scholars such as Iriwati Karve and T. N. Madan, anthropological and sociological scholars who were deeply involved in debates about post-colonial development (Karve 1965; Madan 1962). This narrative of alterity has its roots in British colonial administrators' misapprehensions of family practices on the ground. Early British colonial administrators relied heavily on Hindu textual traditions to generate what they believed to be culturally appropriate laws regarding issues such as property ownership and inheritance. As they examined Hindu legal scriptures, they came across what resembled the joint-property-owning family that had recently begun to decline at home in England as the Industrial Revolution transformed agrarian life. Strongly influenced by contract theorists such as Henry Maine, the colonial administrator and early kinship theorist, they took up the joint family as a "living example" of an evolutionarily earlier family form: the joint family was the ultimate manifestation of a status-based society, fundamentally at odds with, and destined to evolve into, a contract-based society organized around nuclear conjugality (Oldenburg 2002; Uberoi 1993).

10. Scholarship and popular discourse have long depicted the joint family as under threat of disintegration. Yet the joint family has not disappeared as a means to organize households and families, and on-going research continues to show the resilience of multi-generational household patterns and the values of kinship that underlie them (Lamb 2009; Vatuk 1975).

11. *The Discovery of India* is a 600-page genre-bending mix of memoir, history, and nationalist treatise that asks how India ought to draw upon its past in order to imagine its future as a nation-state. Nehru frames his effort to "discover" India precisely in terms of discovering what underlying unity brings something called "India" together in the face of historical complexity and contemporary regional, religious, and socio-economic diversity (see pp. 50–53).

12. Legal structures, such as personal laws that link family law to religious community membership, where women are positioned between state and communal norms, are a legacy of British colonialism (Agnes 2000; Sunder Rajan 2003). This legacy of using "rights" to control and govern leads to active debate about whether rights are, in fact, the best tools for producing gender equality and freedom (for example, see Kapur 2012; Nivedita Menon 2004; Sunder Rajan 2003).

13. The research for *Towards Equality* reflects the longstanding dialogue between transnational organizations and women's organizations in India; the report was undertaken in response to the 1967 United Nations Declaration on the Elimination of Discrimination Against Women, and was brought to the first UN-sponsored conference on women in 1975 (K. Sharma and Sujaya 2012).

14. In the late 1970s, dowry-based violence emerged as a major site for political mobilization and protest among women's groups across northern India. Dowry death and violence was read both as a sign of disordered modern times, leaving violent effects on the bodies of women whose natal families could not satisfy the consumerist desires of their in-laws, and as a result of anachronistic yet resilient patriarchal traditions; both of these arguments were supported by long-standing anxieties about dowry exchange (see Majumdar 2009). The substantial role of representations of dowry pressure in discussions of violence against women in India has had

legislative effects, and for many years, the only criminal law addressing violence ("cruelty" in this case) was Section 498a of the penal code, widely interpreted to specifically address coercive and violent dowry demands (Oldenburg 2002; Basu 2006).

15. See Kowalski 2018 for further discussion of how counselors' activities are transformed from "expert" to "bureaucratic" by the institutional norms of gender-based policies, as well as by dynamics of class inequality that shape counseling centers.

16. In leaving these interviewees anonymous, I respect their requests to have such comments as treated off the record—these debates and distinctions are typically submerged in the service of a larger unified front in sourcing funds, lobbying the state, organizing trainings and events, etc.

17. The English term "neutrality" often appears in humanitarianism, particularly in contexts where alternate dispute resolution, or ADR, is a key tool. This use of "neutrality" has been widely critiqued as depoliticizing by anthropologists who study humanitarianism. Anthropologist Miriam Ticktin quotes the founder of Medecins Sans Frontiers, Bernard Kouchner, as he connects neutrality and care: "'If you are humanitarian . . . this is not politics, you must be neutral, taking care of all.' Neutrality, to reiterate, is the duty to refrain from taking actions that advantage one side of the conflict over another" (2011, 82). For Ticktin, neutrality is a space of silence that one must "leave" in order to "speak out" against the status quo, or risk, in keeping silent, reproducing it (2011, 83).

Chapter 2

1. Like many English terms, ranging from "tension" to "time," "adjustment" and "adjust" are common loan words in Hindi-matrix conversation. It was not clear what, if any, Hindi terms "adjustment" stood in for, or what pathways it took into everyday Hindi usage; there are many words and phrases in Hindi that express ideas about tinkering and adjusting around the edges of fixed relations and realities, such as the term *jugaad* (Jauregui 2014). At times, the use of the English "adjustment" felt slightly clinical, like other clinical loan words like "depression," which take on their own meanings in Hindi matrix worlds (Singh 2017). At other moments, the word felt euphemistic, following a pattern in which English loan words—particularly related to relations and intimacy—serve as polite ways to express what would, in Hindi, feel vulgar or too personal (Hall 2021; Puri 1999).

2. Themes of adjustment and becoming "one's own" after being a stranger are central to studies of the family in India, particularly work that carefully examines how ideas about personhood shape these shifting relations. (See, for example: Cohen 1998; Lamb 2000, 2013; Lambert 2000; U. Menon 2013; Pinto 2008; Trawick 1990; Wadley 1994.)

3. Such narratives of generational inversions in power and authority appear frequently in research on contemporary India as an idiom through which people discuss the moral and material implications of social transformation (Cohen 1998; Gold 2009; Lamb 2009; Vera-Sanso 1999).

4. Even in its grammatical construction, the phrase *ap kya chahti ho?* captures the tricky balance between intimacy and distance that counselors sought: technically grammatically "incorrect" in modern standard Hindi, the question mixes two forms of the second person plural, blending the respectful and formal pronoun *ap* with the more informal conjugated form of the verb, *chahti ho*. This kind of slippage was fairly common in spoken Hindi in Jaipur, and it rendered the tone of the question polite yet informal, literally both respectful and intimate. "*Tum*," the pronoun that matches the conjugation "*chahti ho*," is a more intimate form of address. The

"correct" version of the sentence, from a Hindi homework perspective, would either be "*aap kya chahti hain*," or "*tum kya chahti ho?*"

Chapter 3

1. In line with this approach, in this chapter I describe PWDVA casework primarily through the eyes of counselors, in terms of their understandings of its processes and goals. In some cases, these understandings may be limited or incorrect. However, my goal in this chapter is to analyze how the PWDVA intersected with counseling expertise, rather than to evaluate whether and how counseling expertise deviates from official PWDVA policy goals. Indeed, other scholars have shown that the nature of the PWDVA—its broad definition of violence, its status as a civil law with potential criminal consequences, and its use of a variety of non-state institutions for implementation—means that a variety of institutional actors have sought to deploy the law to creative ends beyond the letter of the law (as with groups in northern India that have sought to use the PWDVA to fight for reproductive rights [Madhok, Unnithan, and Heitmeyer 2014]).

2. The PWDVA is a secular civil law governing family. As a result, it is a departure from most family law in India, which is governed by personal codes that are connected to religious identity. Such laws have historically governed family law concerning divorce, joint property ownership, and inheritance. Women's rights activists in India have long debated whether such personal codes should be replaced with a universal civil code, though such debates align uncomfortably with Hindu fundamentalist calls to replace Muslim personal law with a nation-wide legal code rooted in Hinduism (Agnes 1992; Loomba and Lukose 2012; Nivedita Menon 2004; Sunder Rajan 2003). Legal scholars have suggested that the PWDVA is innovative in the ways that it sidesteps these debates (Lodhia 2009).

3. In working to pass a civil law addressing domestic violence, advocates encountered conflicts around whether the key unit of intervention was to be the family or the female plaintiff. As the bill made its way through Parliament, it encountered competition from a bill drafted by the ruling party at the time, which questioned whether the law should prioritize the stability of the family or the aggrieved woman. These detractors worried that framing the law around women would violate the Indian Constitution's guarantee of gender equality (Jaising 2009). Women's groups, alongside the Lawyers Collective, were ultimately successful in reframing the bill to prioritize the rights and needs of women facing violence, avoiding demands that placed further undue burden on plaintiffs (such as draft language requiring plaintiffs to demonstrate domestic violence was "habitual" to claim support).

4. Significantly, this element of the law—using shared residence rather than official property ownership as a measure of rights to residence—was what saw the most intervention from precedent-setting high-court decisions, which sought to limit this expansive definition, particularly around live-in relationships that were not ratified as marriages (Lawyers Collective 2012).

5. In Rajasthan, state-based efforts to mainstream gender intersected with local women's rights activism to produce a number of state/NGO collaborations, including the Women's Development Programme, women's-only police stations, non-adversarial counseling centers attached to courts and police stations, and fast-track "family" courts, beginning in the early 1980s (Madhok and Rai 2012; Mathur 2004; Moodie 2008). A number of these efforts, especially the Women's Development Programme, were designed to develop interactive strategies that built on genres of interaction that already existed at the village level by creating new venues for interactions between "rural women," NGOs, academic researchers, and the state (Mathur

2004, 135). A number of the activists who ran Source of Strength had been involved in these other efforts at various points in their lives.

6. Counselors and activists in Rajasthan were frustrated by the marked absence of "protection officers," another group of mediators designated by the law. In Rajasthan, protection officers were female state employees. During my year at Source of Strength, I neither met a protection officer nor witnessed a plaintiff, counselor, or activist refer to one. The role and significance of the protection officer varies by state, though even states with more active protection officers face limitations related to budgetary and institutional constraints (see Roychowdhury 2021 for an extended analysis of protection officers in the context of West Bengal).

7. I am not certain whether Simran's father meant that there wasn't a good "fit" between Simran and her husband, or whether her husband wasn't "fit" in the sense of physically fit (which, given the lack of children, would indicate that he was not sexually capable). He himself may have been playing on this ambiguity in describing why the marriage ended.

8. Rhetoric of "manipulation" is common in public discourse around laws designed to protect women from household violence. In public representations of criminal cases under Section 498, for example, people often describe female plaintiffs as "manipulating" the law in order to gain resources or hold their in-laws hostage (for example Oberoi 2008; see Agnes 1995).

Chapter 4

1. In a discussion of the upper-caste politics of *seva* in social reform movements, Srivatsan links the "service" of *seva* to the social hierarchies within which it unfolds, writing, "the term *seva* denotes what is called service in English, but comes to mind in connection with a normally menial, demeaning or polluting act of service which carries no taint in special contexts: in the family, in reparation for wrongs, for community repair, as ethical obligation, establishing the priority of duty, as recognition by god and as the sanctification of an untouchable" (Srivatsan 2006, 427). McGregor's Hindi-English dictionary offers a broad definition that captures the semantic range the term, offering a sense of the array of actions involved in *seva*: "*seva*:1. service. 2. attendance (on); care (of or for a person or an animal); tending. 3. employment, post. 4. worship (as of the feet of a deity); homage. 5. care (of an object: as plants, or the hair). 6. a church service. 7. an administrative or similar service. 8. resort (to): following or taking (a course of medicine, or a drug). *seva karna (ki)*, to serve; to attend (on); to worship; to look after" (1997, 1039).

2. Images of chaotic "large" families and tidy, middle-class "small" families are a product of India's long-standing family planning projects, going back to the mid-twentieth century, when global population control organizations sought to motivate people in the developing world to have fewer children through the promise of consumer goods and leisure products (Connelly 2003; Sreenivas 2021).

3. I use the English "spoiled" because that is the English word that counselors often used in place of *bigarna* when they code-switched, or in Indian English explanations to me. In some ways a better translation might be "ruined," but I have chosen to use the translation I was provided with in the field.

4. This use of "making understand" by a junior person to transform relations differs from other ethnographic findings in northern India, which typically show senior kin making junior kin understand (and thereby using their greater knowledge and education to educate and discipline them into being good family members) (Marrow 2008; Wadley 2010). In my own research,

I found that people described making others understand as an action that flowed both upward and downward along household hierarchies.

5. "Hero Honda Pleasure TVC 2010 Questions," YouTube video of TV advertisement for motor scooter, 0:43, September 7, 2010, https://www.youtube.com/watch?v=z44vMNZwPeA.

6. The noun "*pyar*" is most often translated as "love." But when it is used in the construction "*pyar se*" it doesn't typically have a romantic connotation; it connotes affection and also care, an awareness of how one's words might affect others.

7. Laura Ahearn discusses a similar semantic overlap between "agree," "consent," and "obey" in the related term *mannu* in Nepali, demonstrating how the use of this term in discussions of changing marriage practices reflects shifting conceptions of agency (Ahearn 2010, 249).

8. Hindi has three forms of the second person pronoun: tu, tum, and ap. Tu is both extremely intimate and extremely insulting.

9. Smitha's shy grin in response to the direct use of her husband's name may also have stemmed from practices of name avoidance that are common in many communities in Jaipur. Directly referring to kin by name is seen as inappropriate, and spouses primarily referred to their partners (as well as other family members) with third person pronouns.

10. Strategies of careful speech appear in strategies of political resistance beyond the household. In early 2020, India's federal government passed a law designed to make it easier for some refugees in India to gain citizenship, based on their religious background (the Citizenship Amendment Act, or CAA). Many observers felt that this law violated the secular basis of India's constitution, as Islam was pointedly excluded from the list of acceptable religious backgrounds. Civil liberties advocates suggested that this new law, paired with longstanding plans to develop a National Register of Citizens, seemed designed to potentially strip citizenship from India's Muslim citizens. The concern was that the burdensome documentation demands imposed by the National Register of Citizens would essentially transform many Muslim citizens lacking clear documentation "proving" that they were Indian into "refugees" who were now deportable under the CAA. In the winter of 2020, these paired laws provoked protests across the country. One everyday form of resistance was the suggestion that people should refuse to show the government their documentation when such data was collected for the National Register of Citizens.

In Hindi-language videos that circulated widely on social media, activist Yogendra Yadav coached viewers in how to boycott the collection of their data (Shyam 2020). In coaching viewers in how to speak with officials, he repeatedly urged them to speak "with affection" as a mode of nonviolent resistance. When a government official comes to your house to collect data on household members, he explains, speak to them with affection, serve them tea and snacks. But "if they tell you, it's the law, you have to [share your household information], say affectionately [*pyar se*], Master-ji, I respect you a lot, but what can I do, I respect Mahatma Gandhi even more . . . [and] he said if there is any unconstitutional, unjust law, then resisting that law is not only our right, but our duty." With placating gestures and a gentle, non-confrontational tone, Yadav performed this affectionate speech for viewers, helping them imagine how to occupy a hierarchy even while reminding powerful people of the larger obligations under which they operated.

Part of this performance also involved codeswitching as Yadav discussed rights and duties, as he repeated his point by moving between Hindi words with recognizably Sanskrit roots (*adhikar* and *kartavya* for rights and duties) and Hindi words with recognizably Perso-Arabic

roots (*haq* and *farz,* respectively). All of these words are common in spoken Hindi and recognizable to speakers, even though they are also associated, in some contexts, with different religious
communities. In so doing, he modeled how careful speech can order difference, now in the
body politic of the nation rather than the household. Through careful speech, Yadav's imagined
speaker resists one set of top-down legal imperatives with an argument about a different set
of rights and duties, authorized by a vision of national order organized around the everyday
actions of citizens.

Chapter 5

1. Counselors' understanding of the potentially disruptive power of labels like "violence"
reflect an institutional phenomenon that Amy Sousa has called "diagnostic neutrality" (Sousa
2016, 43). At a psychiatric hospital in northern India, Sousa found that doctors rarely shared
the diagnostic label of schizophrenia with patients and their families, merely giving instructions
about how to treat and support the patient. While such an approach initially appears highly
paternalistic, Sousa suggests that "by de-emphasizing diagnoses, doctors prevent the development of negative stereotypes that encumber social recovery . . . The distressing symptoms of
schizophrenia become signs of a temporary condition, rather than "who a person is" (43). While
"violence" is a feature not of persons but relations, counselors take a similar approach.

2. Hindi, like English, incorporates vocabulary from a diverse range of linguistic sources,
including Indic languages, Sanskrit, Perso-Arabic, and, increasingly, English. Much as Latinate
words often indicate a higher register of English, words sourced from Sanskrit often have the
feel of higher-register Hindi, as opposed to "everyday" Hindi, with its Perso-Arabic roots. *Haq*
originates with Perso-Arabic languages, while *adhikar* derives from Sanskrit (Madhok 2009).

3. Another layer of productive misunderstandings, one focused on differing ideas about
individuals, relations, and diagnosis, shapes interactions between long-standing northern Indian
grassroots projects addressing violence, and transnationally driven approaches that appear to
build on such projects—dynamics addressed in, for example, Madhok 2015; Sharma 2008; and
Unnithan and Heitmeyer 2014.

4. Observers of these phenomena have long expressed skepticism about such labeling activities. Paul Farmer's *Pathologies of Power,* for example, opens with a somewhat scathing description of a gender sensitivity workshop hosted in Chiapas by women from Guatemala City: "It
seemed to us that the exercise was demeaning—the participants, having survived genocide and
displacement, were now being treated like children. They were being asked to respond to an
agenda imported from capital cities, from do-gooder organizations like ours, from U.S. univer-
sities with the 'right' answers to their every question" (Farmer 2005, 3–4). Farmer's larger point,
in starting with this episode, is that the workshop offered no space for the workshop participants
to offer their own accounting of the violence they experienced; its pedagogical aims served to
erase, rather than amplify, a dialogue between equals about the causes and effects of structural
violence.

5. I draw heavily on Mathur's scholarship in this section, because it concisely crystallizes
many concerns I observed among activists and organizers in Jaipur and, due to Mathur's participation within the larger institutional network that supported counseling centers, represents
a line of reasoning that shaped the perspectives of many organizers who ran counseling centers
and worried about their effects. Because of her position as a scholar at an academic institution,
Mathur is able to express some of these concerns without worrying about the inter-institutional

politics that shaped many of my interviews with organizers. Throughout the book, which carefully details a variety of projects in the state going back to the 1970s, Mathur builds on her own longstanding experience in activism, along with observations of other sites and interviews, in order to emphasize that gendered violence emerged as a key category for activism in Rajasthan because it was the primary concern that rural and working-class women voiced when they came together with activists in grassroots, solidarity-building groups.

6. Although the moment of naming violence is a central part of Mathur's argument, the book does not share what specific vernacular terms participants in these projects used; while she presents Rajasthani Hindi labels for harmful traditional practices like *sati*, we do not see what "naming violence" looks like in Hindi, Marwari, or other languages spoken across the state of Rajasthan. Other work on northern Indian women's movements, however, suggest that these moments of translation are in fact central to generating social transformation. For example, Richa Nagar and the Sangatin Writers Collective describes the careful multilinguistic work in collaboratively producing narratives across Awadhi, modern standard Hindi (with its politics around distinctions between "Hindi" and "Urdu"), and English (Sangatin Writers Collective and Nagar 2006; Nagar 2017). Mathur's approach, in leaving "violence" in English, suggests that the term needs no translation, perhaps due to its prelinguistic truth.

7. While treating "violence" as if its meaning is transparent and permanent is politically strategic, activists and scholars are of course viscerally aware of the tremendous political labor that was needed to bring the label "violence" into the conversation around gendered harms, as such work is ongoing, historically recent, and subject to continual negotiation (see Abu-Lughod 2013; Adelman and Coker 2016; Bumiller 2008; Grewal 2005; Nivedita Menon 2004; Merry 2009; Riles 1998 for further elaboration of these dynamics).

8. In one Hindi dictionary, *pareshan* is defined as "agitated because of sadness or suffering; troubled; confused or perturbed;" the noun *pareshani* is described as "distress, anxiousness, agitation, a great deal of confusion or worry" (S. S. Das 1975, 2876; translation mine). McGregor glosses this in English as "trouble, distress; embarrassment; perplexity" (McGregor 1997, 611).

9. I focus on the English label violence rather than the Hindi word *himsa* here because it was most frequently the English label that circulated. Uses of *himsa*, for example, in Hindi language versions of women's rights outreach materials or in legislation seems most frequently to be a direct translation of the English "violence." *Himsa*—familiar to many English speakers in its negative form, *ahimsa*, or non-violence, a central piece of Gandhian philosophy—is itself an enormously complex moral and ethical term, with roots in religious and political traditions in India.

10. Hema and Indu saw Anju's inability to make sense of the interactional style in her household as a result of being from a neighboring state in India, where people didn't speak straight but instead concealed their intentions. They were not the only people I knew who discussed regional distinctions in terms of differences in speaking style; I was told, for example, that when people from Agra (in Uttar Pradesh) spoke, it was like "they were throwing stones."

11. Discussions of "straight speech" (*sidhe bolna*) also reflect ideologies of inner reference, similar to those at play in labeling violence strategies. However, as Hema goes on to suggest, here, the "straightness" of inner reference is less about revealing what is inside oneself, and more about straightforward dealing within relations.

Conclusion

1. "*Sasural paksh ki zyaada dakhlandaji se tutti hain shadiyan, mobile phone bana ek bari vajah*," Newstrack, accessed 18 November 2021, https://newstrack.com/uttar-pradesh

/bundelkhand/jhansi/jhansi-latest-news-in-hindi-today-parivar-paramarsh-kendra-family
-counselor-parivarik-vivad-taja-khabar-aaj-ki-uttar-pradesh-2021-293641.

2. "*Dampatya bachane ko nau jagahon par khulega counseling center*," Jagran Prakashan, accessed 18 November 2021, https://www.jagran.com/bihar/patna-city-nine-counsiling-center -open-in-state-22198263.html.

WORKS CITED

Abbott, Andrew. 1995. "Boundaries of Social Work or Social Work of Boundaries? The Social Service Review Lecture." *Social Service Review* 69 (4): 545–62.

Abu-Lughod, Lila. 1990. "The Romance of Resistance: Tracing Transformations of Power Through Bedouin Women." *American Ethnologist* 17 (1): 41–55.

———. 2010. "Against Universals: The Dialects of (Women's) Human Rights and Human Capabilities." In *Rethinking the Human*, edited by J. Michelle Molina and Donald K. Swearer, 67–93. Cambridge, MA: Harvard University Press.

———. 2013. *Do Muslim Women Need Saving?* Cambridge, MA.: Harvard University Press.

Abu-Lughod, Lila, and Catherine A. Lutz. 1990. "Introduction: Emotion, Discourse, and the Politics of Everyday Life." In *Language and the Politics of Emotion*, edited by Lila Abu-Lughod and Catherine A. Lutz, 1–24. Cambridge University Press Cambridge.

Adelman, Madelaine. 2004. "The Battering State: Towards a Political Economy of Domestic Violence." *Journal of Poverty* 8 (3): 45–64.

Adelman, Madelaine, and Donna Coker. 2016. "Introduction: Pedagogies of Domestic Violence." *Violence Against Women* 22 (12): 1419–25.

Agarwal, Bina. 1994. *A Field of One's Own: Gender and Land Rights in South Asia*. Cambridge: Cambridge University Press.

Agha, Asif. 2005. "Voice, Footing, Enregisterment." *Journal of Linguistic Anthropology* 15 (1): 38–59.

———. 2007. *Language and Social Relations*. Cambridge: Cambridge University Press.

Agnes, Flavia. 1992. "Protecting Women against Violence? Review of a Decade of Legislation, 1980–89." *Economic and Political Weekly* 27 (17): WS 19–WS 33.

———. 1995. "Protective Legislations: Myth of Misuse." *Economic and Political Weekly* 30 (16): 865–66.

———. 2000. "Women, Marriage, and the Subordination of Rights." In *Subaltern Studies XI: Community, Gender, and Violence*, edited by Partha Chatterjee and Pradeep Jeganathan, 106–37. New York: Columbia University Press.

Ahearn, Laura M. 2001. "Language and Agency." *Annual Review of Anthropology* 30: 109–37.

———. 2010. *Invitations to Love: Literacy, Love Letters, and Social Change in Nepal*. Ann Arbor: University of Michigan Press.

Asad, Talal. 2003. *Formations of the Secular: Christianity, Islam, Modernity*. Stanford, CA: Stanford University Press.

Aulino, Felicity. 2016. "Rituals of Care for the Elderly in Northern Thailand: Merit, Morality, and the Everyday of Long-Term Care." *American Ethnologist* 43 (1): 91–102.

Bacchi, Carol. 2012. "Why Study Problematizations? Making Politics Visible." *Open Journal of Political Science* 2 (1): 1–8.

Bakhtin, M. M. 2010. *The Dialogic Imagination: Four Essays*. Austin: University of Texas Press.

Ball, Christopher. 2018. "Language of Kin Relations and Relationlessness." *Annual Review of Anthropology* 47 (1): 47–60.

Basu, Srimati. 1999. *She Comes to Take Her Rights: Indian Women, Property, and Propriety*. Albany, NY: State University of New York Press.

———. 2006. "Playing off Courts: The Negotiation of Divorce and Violence in Plural Legal Settings in Kolkata." *Journal of Legal Pluralism and Unofficial Law* 38 (52): 41–75.

———. 2012. "Judges of Normality: Mediating Marriage in the Family Courts of Kolkata, India." *Signs: Journal of Women in Culture and Society* 37 (2): 469–92.

———. 2015. *The Trouble with Marriage: Feminists Confront Law and Violence in India*. Berkeley: University of California Press.

Bauman, Richard, and Charles L. Briggs. 2000. "Language Philosophy as Language Ideology: John Locke and Johann Gottfried Herder." In *Regimes of Language: Ideologies, Polities, and Identities*, edited by Paul Kroskrity, 139–204. Santa Fe, NM: School for Advanced Research Press.

Bear, Laura. 2013. "'This Body Is Our Body': Vishwakarma Puja, the Social Debts of Kinship, and Theologies of Materiality in a Neoliberal Shipyard." In *Vital Relations: Modernity and the Persistent Life of Kinship*, edited by Susan McKinnon and Fenella Cannell, 155–79. Santa Fe, NM: School for Advanced Research Press.

Bear, Laura, Karen Ho, Anna Lowenhaupt Tsing, and Sylvia Yanagisako. 2015. "Gens: A Feminist Manifesto for the Study of Capitalism." Theorizing the Contemporary, *Fieldsights*, March 30. https://culanth.org/fieldsights/gens-a-feminist-manifesto-for-the-study-of-capitalism.

Benjamin, Ruha. 2018. "Black Afterlives Matter: Cultivating Kinfulness as Reproductive Justice." In *Making Kin Not Population*, edited by Adele E. Clarke and Donna Jeanne Haraway, 41–66. Chicago: Prickly Paradigm Press.

Berman, Elise. 2018. "Force Signs: Ideologies of Corporal Discipline in Academia and the Marshall Islands." *Journal of Linguistic Anthropology* 28 (1): 22–42.

———. 2019. *Talking Like Children: Language and the Production of Age in the Marshall Islands*. Oxford: Oxford University Press.

Bernal, Victoria, and Inderpal Grewal. 2014a. "The NGO Form: Feminist Struggles, States, and Neoliberalism." In *Theorizing NGOs: States, Feminisms, and Neoliberalism*, edited by Victoria Bernal and Inderpal Grewal, 1–18. Durham, NC: Duke University Press.

———, eds. 2014b. *Theorizing NGOs: States, Feminisms, and Neoliberalism*. Durham, NC: Duke University Press.

Bhate-Deosthali, Padma, Sangeeta Rege, and Padma Prakash, eds. 2016. "Introduction." In *Feminist Counselling and Domestic Violence in India*, 1–15. London: Routledge.

Biruk, Crystal. 2016. "Studying up in Critical NGO Studies Today: Reflections on Critique and the Distribution of Interpretive Labour." *Critical African Studies* 8 (3): 291–305.

Blommaert, Jan. 2001. "Investigating Narrative Inequality: African Asylum Seekers' Stories in Belgium." *Discourse and Society* 12 (4): 413–49.

Borneman, John. 1997. "Caring and Being Cared for: Displacing Marriage, Kinship, Gender and Sexuality." *International Social Science Journal* 49 (154): 573–84.

Bornstein, Erica. 2012. *Disquieting Gifts: Humanitarianism in New Delhi*. Stanford, CA: Stanford University Press.

Bornstein, Erica, and Aradhana Sharma. 2016. "The Righteous and the Rightful: The Techno-moral Politics of NGOs, Social Movements, and the State in India." *American Ethnologist* 43 (1): 76–90.

Borovoy, Amy, and Kristen Ghodsee. 2012. "Decentering Agency in Feminist Theory: Recuperating the Family as a Social Project." *Women's Studies International Forum* 35 (3): 153–65.

Bourdieu, Pierre. 1977. *Outline of a Theory of Practice*. Translated by Richard Nice. Cambridge: Cambridge University Press.

Brenneis, Donald. 1984. "Grog and Gossip in Bhatgaon." *American Ethnologist* 11 (3): 487–506.

Briggs, Charles L. 1997. "Notes on a" Confession": On the Construction of Gender, Sexuality, and Violence in an Infanticide Case." *Pragmatics* 7 (4): 519–46.

Brodwin, Paul. 2013. *Everyday Ethics: Voices from the Front Line of Community Psychiatry*. Berkeley: University of California Press.

Brown, Wendy. 1995. *States of Injury: Power and Freedom in Late Modernity*. Princeton, NJ: Princeton University Press.

Buch, Elana. 2015. "Aging and Care." *Annual Review of Anthropology* 44 (1): 277–93.

———. 2018. *Inequalities of Aging: Paradoxes of Independence in American Home Care*. New York: New York University Press.

Bumiller, Kristin. 2008. *In an Abusive State: How Neoliberalism Appropriated the Feminist Movement against Sexual Violence*. Durham, NC: Duke University Press.

Bunch, Charlotte. 1990. "Women's Rights as Human Rights: Toward a Re-Vision of Human Rights." *Human Rights Quarterly* 12 (4): 486–98.

Burte, Aruna. 2016. "The Spirit of Resistance." In *Feminist Counselling and Domestic Violence in India*, edited by Padma Bhate-Deosthali, Sangeeta Rege, and Padma Prakash. London: Routledge.

Butler, Judith. 1997. *The Psychic Life of Power: Theories in Subjection*. Stanford, CA: Stanford University Press.

———. 2020. *The Force of Nonviolence: An Ethico-Political Bind*. London: Verso Books.

Carr, E. Summerson. 2010a. "Enactments of Expertise." *Annual Review of Anthropology* 39 (1): 17–32.

———. 2010b. *Scripting Addiction: The Politics of Therapeutic Talk and American Sobriety*. Princeton, NJ: Princeton University Press.

———. 2015. "Occupation Bedbug: Or, the Urgency and Agency of Professional Pragmatism." *Cultural Anthropology* 30 (2): 257–85.

Carsten, Janet. 2000. Introduction to *Cultures of Relatedness: New Approaches to the Study of Kinship*, edited by Janet Carsten, 1–36. Cambridge: Cambridge University Press.

———. 2004. *After Kinship*. Cambridge: Cambridge University Press.

———. 2017. "Kinship and Gender as Legacy and Future." *Journal of the Royal Anthropological Institute (N.S.)* 23 (1): 189–92.

Carsten, Janet, and Stephen Hugh-Jones. 1995. Introduction to *About the House: Lévi-Strauss and Beyond*, edited by Janet Carsten and Stephen Hugh-Jones,1–46. Cambridge: Cambridge University Press.

Chatterjee, Indrani. 2004. Introduction to *Unfamiliar Relations: Family and History in South Asia*, edited by Indrani Chatterjee, 1–45. New Brunswick, NJ: Rutgers University Press.

Chatterjee, Nilanjana, and Nancy E. Riley. 2001. "Planning an Indian Modernity: The Gendered Politics of Fertility Control." *Signs*, 811–45.

Chatterjee, Partha. 1993. *The Nation and Its Fragments: Colonial and Postcolonial Histories*. Princeton, NJ: Princeton University Press.

Chidambaram, Soundarya. 2012. "The Right Kind of Welfare in South India's Urban Slums: *Seva* vs. Patronage and the Success of Hindu Nationalist Organizations." *Asian Survey* 52 (2): 298–320.

Chowdhry, Prem. 2009. "'First Our Jobs Then Our Girls': The Dominant Caste Perceptions on the 'Rising' Dalits." *Modern Asian Studies* 43 (2): 437–79.

Chua, Jocelyn Lim. 2012. "The Register of Complaint: Psychiatric Diagnosis and the Discourse of Grievance in the South Indian Mental Health Encounter." *Medical Anthropology Quarterly* 26 (2): 221–40.

Ciotti, Manuela. 2011. "Resurrecting *Seva* (Social Service): Dalit and Low-Caste Women Party Activists as Producers and Consumers of Political Culture and Practice in Urban North India." *Journal of Asian Studies* 71 (01): 149–70.

Clarke, Adele E. 2018. "Introducing Making Kin Not Population." In *Making Kin Not Population*, edited by Adele E. Clarke and Donna Jeanne Haraway, 41–66. Chicago: Prickly Paradigm Press.

Cohen, Lawrence. 1998. *No Aging in India: Alzheimer's, the Bad Family, and Other Modern Things*. Berkeley: University of California Press.

Cole, Jennifer. 2014. "Working Mis/Understandings: The Tangled Relationship between Kinship, Franco-Malagasy Binational Marriages, and the French State." *Cultural Anthropology* 29 (3): 527–51.

Cole, Jennifer, and Deborah Lynn Durham. 2007. "Age, Regeneration, and the Intimate Politics of Globalization." In *Generations and Globalization: Youth, Age, and Family in the New World Economy*, edited by Jennifer Cole and Deborah Lynn Durham, 1–29. Bloomington: Indiana University Press.

Collier, Jane Fishburne. 1997. *From Duty to Desire: Remaking Families in a Spanish Village*. Princeton, NJ: Princeton University Press.

Collier, Jane, Michelle Rosaldo, Sylvia Junko Yanagisako, Barrie Thorne, and Marilyn Yalom. 1992. "Is There a Family? New Anthropological Views." In *Rethinking the Family: Some Feminist Questions*, rev. ed., 31–51. Boston: Northeastern University Press.

Comaroff, Jean, and John L. Comaroff. 1991. *Of Revelation and Revolution, Volume 1: Christianity, Colonialism, and Consciousness in South Africa*. Chicago: University of Chicago Press.

Connelly, Matthew. 2003. "Population Control is History: New Perspectives on the International Campaign to Limit Population Growth." *Comparative Studies in Society and History* 45 (1): 122–47.

———. 2006. "Population Control in India: Prologue to the Emergency Period." *Population and Development Review* 32 (4): 629–67.

Counts, Dorothy Ayers, Judith K. Brown, and Jacquelyn Campbell. 1999. *To Have and to Hit: Cultural Perspectives on Wife Beating*. Urbana: University of Illinois Press.

Daly, M. 2005. "Gender Mainstreaming in Theory and Practice." *Social Politics: International Studies in Gender, State and Society* 12 (3): 433–50.

Das, Shyam Sundar. 1975. *Hindi Shabd Sagar*. Kasi: Nagari Pracarini Sabha.

Das, Veena. 1976. "Masks and Faces: An Essay on Punjabi Kinship." *Contributions to Indian Sociology* 10 (1): 1–30.

———. 2007. *Life and Words: Violence and the Descent into the Ordinary*. University of California Press.

———. 2008. "Violence, Gender, and Subjectivity." *Annual Review of Anthropology* 37 (1): 283–99.

———. 2010. "Engaging the Life of the Other: Love and Everyday Life." In *Ordinary Ethics: Anthropology, Language, and Action*, edited by Michael Lambek, 376–99. New York: Fordham University Press.

Das, Veena, and Renu Addlakha. 2001. "Disability and Domestic Citizenship: Voice, Gender, and the Making of the Subject." *Public Culture* 13 (3): 511–31.

Dickey, Sara. 2000. "Permeable Homes: Domestic Service, Household Space, and the Vulnerability of Class Boundaries in Urban India." *American Ethnologist* 27 (2): 462–89.

Dore, Martha Morrison. 2008. "Family Systems Theory." In *Comprehensive Handbook of Social Work and Social Welfare*. New York: John Wiley and Sons.

Duranti, Alessandro. 1993. "Truth and Intentionality: An Ethnographic Critique." *Cultural Anthropology* 8 (2): 214–45.

El Ouardani, Christine Nutter. 2018. "Care or Neglect?: Corporal Discipline Reform in a Rural Moroccan Classroom." *Anthropology and Education Quarterly* 49 (2): 129–45.

Ellison, Susan Helen. 2018. *Domesticating Democracy: The Politics of Conflict Resolution in Bolivia*. Durham, NC: Duke University Press.

Elman, Benjamin, and Sheldon Pollock. 2018. *What China and India Once Were: The Pasts That May Shape the Global Future*. New York: Columbia University Press.

Enfield, N. J. 2017. "Elements of Agency." In *Distributed Agency*. New York: Oxford University Press.

Englund, Harri. 2006. *Prisoners of Freedom: Human Rights and the African Poor*. Berkeley: University of California Press.

Farmer, Paul. 2005. *Pathologies of Power: Health, Human Rights, and the New War on the Poor*. Berkeley: University of California Press.

Ferguson, James. 2013. "Declarations of Dependence: Labour, Personhood , and Welfare in Southern Africa." *Journal of the Royal Anthropological Institute* 19 (2): 223–42.

Foucault, Michel. 1980. *The History of Sexuality: Volume 1*. 1st Vintage Books ed. New York: Vintage Books.

———. 1991. "Governmentality." In *The Foucault Effect: Studies in Governmentality*, edited by Graham Burchell, Colin Gordon, and Peter Miller, 87–104. Chicago: University of Chicago Press.

Franklin, Sarah, and Susan McKinnon. 2001. Introduction to *Relative Values: Reconfiguring Kinship Studies*, edited by Sarah Franklin and Susan McKinnon, 1–28. Durham, NC: Duke University Press.

Fraser, Nancy, and Linda Gordon. 1994. "A Genealogy of Dependency: Tracing a Keyword of the U.S. Welfare State." *Signs* 19 (2): 309–36.

Fuller, C.J. J., and Haripriya Narasimhan. 2008. "Companionate Marriage in India: The Changing Marriage System in a Middle-Class Brahman Subcaste." *Journal of the Royal Anthropological Institute* 14 (4): 736–54.

Gal, Susan. 1991. "Between Speech and Silence: The Problematics of Research on Language and Gender." In *Gender at the Crossroads of Knowledge: Feminist Anthropology in the Postmodern Era*, edited by Micaela Di Leonardo, 175–203. Berkeley: University of California Press.

———. 2003. "Movements of Feminism: The Circulation of Discourses about Women." In *Recognition Struggles and Social Movements: Contested Identities, Agency, and Power*, edited by Barbara Hobson, 93–118. Cambridge: Cambridge University Press.

———. 2013. "Tastes of Talk: Qualia and the Moral Flavor of Signs." *Anthropological Theory* 13 (1–2): 31–48.

———. 2018. "Registers in Circulation: The Social Organization of Interdiscursivity." *Signs and Society* 6 (1): 1–24.

Gal, Susan, Julia Kowalski, and Erin Moore. 2015. "Rethinking Translation in Feminist NGOs: Rights and Empowerment Across Borders." *Social Politics* 22 (4): 610–35.

Garcia, Angela. 2010. *The Pastoral Clinic: Addiction and Dispossession Along the Rio Grande*. Berkeley: University of California Press.

Gilbertson, Amanda. 2018. *Within the Limits: Moral Boundaries of Class and Gender in Urban India*. New edition. New Delhi, India: Oxford University Press.

Gold, Ann Grodzins. 2009. "Tasteless Profits and Vexed Moralities: Assessments of the Present in Rural Rajasthan." *Journal of the Royal Anthropological Institute* 15 (2): 365–85.

Goldfarb, Kathryn E. 2016. "'Coming to Look Alike': Materializing Affinity in Japanese Foster and Adoptive Care." *Social Analysis* 60 (2): 47–64.

Goldfarb, Sally. 2011. "A Clash of Cultures: Women, Domestic Violence, and Law in the United States." In *Gender and Culture at the Limit of Rights*, edited by Dorothy Louise Hodgson, 55–80. Philadelphia: University of Pennsylvania Press.

Goldstein, Daniel. 2013. "Whose Vernacular? Translating Human Rights Across Local Contexts." In *Human Rights at the Crossroads*, edited by Mark Goodale, 111–21. Oxford: Oxford University Press.

Goldstein, Donna. 2003. *Laughter Out of Place: Race, Class, Violence and Sexuality in a Rio Shantytown*. Berkeley: University of California Press.

Goodale, Mark. 2006. "Toward a Critical Anthropology of Human Rights." *Current Anthropology* 47 (3): 485–511.

Goode, William Josiah. 1963. *World Revolution and Family Patterns*. New York: Free Press of Glencoe.

Govindrajan, Radhika. 2018. *Animal Intimacies: Interspecies Relatedness in India's Central Himalayas*. Chicago: University of Chicago Press.

Grewal, Inderpal. 1999. "'Women's Rights as Human Rights': Feminist Practices, Global Feminism, and Human Rights Regimes in Transnationality." *Citizenship Studies* 3 (3): 337–54.

———. 2005. *Transnational America: Feminisms, Diasporas, Neoliberalisms*. Durham, NC: Duke University Press.

Grover, Shalini. 2009. "Lived Experiences: Marriage, Notions of Love, and Kinship Support amongst Poor Women in Delhi." *Contributions to Indian Sociology* 43 (1): 1–33.

———. 2011. *Marriage, Love, Caste, and Kinship Support: Lived Experiences of the Urban Poor in India*. New Delhi: Social Science Press.

Gupte, Manisha. 2016. "Why Feminism Should Inform Our Routine Interventions in Domestic Violence." In *Feminist Counselling and Domestic Violence in India*, edited by Padma Bhate-Deosthali, Sangeeta Rege, and Padma Prakash. London: Routledge.

Hall, Kira. 2021. "Language in the Middle: Class and Sexuality on the Hinglish Continuum." *Journal of Sociolinguistics* 25 (3): 303–23.

Han, Clara. 2012. *Life in Debt: Times of Care and Violence in Neoliberal Chile*. Berkeley: University of California Press.

Haraway, Donna J. 1981. "In the Beginning Was the Word: The Genesis of Biological Theory." *Signs* 6 (3): 469–81.

———. 2016. *Staying with the Trouble: Making Kin in the Chthulucene*. Durham, NC: Duke University Press.

Hautzinger, Sarah J. 2007. *Violence in the City of Women: Police and Batterers in Bahia, Brazil.* Berkeley: University of California Press.

Hemment, Julie. 2004. "Global Civil Society and the Local Costs of Belonging: Defining Violence against Women in Russia." *Signs: Journal of Women in Culture and Society* 29 (3): 815–40.

———. 2007. *Empowering Women in Russia: Activism, Aid, and NGOs.* Bloomington: Indiana University Press.

Hemmings, Clare. 2011. *Why Stories Matter: The Political Grammar of Feminist Theory.* Durham, NC: Duke University Press.

Hill, Jane. 1995. "The Voices of Don Gabriel: Responsibility and Self in a Modern Mexicano Narrative." In *The Dialogic Emergence of Culture*, edited by Dennis Tedlock and Bruce Mannheim, 97–147. Urbana: University of Illinois Press.

———. 2009. *The Everyday Language of White Racism.* New York: John Wiley and Sons.

Hochschild, Arlie Russel. 2000. "Global Care Chains and Emotional Surplus Value." In *Global Capitalism*, edited by Will Hutton and Anthony Giddens. New York: New Press.

Hodgson, Dorothy Louise, ed. 2011. *Gender and Culture at the Limit of Rights.* 1st ed. Pennsylvania Studies in Human Rights. Philadelphia: University of Pennsylvania Press.

Hodžić, Saida. 2016. *The Twilight of Cutting: African Activism and Life after NGOs.* Berkeley: University of California Press.

hooks, bell. 2015. *Feminist Theory: From Margin to Center.* 3rd ed. New York: Routledge.

Hull, Matthew S. 2011. "Communities of Place, Not Kind: American Technologies of Neighborhood in Postcolonial Delhi." *Comparative Studies in Society and History* 53 (4): 757–90.

———. 2012. *Government of Paper: The Materiality of Bureaucracy in Urban Pakistan.* Berkeley: University of California Press.

International Institute for Population Sciences and Macro International. 2008. *National Family Health Survey (NFHS-3), India, 2005–06: Rajasthan.* Mumbai: IIPS.

Irvine, Judith T. 1989. "When Talk Isn't Cheap: Language and Political Economy." *American Ethnologist* 16 (2): 248–67.

Irvine, Judith T., and Susan Gal. 2000. "Language Ideology and Linguistic Differentiation." In *Regimes of Language: Ideologies, Polities, and Identities*, edited by Paul Kroskrity, 35–84. Santa Fe, NM: School for Advanced Research Press.

Jaising, Indira. 2009. "Bringing Rights Home: Review of the Campaign for a Law on Domestic Violence." *Economic and Political Weekly* 44 (44): 50–57.

Jaising, Indira, and Monica Sakhrani. 2007. *Law of Domestic Violence: A User's Manual for Women.* 2nd ed. New Delhi: Universal Law Pub. Co.

Jakobson, Roman. 1960. "Closing Statement: Linguistics and Poetics." In *Style in Language*, edited by Thomas A. Sebeok, 350–77. Cambridge: MIT Press.

Jarrín, Alvaro. 2017. *The Biopolitics of Beauty: Cosmetic Citizenship and Affective Capital in Brazil.* Berkeley: University of California Press.

Jauregui, Beatrice. 2014. "Provisional Agency in India: *Jugaad* and Legitimation of Corruption." *American Ethnologist* 41 (1): 76–91.

Jeffery, Patricia, and Roger Jeffery. 1994. "Killing My Heart's Desire: Education and Female Autonomy in Rural India." In *Women as Subjects: South Asian Histories*, edited by Nita Kumar, 125–71. Charlottesville: University Press of Virginia.

Jhamb, Bhumika. 2011. "The Missing Link in the Domestic Violence Act." *Economic and Political Weekly* 46 (33): 45–50.

Kalokhe, Ameeta, Carlos del Rio, Kristin Dunkle, Rob Stephenson, Nicholas Metheny, Anuradha Paranjape, and Seema Sahay. 2017. "Domestic Violence against Women in India: A Systematic Review of a Decade of Quantitative Studies." *Global Public Health* 12 (4): 498–513.

Kandiyoti, Deniz. 1988. "Bargaining with Patriarchy." *Gender and Society* 2 (3): 274–90.

———. 1998. "Gender, Power and Contestation: Rethinking Bargaining with Patriarchy." In *Feminist Visions of Development: Gender Analysis and Policy*, edited by Cecile Jackson and Ruth Pearson, 138–55. New York: Routledge.

Kantor, Hayden S. 2019. "A Body Set between Hot and Cold: Everyday Sensory Labor and Attunement in an Indian Village." *Food, Culture and Society* 22 (2): 237–52.

Kapadia, K. M. 1955. *Marriage and Family in India*. Bombay: Oxford University Press.

Kapur, Ratna. 2012. "Hecklers to Power? The Waning of Liberal Rights and Challenges to Feminism in India." In *South Asian Feminisms*, edited by Ania Loomba and Ritty A. Lukose, 333–55. Durham, NC: Duke University Press.

Karlekar, Malavika. 1998. "Domestic Violence." *Economic and Political Weekly* 33 (27): 1741–51.

Karve, Irawati Karmarkar. 1965. *Kinship Organization in India*. New Delhi: Asia Publishing House.

Kashyap, Lina. 2009. "Training Family Counsellors in Contemporary India." *Indian Journal of Social Work* 70 (2): 133.

Keane, Webb. 1997. "From Fetishism to Sincerity: On Agency, the Speaking Subject, and their Historicity in the Context of Religious Conversion." *Comparative Studies in Society and History* 39 (4): 674–93.

———. 1999. "Voice." *Journal of Linguistic Anthropology*, 271–73.

———. 2003. "Semiotics and the Social Analysis of Material Things." *Language and Communication* 23 (2003): 409–25.

———. 2011. "Indexing Voice: A Morality Tale." *Journal of Linguistic Anthropology* 21 (2): 166–78.

Keck, Margaret E., and Kathryn Sikkink. 1998. *Activists Beyond Borders: Advocacy Networks in International Politics*. Ithaca, NY: Cornell University Press.

Khullar, Mala. 2005. Introduction to *Writing the Women's Movement: A Reader*, edited by Mala Khullar, 1–43. New Delhi: Zubaan.

Kittay, Eva Feder. 2013. *Love's Labor: Essays on Women, Equality and Dependency*. Routledge.

Kowalski, Julia. 2016. "Ordering Dependence: Care, Disorder, and Kinship Ideology in North Indian Antiviolence Counseling." *American Ethnologist* 43 (1): 63–75.

———. 2018. "Bureaucratizing Sensitivity: Documents and Expertise in North Indian Antiviolence Counseling." *PoLAR: Political and Legal Anthropology Review* 41 (1): 108–23.

———. 2021. "Between Gender and Kinship: Mediating Rights and Relations in North Indian NGOs." *American Anthropologist* 123 (2): 330–342.

Kumar, Nita. 2017. "Mai: A Discussion." Afterword to *Mai*, by Geetanjali Shree, 171–223. New Delhi: Niyogi Books.

Kumar, Radha. 1997. *The History of Doing: An Illustrated Account of Movements for Women's Rights and Feminism in India 1800–1990*. Delhi: Zubaan.

Kunreuther, Laura. 2006. "Technologies of the Voice: FM Radio, Telephone, and the Nepali Diaspora in Kathmandu." *Cultural Anthropology* 21 (3): 323–53.

Lamb, Sarah. 2000. *White Saris and Sweet Mangoes: Aging, Gender, and Body in North India*. Berkeley: University of California Press.

———. 2009. *Aging and the Indian Diaspora*. Bloomington: Indiana University Press.

———. 2013. "Personhood, Appropriate Dependence, and the Rise of Eldercare Institutions in India." In *Transitions and Transformations: Cultural Perspectives on Aging and the Life Course*, 172–87. New York: Berghahn Books.

———. 2018. "Being Single in India: Gendered Identities, Class Mobilities, and Personhoods in Flux." *Ethos* 46 (1): 49–69.

Lambert, Helen. 2000. "Sentiment and Substance in North Indian Forms of Relatedness." In *Cultures of Relatedness: New Approaches to the Study of Kinship*, edited by Janet Carsten, 73–89. Cambridge: Cambridge University Press.

Lang, Sabine. 1997. "The NGOization of Feminism." In *Transitions, Environments, Translations: Feminisms in International Politics*, edited by Cora Kaplan, Joan Wallach Scott, and Debra Keates, 101–20. New York: Routledge.

Lawyers Collective. 2012. *Staying Alive: Fifth Monitoring and Evaluation Report 2012 on the Protection of Women from Domestic Violence Act, 2005*. Delhi: Lawyer's Collective in collaboration with The International Center for Research on Women.

———. 2013. *Staying Alive: Evaluating Court Orders; Sixth Monitoring and Evaluation Report 2013 on the Protection of Women from Domestic Violence Act, 2005*. New Delhi: Lawyers Collective.

Lazarus-Black, Mindie. 2007. *Everyday Harm: Domestic Violence, Court Rites, and Cultures of Reconciliation*. Urbana: University of Illinois Press.

Lemons, Katherine. 2016. "The Politics of Livability: Tutoring Kinwork in a New Delhi Women's Arbitration Center." *PoLAR: Political and Legal Anthropology Review* 39 (2): 244–60.

Levitt, Peggy, and Sally Merry. 2009. "Vernacularization on the Ground: Local Uses of Global Women's Rights in Peru, China, India and the United States." *Global Networks* 9 (4): 441–61.

Lipsky, Michael. 2010. *Street-Level Bureaucracy: Dilemmas of the Individual in Public Services*. New York: Russell Sage Foundation.

Livingston, Julie. 2005. *Debility and Moral Imagination in Botswana: Disability, Chronic Illness, and Aging*. Bloomington: Indiana University Press.

———. 2007. "Productive Misunderstandings and the Dynamism of Plural Medicine in Mid-Century Bechuanaland." *Journal of Southern African Studies* 33 (4): 801–10.

Lodhia, Sharmila. 2009. "Legal Frankensteins and Monstrous Women: Judicial Narratives of the 'Family in Crisis.'" *Meridians: Feminism, Race, Transnationalism* 9 (2): 102–29.

Loomba, Ania, and Ritty Lukose. 2012. "South Asian Feminisms: Contemporary Interventions." In *South Asian Feminisms*, edited by Ania Loomba and Ritty A. Lukose, 1–32. Durham, NC: Duke University Press.

Madan, T. N. 1962. "The Hindu Joint Family." *Man* 62: 88–89.

Madhok, Sumi. 2009. "Five Notions of Haq: Exploring Vernacular Rights Cultures in South Asia." *LSE Gender Institute. New Working Paper Series*, no. 25: 3.

———. 2010. "Rights Talk and the Feminist Movement in India." In *Women's Movements in Asia: Feminisms and Transnational Activism*, edited by Mina Roces and Mina Edwards, 224–41. New York: Routledge.

———. 2012. *Rethinking Agency: Developmentalism, Gender and Rights*. New York: Routledge.

———. 2015. "Developmentalism, Human Rights, and Gender Politics: From a Politics of Origins to a Politics of Meanings." In *Human Rights: India and the West*, edited by Ashwani Peetush and Jay Drydak, 95–121. New Delhi: Oxford University Press.

Madhok, Sumi, and Shirin M. Rai. 2012. "Agency, Injury, and Transgressive Politics in Neoliberal Times." *Signs* 37 (3): 645–69.

Madhok, Sumi, Maya Unnithan, and Carolyn Heitmeyer. 2014. "On Reproductive Justice: 'Domestic Violence', Rights and the Law in India." *Culture, Health and Sexuality* 16 (10): 1231–44.

Mahapragya, Acharya, and Avul Pakir Jainulabdeen Abdul Kalam. 2008. *The Family and the Nation*. New Delhi: Harper Collins Publishers India.

Mahmood, Saba. 2001. "Feminist Theory, Embodiment, and the Docile Agent: Some Reflections on the Egyptian Islamic Revival." *Cultural Anthropology* 16 (2): 202–36.

———. 2005. *Politics of Piety: The Islamic Revival and the Feminist Subject*. Princeton, NJ: Princeton University Press.

Majumdar, Rochona. 2007. "Family Values in Transition: Debates around the Hindu Code." In *From the Colonial to the Postcolonial: India and Pakistan in Transition*, edited by Dipesh Chakrabarty, Rochona Majumdar, and Andrew Sartori, 223–40. New Delhi: Oxford University Press.

———. 2009. *Marriage and Modernity: Family Values in Colonial Bengal*. Durham, NC: Duke University Press.

Mani, Lata. 1998. *Contentious Traditions: The Debate on Sati in Colonial India*. Berkeley: University of California Press.

Mankekar, Purnima. 1999. *Screening Culture, Viewing Politics: An Ethnography of Television, Womanhood, and Nation in Postcolonial India*. Durham, NC: Duke University Press.

Marrow, Jocelyn. 2008. "Psychiatry, Modernity and Family Values: Clenched Teeth Illness in North India." PhD diss., University of Chicago.

———. 2013. "The Rhetoric of Women and Children's Rights in Indian Psychiatry." *Anthropology and Medicine* 20 (1): 37–41.

Mathur, Kanchan. 1999. "The Emergence of Violence Against Women as an Issue in the Women's Development Programme, Rajasthan." In *Institutions, Relations, and Outcomes: A Framework and Case Studies for Gender-aware Planning*, edited by Naila Kabeer and Ramya Subrahmanian, 288–311. Delhi: Kali for Women.

———. 2004. *Countering Gender Violence: Initiatives Towards Collective Action in Rajasthan*. New Delhi: Sage Publications.

Matoesian, Gregory. 1999. "The Grammaticalization of Participant Roles in the Constitution of Expert Identity." *Language in Society* 28 (4): 491–521.

———. 2005. "Nailing Down an Answer: Participants of Power in Trial Talk." *Discourse Studies* 7 (6): 733–59.

Maunaguru, Sidharthan. 2019. *Marrying for a Future: Transnational Sri Lankan Tamil Marriages in the Shadow of War*. Seattle: University of Washington Press.

McClusky, Laura J. 2001. *"Here, Our Culture Is Hard": Stories of Domestic Violence from a Mayan Community in Belize*. Austin: University of Texas Press.

McGregor, Ronald Stuart. 1997. *The Oxford Hindi-English Dictionary*. Oxford: Oxford University Press.

McKinnon, Susan. 2001. "The Economies in Kinship and the Paternity of Culture: Origin Stories in Kinship Theory." In *Relative Values: Reconfiguring Kinship Studies*, edited by Susan McKinnon and Sarah Franklin, 277–301. Durham, NC: Duke University Press.

———. 2013. "Kinship Within and Beyond the 'Movement of Progressive Societies.'" In *Vital Relations: Modernity and the Persistent Life of Kinship*, edited by Susan McKinnon and Fenella Cannell, 39–62. Santa Fe, NM: School for Advanced Research Press.

———. 2016. "Temperamental Differences: The Shifting Political Implications of Cousin Marriage in Nineteenth-Century America." *Social Analysis* 60 (2): 31–46.

McKinnon, Susan, and Fenella Cannell. 2013a. "The Difference Kinship Makes." In *Vital Relations: Modernity and the Persistent Life of Kinship*, edited by Susan McKinnon and Fenella Cannell, 3–38. Santa Fe, NM: School for Advanced Research Press.

———, eds. 2013b. *Vital Relations: Modernity and the Persistent Life of Kinship*. Santa Fe, NM: School for Advanced Research Press.

Menon, Nikhil. 2021. "Developing Histories of Indian Development." *History Compass* 19(10): e12689.

Menon, Nivedita. 2004. *Recovering Subversion: Feminist Politics Beyond the Law*. Urbana: University of Illinois Press.

Menon, Usha. 2013. *Women, Wellbeing, and the Ethics of Domesticity in an Odia Hindu Temple Town*. Heidelberg: Springer India.

Merry, Sally Engle. 2003. "Rights Talk and the Experience of Law : Implementing Women ' s Human Rights to Protection from Violence." *Human Rights Quarterly* 25 (2): 343–81.

———. 2006. *Human Rights and Gender Violence: Translating International Law into Local Justice*. Chicago: University of Chicago Press.

———. 2009. *Gender Violence: A Cultural Perspective*. Introductions to Engaged Anthropology. Chichester, West Sussex, UK: Wiley-Blackwell.

———. 2016. *The Seductions of Quantification: Measuring Human Rights, Gender Violence, and Sex Trafficking*. Chicago: University of Chicago Press.

Mol, Annemarie. 2008. *The Logic of Care: Health and the Problem of Patient Choice*. New York: Routledge.

Moodie, Megan. 2008. "Enter Microcredit: A New Culture of Women's Empowerment in Rajasthan?" *American Ethnologist* 35 (3): 454–65.

Moore, Henrietta. 1994. "The Problem of Explaining Violence in the Social Sciences." In *Sex and Violence: Issues in Representation and Experience*, edited by Penelope Harvey and Peter Gow, 138–55. London: Routledge.

Morreira, Shannon. 2016. *Rights after Wrongs: Local Knowledge and Human Rights in Zimbabwe*. Stanford, CA: Stanford University Press.

Mukhopadhyay, Amrita. 2019. "Found and Lost in Translation: Exploring the Legal Protection of Women from the Domestic Violence Act 2005 Through the Social Public Space of Kolkata." *Social and Legal Studies* 28 (3): 349–69.

Mulla, Sameena. 2014. *The Violence of Care: Rape Victims, Forensic Nurses, and Sexual Assault Intervention*. New York: New York University Press.

Nagar, Richa. 2017. *Muddying the Waters: Coauthoring Feminisms across Scholarship and Activism*. Urbana: University of Illinois Press.

Nagaraj, Vasudha. 2010. "Local and Customary Forums Adapting and Innovating Rules of Formal Law." *Indian Journal of Gender Studies* 17 (3): 429–50.

Nehru, Jawaharlal. 2004. *The Discovery of India*. New Delhi: Penguin Books.

Newbigin, Eleanor. 2010. "A Post-Colonial Patriarchy? Representing Family in the Indian Nation-State." *Modern Asian Studies* 44 (1): 121–44.

———. 2013. *The Hindu Family and the Emergence of Modern India: Law, Citizenship and Community*. Cambridge: Cambridge University Press.

Oberoi, Radhika. 2008. "How Fair Is Dowry Law?" *Times of India*, Sept. 8, 2008.

Ochs, Elinor. 2004. "Narrative Lessons." In *A Companion to Linguistic Anthropology*, edited by Alessandro Duranti, 269–89. New York: Oxford University Press.

Oldenburg, Veena Talwar. 2002. *Dowry Murder: The Imperial Origins of a Cultural Crime*. Oxford: Oxford University Press.

Ortner, Sherry B. 2005. "Subjectivity and Cultural Critique." *Anthropological Theory* 5 (1): 31–52.

———. 2006. *Anthropology and Social Theory: Culture, Power, and the Acting Subject*. Durham, NC: Duke University Press.

Pandian, Anand. 2009. *Crooked Stalks: Cultivating Virtue in South India*. Durham, NC: Duke University Press.

Pandian, Anand, and Daud Ali. 2010. Introduction to *Ethical Life in South Asia*, edited by Anand Pandian and Daud Ali, 1–20. Bloomington: Indiana University Press.

Parmentier, Richard J. 1994. *Signs in Society: Studies in Semiotic Anthropology*. Bloomington: Indiana University Press.

Mishra, Paro. 2013. "Sex Ratios, Cross-Region Marriages and the Challenge to Caste Endogamy in Haryana." *Economic and Political Weekly* 48 (35): 70–78.

Parreñas, Rhacel. 2008. *The Force of Domesticity: Filipina Migrants and Globalization*. New York: New York University Press.

Parson, Nia. 2010. "'I Am Not [Just] a Rabbit Who Has a Bunch of Children!': Agency in the Midst of Suffering at the Intersections of Global Inequalities, Gendered Violence, and Migration." *Violence Against Women* 16 (8): 881–901.

Peirce, Charles. 1956. "Logic as Semiotic: The Theory of Signs." In *Philosophical Writings of Peirce*, edited by Justus Buchler, 98–119. New York: Dover Publications.

Pinto, Sarah. 2008. *Where There Is No Midwife: Birth and Loss in Rural India*. New York: Berghahn Books.

———. 2011. "Rational Love, Relational Medicine: Psychiatry and the Accumulation of Precarious Kinship." *Culture, Medicine, and Psychiatry* 35: 376–95.

———. 2014. *Daughters of Parvati: Women and Madness in Contemporary India*. Philadelphia: University of Pennsylvania Press.

Plesset, Sonja. 2006. *Sheltering Women: Negotiating Gender and Violence in Northern Italy*. Stanford, CA: Stanford University Press.

Post News Network. 2019. "UP Man Divorces Wife for Feeding 'Laddoos' Day and Night." *OrissaPOST*, August 20, 2019. https://www.orissapost.com/up-man-divorces-wife-for -feeding-laddoos-day-and-night/.

Povinelli, Elizabeth A. 2002. "Notes on Gridlock: Genealogy, Intimacy, Sexuality." *Public Culture* 14 (1): 215–38.

———. 2006. *The Empire of Love: Toward a Theory of Intimacy, Genealogy, and Carnality*. Durham, NC: Duke University Press.

Price, Joshua M. 2002. "The Apotheosis of Home and the Maintenance of Spaces of Violence." *Hypatia* 17 (4): 39–70.

Puri, Jyoti. 1999. *Woman, Body, Desire in Post-Colonial India: Narratives of Gender and Sexuality*. New York: Routledge.

Raheja, Gloria Goodwin. 1995. "Crying When She's Born and Crying When She Goes Away: Marriage and the Idiom of the Gift in Pahansu Song Performance." In *From the Margins of Hindu Marriage: Essays on Gender, Religion, and Culture*, edited by Lindsey Harlan and Paul Courtwright, 18–59. Oxford: Oxford University Press.

Raheja, Gloria Goodwin, and Ann Grodzins Gold. 1994. *Listen to the Heron's Words: Reimagining Gender and Kinship in North India*. Berkeley: University of California Press.

Ramberg, Lucinda. 2013. "Troubling Kinship: Sacred Marriage and Gender Configuration in South India." *American Ethnologist* 40 (4): 661–75.

Rao, S. N. 2002. *Counselling and Guidance*. New Delhi: Tata McGraw-Hill Education.

Raychaudhuri, Tapan. 2000. "Love in a Colonial Climate: Marriage , Sex and Romance in Nineteenth-Century Bengal." *Modern Asian Studies* 34 (2): 349–78.

Richland, Justin B. 2007. "Pragmatic Paradoxes and Ironies of Indigeneity at the Edge of Hopi Sovereignty." *American Ethnologist* 34 (3): 540–57.

Riles, Annelise. 1998. "Infinity within the Brackets." *American Ethnologist* 25 (3): 378–98.

———. 2006. "Anthropology, Human Rights, and Legal Knowledge: Culture in the Iron Cage." *American Anthropologist* 108 (1): 52–65.

Robbins, Jessica C. 2020. *Aging Nationally in Contemporary Poland: Memory, Kinship, and Personhood*. New Brunswick, NJ: Rutgers University Press.

Rook-Koepsel, Emily. 2021. "Social Work and Political Visibility: Activism, Education and the Disciplining of Social Service." *South Asia: Journal of South Asian Studies* 44 (2): 329–43.

Rosaldo, Michelle. 1982. "The Things We Do with Words: Ilongot Speech Acts and Speech Act Theory in Philosophy." *Language in Society* 11 (2): 203–37.

Roychowdhury, Poulami. 2016. "Desire, Rights, Entitlements: Organizational Strategies in the War on Violence." *Signs: Journal of Women in Culture and Society* 41 (4): 793–820.

———. 2021. *Capable Women, Incapable States: Negotiating Violence and Rights in India*. New York: Oxford University Press.

Rubin, Gayle. 1975. "The Traffic in Women: Notes on the 'Political Economy' of Sex." In *Toward an Anthropology of Women*, edited by Rayna R. Reiter, 157–210. New York: Monthly Review Press.

Sahlins, Marshall David. 1981. *Historical Metaphors and Mythical Realities: Structure in the Early History of the Sandwich Islands Kingdom*. Ann Arbor: University of Michigan Press.

Sangatin Writers Collective and Richa Nagar. 2006. *Playing with Fire: Feminist Thought and Activism through Seven Lives in India*. Minneapolis: University of Minnesota Press.

Sargent, Adam. 2020. "Working against Labor: Struggles for Self in the Indian Construction Industry." *Anthropology of Work Review* 41 (2): 76–85.

Sarkar, Tanika. 2000. "A Prehistory of Rights: The Age of Consent Debate in Colonial Bengal." *Feminist Studies* 26 (3): 601.

Schneider, David Murray. 1984. *A Critique of the Study of Kinship*. Ann Arbor: University of Michigan Press.

Sen, Uditi. 2018. *Citizen Refugee: Forging the Indian Nation after Partition*. Cambridge: Cambridge University Press.

Sewell, William Hamilton. 2005. *Logics of History: Social Theory and Social Transformation*. Chicago: University of Chicago Press.

Shah, A. M. 1968. "Changes in the Indian Family: An Examination of Some Assumptions." *Economic and Political Weekly* 3 (1/2): 127–34.

Sharma, Aradhana. 2006. "Crossbreeding Institutions, Breeding Struggle: Women's Empowerment, Neoliberal Governmentality, and State (Re)Formation in India." *Cultural Anthropology* 21 (1): 60–95.

———. 2008. *Logics of Empowerment: Development, Gender, and Governance in Neoliberal India*. Minneapolis: University of Minnesota Press.

Sharma, Kumud, and C. P. Sujaya. 2012. "Introducing Towards Equality." In *Towards Equality: Report of the Committee on the Status of Women in India*, 1st ed., edited by Kumud Sharma and C.P. Sujaya. Delhi: Pearson Education India.

Sharma, Kumud, C. P. Sujaya, and C. P. Sujaya, eds. 2012. *Towards Equality: Report of the Committee on the Status of Women in India*. New Delhi: Centre for Women's Development Studies; Pearson.

Sherman, Taylor C. 2018. "'A New Type of Revolution': Socialist Thought in India, 1940s–1960s." *Postcolonial Studies* 21 (4): 485–504.

———. 2021. "Not Part of the Plan? Women, State Feminism and Indian Socialism in the Nehru Years." *South Asia: Journal of South Asian Studies* 44 (2): 298–312.

Shever, Elana. 2008. "Neoliberal Associations: Property, Company, and Family in the Argentine Oil Fields." *American Ethnologist* 35 (4): 701–16.

Shree, Geetanjali. 2017. *Mai*. Translated by Nita Kumar. New Delhi: Niyogi Books.

Shyam, Kumar. 2020. "The 5 Step Game of NPR+CAA+NRC by Yogendra Yadav." February 14, 2020. YouTube video, 7:56. https://www.youtube.com/watch?v=tAURBzy-Yu4.

Silverstein, Leni M., and Ellen Lewin. 2016. "Introduction: Anthropologies and Feminisms: Mapping Our Intellectual Journey." In *Mapping Feminist Anthropology in the Twenty-First Century*, edited by Ellen Lewin and Leni M. Silverstein, 6–38. New Brunswick: Rutgers University Press.

Silverstein, Michael. 1976. "Shifters, Linguistic Categories, and Cultural Description." In *Meaning in Anthropology*, edited by Keith H. Basso and Henry A. Selby, 11–55. Albuquerque: University of New Mexico Press.

———. 2003. "Indexical Order and the Dialectics of Sociolinguistic Life." *Language and Communication* 23: 193–229.

Silverstein, Michael, and Greg Urban. 1996. "Natural History of Discourse." In *Natural Histories of Discourse*, edited by Michael Silverstein and Greg Urban, 1–17. Chicago: University of Chicago Press.

Singh, Bhrigupati. 2017. "Depression." *South Asia: Journal of South Asian Studies* 40 (2): 297–300.

Sinha, Mrinalini. 2006. *Specters of Mother India: The Global Restructuring of an Empire*. Durham, NC: Duke University Press.

Sousa, Amy. 2016. "Diagnostic Neutrality in Psychiatric Treatment in North India." In *Our Most Troubling Madness: Case Studies in Schizophrenia across Cultures*, edited by T. M. Luhrmann and Jocelyn Marrow, 42–55. Berkeley: University of California Press.

Sreenivas, Mytheli. 2008. *Wives, Widows, and Concubines: The Conjugal Family Ideal in Colonial India*. Bloomington: Indiana University Press.

———. 2021. *Reproductive Politics and the Making of Modern India*. Seattle: University of Washington Press.

Sreenivasan, Ramya. 2004. "Honoring the Family: Narratives and Politics of Kinship in Pre-Colonial Rajasthan." In *Unfamiliar Relations: Family and History in South Asia*, edited by Indrani Chatterjee, 46–72. New Brunswick, N.J.: Rutgers University Press.

Srivatsan, R. 2006. "Concept of 'Seva' and the 'Sevak' in the Freedom Movement." *Economic and Political Weekly* 41 (5): 427–38.

Stephen, Lynn. 1995. "Women's Rights Are Human Rights: The Merging of Feminine and Feminist Interests among El Salvador's Mothers of the Disappeared (CO-MADRES)." *American Ethnologist* 22 (4): 807–27.

Stevenson, Lisa. 2014. *Life Beside Itself: Imagining Care in the Canadian Arctic*. Berkeley: University of California Press.

Strathern, Marilyn. 1987. "An Awkward Relationship: The Case of Feminism and Anthropology." *Signs* 12 (2): 276–92.

———. 1992. *After Nature: English Kinship in the Late Twentieth Century*. Cambridge: Cambridge University Press.

Sturman, Rachel. 2012. *The Government of Social Life in Colonial India: Liberalism, Religious Law, and Women's Rights*. Cambridge: Cambridge University Press.

Sufrin, Carolyn. 2017. *Jailcare: Finding the Safety Net for Women behind Bars*. Berkeley: University of California Press.

Sunder Rajan, Rajeswari. 2003. *The Scandal of the State: Women, Law, Citizenship in Postcolonial India*. New Delhi: Permanent Black.

———. 2004. "Rethinking Law and Violence: The Domestic Violence (Prevention) Bill in India, 2002." *Gender and History* 16 (3): 769–93.

Suneetha, A., and Vasudha Nagaraj. 2010. "Dealing with Domestic Violence: Towards Complicating the Rights Discourse." *Indian Journal of Gender Studies* 17 (3): 451–78.

TallBear, Kim. 2019. "Caretaking Relations, Not American Dreaming." *Kalfou* 6 (1): 24–41.

Tarlo, Emma. 2003. *Unsettling Memories: Narratives of the Emergency in Delhi*. London: C. Hurst.

Thelen, T. 2015. "Care as Social Organization: Creating, Maintaining and Dissolving Significant Relations." *Anthropological Theory* 15 (4): 497–515.

Thomas, Dorothy Q., and Michele E. Beasley. 1993. "Domestic Violence as a Human Rights Issue." *Human Rights Quarterly* 15 (1): 36–62.

Ticktin, Miriam. 2011. *Casualties of Care: Immigration and the Politics of Humanitarianism in France*. Berkeley: University of California Press.

Trautmann, Thomas. 1987. *Lewis Henry Morgan and the Invention of Kinship*. Berkeley: University of California Press.

Trawick, Margaret. 1990. *Notes on Love in a Tamil Family*. Berkeley: University of California Press.

Trinch, Shonna L. 2001. "The Advocate as Gatekeeper: The Limits of Politeness in Protective Order Interviews with Latina Survivors of Domestic Abuse." *Journal of Sociolinguistics* 5 (4): 475–506.

———. 2007. "Deconstructing the Stakes in High Stakes Gatekeeping Interviews: Battered Women and Narration." *Journal of Pragmatics* 39 (11): 1895–1918.

Tronto, Joan. 2014. "Care as a Basis for Radical Political Judgments." *Hypatia* 10 (2): 141–49.

Tsing, Anna Lowenhaupt. 2005. *Friction: An Ethnography of Global Connection*. Princeton, NJ: Princeton University Press.

———. 2015. *The Mushroom at the End of the World: On the Possibility of Life in Capitalist Ruins*. Princeton, NJ: Princeton University Press.

Uberoi, Patricia. 1993. *Family, Kinship, and Marriage in India*. Delhi: Oxford University Press.

———. 1996. "The Family in Official Discourse." *India International Centre Quarterly* 23 (3): 134–55.

———. 1998. "The Diaspora Comes Home: Disciplining Desire in DDLJ." *Contributions to Indian Sociology* 32 (2): 305–36.

———. 2005. "The Family in India: Beyond the Nuclear versus Joint Debate." In *Writing the Women's Movement: A Reader*, edited by Mala Khullar, 361–96. New Delhi: Zubaan.

United Nations. 2010. *Handbook for Legislation on Violence against Women*. New York: United Nations.

United Nations General Assembly. 1994. *Declaration on the Elimination of Violence against Women*. New York: United Nations Department of Public Information.

Unnithan, Maya, and Carolyn Heitmeyer. 2012. "Global Rights and State Activism: Reflections on Civil Society–State Partnerships in Health in NW India." *Contributions to Indian Sociology* 46 (3): 283–310.

———. 2014. "Challenges in 'Translating' Human Rights: Perceptions and Practices of Civil Society Actors in Western India." *Development and Change* 45 (6): 1361–84.

Van Vleet, Krista E. 2008. *Performing Kinship: Narrative, Gender, and the Intimacies of Power in the Andes.* Austin: University of Texas Press.

Varadappan, Sarojini. 1975. "Future Vision of the Activities of the CSWB." *Social Welfare* 22 (6–7): 104–7.

Vatuk, Silvia. 1975. "Gifts and Affines in North India." *Contributions to Indian Sociology* 9 (2): 155–96.

———. 1990. "'To Be a Burden on Others': Dependency Anxiety among the Elderly in India." In *Divine Passions: The Social Construction of Emotion in India*, edited by Owen M. Lynch, 64–90. Berkeley: University of California Press.

———. 2017. *Marriage and Its Discontents: Women, Islam and the Law in India.* Delhi: Women Unlimited, an associate of Kali for Women.

Vera-Sanso, Penny. 1999. "Dominant Daughters-in-Law and Submissive Mothers-in-Law? Cooperation and Conflict in South India." *Journal of the Royal Anthropological Institute* 5 (4): 577–93.

Visweswaran, Kamala. 2004. "Gendered States: Rethinking Culture as a Site of South Asian Human Rights Work." *Human Rights Quarterly* 26 (2): 483–511.

Wadley, Susan Snow. 1994. *Struggling with Destiny in Karimpur, 1925–1984.* Berkeley: University of California Press.

———. 2010. "One Straw from a Broom Cannot Sweep: The Ideology and Practice of the Joint Family in India." In *Everyday Life in South Asia, Second Edition*, edited by Diane P. Mines and Sarah E. Lamb, 14–25. Bloomington: Indiana University Press.

Walters, Kimberly. 2016. "The Stickiness of Sex Work: Pleasure, Habit, and Intersubstantiality in South India." *Signs: Journal of Women in Culture and Society* 42 (1): 99–121.

Wardlow, Holly. 2006. *Wayward Women: Sexuality and Agency in a New Guinea Society.* Berkeley: University of California Press.

Watkins, Susan Cotts, and Ann Swidler. 2013. "Working Misunderstandings: Donors, Brokers, and Villagers in Africa's AIDS Industry." *Population and Development Review* 38 (s1): 197–218.

Watkins, Susan Cotts, Ann Swidler, and Thomas Hannan. 2012. "Outsourcing Social Transformation: Development NGOs as Organizations." *Annual Review of Sociology* 38 (1): 285–315.

Watt, Carey A. 2006. "Envisioning 'Seva.'" *Economic and Political Weekly* 41 (48): 4958–61.

Weidman, Amanda. 2014. "Anthropology and Voice." *Annual Review of Anthropology* 43 (1): 37–51.

Weiner, Annette B. 1980. "Reproduction: A Replacement for Reciprocity." *American Ethnologist* 7 (1): 71–85.

Weinstein, Deborah F. 2004. "Culture at Work: Family Therapy and the Culture Concept in Post-World War II America." *Journal of the History of the Behavioral Sciences* 40 (1): 23–46.

Wies, Jennifer R., and Hillary J. Haldane. 2011. "Ethnographic Notes from the Front Lines of Gender-Based Violence." In *Anthropology at the Front Lines of Gender-Based Violence*, edited by Jennifer R. Wies and Hillary J. Haldane, 1–18. Nashville, TN: Vanderbilt University Press.

Wilce, James MacLynn. 1998. *Eloquence in Trouble: The Poetics and Politics of Complaint in Rural Bangladesh*. New York: Oxford University Press.

Wilson, Kalpana. 2013. "Agency as 'Smart Economics': Neoliberalism, Gender and Development." In *Gender, Agency and Coercion*, edited by Sumi Madhok, Anne Phillips, and Kalpana Wilson, 84–101. Basingstoke, UK: Palgrave Macmillan.

Wilson, Richard. 2007. "Tyrannosaurus Lex." In *The Practice of Human Rights: Tracking Law between Local and Global*, edited by Mark Goodale and Sally Engle Merry, 342–70. Cambridge: Cambridge University Press.

Woolard, Kathryn. 1998. "Introduction: Language Ideology as a Field of Inquiry." In *Language Ideologies: Practice and Theory*, edited by Bambi Schieffelin, Kathryn Woolard, and Paul Kroskrity, 3–47. Oxford: Oxford University Press.

Wortham, Stanton. 2001. *Narratives in Action: A Strategy for Research and Analysis*. New York: Teachers College Press.

Wright, Andrea. 2020. "Making Kin from Gold: Dowry, Gender, and Indian Labor Migration to the Gulf." *Cultural Anthropology* 35 (3): 435–61.

Yanagisako, Sylvia Junko. 1975. "Two Processes of Change in Japanese-American Kinship." *Journal of Anthropological Research* 31 (3): 196–224.

———. 2002. *Producing Culture and Capital: Family Firms in Italy*. Princeton, NJ: Princeton University Press.

———. 2015. "Kinship: Still at the Core." *HAU: Journal of Ethnographic Theory* 5 (1): 489–94.

Yanagisako, Sylvia Junko, and Jane Fishburne Collier. 1987. *Gender and Kinship: Essays toward a Unified Analysis*. Stanford, CA: Stanford University Press.

Yanagisako, Sylvia Junko, and Carol Delaney. 1995. "Naturalizing Power." In *Naturalizing Power: Essays in Feminist Cultural Analysis*, edited by Sylvia Junko Yanagisako and Carol Delaney, 1–24. New York: Routledge.

Yarris, Kristin E. 2017. *Care Across Generations: Solidarity and Sacrifice in Transnational Families*. Stanford, CA: Stanford University Press.

INDEX

adjustment: ambiguities associated with, 71–73; of *bahus*, 52, 69–71, 74, 85; capacities for, 70–71; coercion vs., 44, 45, 62; as counseling strategy and goal, 60–61, 67–68, 72–73, 75; criticisms of, 71–72; in family relations, 23, 26–27, 44, 68–71, 82–83; meanings of, 68, 187n1; personhood and, 70, 187n2; possibilities and limitations of, 72; to social transformations, 47, 71, 74–75, 85; in speech, 135

affection, speaking with, 132–35, 190n10

age at marriage, 70

agency: liberal conception of relations as hindrance to, 5, 15, 25, 176–77; relations as medium for exercise of, 5, 25–26. *See also* generative agency; personhood

Ahearn, Laura, 180n7

alternate dispute resolution, 28, 182n18, 187n17

anticipatory structures, 33, 91–92, 99, 102–15, 153

asking-and-giving, 117, 129–37, 161, 164

bahus (daughters-in-law): adjustments expected of, 52, 69–71, 74, 85; careful speech of, 136; conflicts faced by, 73–74; education of, 74; expectations regarding care for elders, 119–20, 154–55; family roles of, 123–24; as new mothers, 115–17, 138

Basu, Srimati, 13, 113, 145, 182n18

Beijing Declaration and Platform for Action (UN), 96

Benjamin, Ruha, 23, 168

Bunch, Charlotte, 146–48

Butler, Judith, 177

Cannell, Fenella, 18

care, 24–25, 91, 119, 168, 176, 181n11. *See also* careful speech; *seva*

careful speech, 117–40; agency exercised through, 32, 118, 137; characteristics of, 30, 117; and family relations, 30, 33, 117–18, 129–40, 168; labeling contrasted with, 31–32, 34, 139–40, 145, 165–66, 172–74; material actions linked to, 130–31; and overt violence, 141; political aspect of, 174; in political contexts, 190n10; strategies of, 30, 34, 118, 129, 133–36, 139–40, 153, 156–57, 165, 168; and terminology related to violence, 31–32; tips for, 132–36. See also *seva*

Carr, Summerson, 173–74

caste organizations, 40–41

Central Social Welfare Board, 9, 52, 55

Chopra, Priyanka, 131

class/status, 126–27

coercion: avoidance of, 10, 38, 45, 46, 49–51, 60, 62; compromise vs., 44, 45, 62; in family relations, 28, 30, 38, 48–51; verbal controlling behavior and, 131–32

Cohen, Lawrence, 121

Cold War, 48

Cole, Jennifer, 16–17, 171

communication. *See* language and interaction

compromise. *See* adjustment

consent, 180n8

contaminated diversity, 7, 179n4

Convention on the Elimination of Discrimination Against Women (UN), 96

counseling: ambiguities/contradictions of, 6–7, 13–16, 24, 27, 34, 37–38, 44, 46–47, 53–55, 57–59, 63–64, 166–69, 172–73, 177–78; class/status of clients for, 126–27; description of sessions, 11, 42, 43, 61, 77–78, 79–86, 164; documentation process in, 76–78, 88, 91, 100–110; family courts compared to, 41–42; family/kinship relations as focus of, 3–7, 13–18, 26–27, 30,

100, 102, 111; help sought from, 39–40;
   language use in, 31
liberal theory, 17–19, 25, 169, 175–77. *See
   also* personhood; women's rights
linguistic anthropology, 29
Lipsky, Michael, 37, 58
Livingston, Julie, 72, 171

ma'ams: administrative duties of, 56, 172–73;
   counselors in relation to, 11, 55, 56,
   172–73; expertise of, 57; participation of,
   in counseling sessions, 56; respect given
   to, 56; *seva* performed by, 120; social
   status and personal characteristics of, 11,
   42, 56; voluntary service of, 56
Madhok, Sumi, 182n17
Mahapragya, Acharya, 51
mahila thana. See women's police stations
Mahmood, Saba, 25–26, 182n16
Maintenance and Welfare of Parents and
   Senior Citizens Act, 49
Mathur, Kanchan, 148, 191n5, 192n6
Matoesian, Gregory, 31
McKinnon, Susan, 17–18
mediation. *See* alternate dispute resolution;
   counseling
Merry, Sally Engle, 19, 150, 183n21
modernity: family's role in, 6–7, 46, 48;
   India's social order and, 47; liberal models
   of, 17–18; personhood in, 18; women's
   role in, 6–7. *See also* development
money problems: extended family responsibilities as source of, 2–3, 20, 65, 82–83; in
   marriages, 1–2, 82–84, 134
morality: and dilemmas of interdependence,
   16–17, 63; gender violence as violation
   of, 30; imagination of improved family
   relations, 23, 24, 26, 39, 70, 72, 120–29;
   language's constitutive role in, 168;
   popular conception of decline in, 85. See
   also *seva*
Mulla, Sameena, 31, 91–92
multi-generational families. *See* joint
   families
Muslims, 190n10

Nagaraj, Vasudha, 14
natal families: dangers posed by, 21; help
   sought from, 40; interference from, 20,
   74, 76, 82, 170; post-birth recovery with,
   115–17, 138; role of, 20

National Register of Citizens, 190n10
Nehru, Jawaharlal, *Discovery of India*, 49–50,
   186n11
neutrality: avoidance of labeling as
   outgrowth of, 191n1; as chief value in
   counseling, 11, 32, 36, 41, 45, 75, 93, 107;
   goals of, 38–39, 45, 58; in humanitarianism, 187n17; interactive practice as means
   to, 38, 45, 58–59; performances of, 42;
   promise and limits of, 45; types of, 45
non-governmental organizations (NGOs): 9,
   28–29, 188n5; and counseling expertise,
   36; process of NGOization, 8, 181n12; and
   role of talk/interaction, 29, 171, 183n19
nurses, 91–92

Odissa Post (newspaper), 35
order/disorder. *See* hierarchy; India and
   the social order of the state; joint family;
   kinship; *seva*

pareshani (harassment), 2, 152–53
Partition, 47
patriarchy: accommodation of, 7; critiques
   of, 5, 8, 52–53; gender inequality linked
   to, 20; gender violence attributed to, 3, 5;
   interdependent ties in, 19–20, 74. *See also*
   gender inequality
personhood: adjustment as aspect of, 70,
   187n2; individual vs. social-relational
   conceptions of, 5, 7, 14, 17–19, 27–28, 43,
   47, 175–78; liberal conception of, 17–19,
   169, 175–77; models of language in relation to, 149–51; relational and dynamic
   conception of, 26, 43–44; voice linked to,
   63; women as rights-bearing subjects, 15,
   19, 53–54, 63, 142, 174. *See also* agency
Pinto, Sarah, 20, 68, 174
police: counseling centers in relation to, 9,
   41, 60; criticisms of, 23; help sought from,
   39–40; women's treatment by, 40. *See also*
   women's police stations
Povinelli, Elizabeth, 169
power: in family relations, 15, 26, 61, 70–71,
   73; gender and, 147–48. *See also* women:
   empowerment of
productive misunderstandings, 171–73
protection officers, 97, 110, 189n6
Protection of Women from Domestic
   Violence Act (PWDVA), 12, 40, 89–95,
   97–114, 145, 188nn1–3

ACKNOWLEDGMENTS

This book examines how people debate reciprocity, support, and obligation as they sustain selves and relations into an uncertain future. In much the same way, this book was sustained by many people, through multiple uncertain cycles of academic life, across three cross-country moves and four academic institutions.

This book could not have been written without the support of the organizations that ran the family counseling centers where I conducted research. I am particularly grateful for the enthusiastic support of the counselors whose work I discuss here, in spite of busy rosters of counseling cases, paperwork, and unpleasantly hot weather. I am also indebted to their bosses, who granted me permission to spend a great deal of time on site, gave me access to case file archives, and invited me to meetings and outreach programs. Without the participation and permission of these women, this project would not have been possible. I am particularly grateful for the support and friendship of the two counselors I call Hema and Indu.

Beyond fieldwork, I was fortunate to connect with Jaipur's Institute of Development Studies (IDS). I am grateful for conversations with IDS scholar Kanchan Mathur concerning counseling in Rajasthan. At IDS, I had the good fortune to coincide with Maya Unnithan and Carrie Heitmeyer, who offered sage advice about negotiating fieldwork among Jaipur's women's rights organizations, and offered a great deal of background information about recent changes to NGO work and women-oriented legislation. Professors Bela Kothari and Kumud Sharma provided logistical support as well as visa sponsorship at the University of Rajasthan. Everyday life in Jaipur was made possible by the offices of the American Institute of Indian Studies (AIIS) in Jaipur. In addition to guiding my Hindi away from books and into spoken interaction, AIIS also helped with everything from finding a place to live to registering and renewing a research visa. Kumar Janyani, in particularly, caused much important work to be done on my behalf. The Aroras provided a landing place during early Hindi studies. The Gaur family took enormously good care of my partner and I during the bulk of fieldwork, doing everything from keeping us fed to making sure our birthdays were feted to setting broken bones (or at least taking us to the correct hospital to do so). More recently, the Gangwal family has provided a welcoming home away from home for my visits to Jaipur.

In both India and the United States, Abhishek Jain, Pooja Ranade, Purun Singh, and Suman Tank provided invaluable assistance with designing, transcribing, and discussing interviews, as well as providing more intangible conversation and intellectual support.

Whatever Hindi skills I have are owed to many patient and skilled teachers in Chicago and in Jaipur: Sayeed Ayub, Vidhu Shekhar Chaturvedi, Jason Grunebaum, Valerie Ritter, Dr. Achyuta Nand Singh, and Ulrike Stark, *apke sikhaane ke liye jitne abhari hun utne hi nahin bata sakti hun.*

I spent many years as a student in the Department of Comparative Human Development at the University of Chicago, first as an undergraduate and then as a PhD student. A unique interdisciplinary space, it shaped my training as an anthropologist and my attention to the social world, and I continue to be grateful for the cross-disciplinary provocations it provided. This book has been profoundly shaped by Jennifer Cole's ability to locate global processes in the everyday politics of intimate life, as well her keen editorial eye, expectation that ethnographic prose be both sophisticated and clear, and encouragement to cultivate close ties with fellow ethnographic writers. Susan Gal literally welcomed me into the linguistic anthropological fold when I returned from the field with a heap of interactive material that I was struggling to explain to others, and has been a source of intellectual generativity since I first turned up in her anthropology of gender course. This book only scratches the surface of the historical questions that Rochona Majumdar raised throughout the dissertation process, and the analytic questions I asked of my ethnographic materials were profoundly impacted by her research on family, marriage, and gender. Eugene Raikhel has been a generous and thoughtful interlocutor about care, violence, and medical anthropology.

My years at Chicago were shaped by the leadership of the late Richard Taub and John Lucy, as well as Janie Lardner, Stephanie Dering, and, in the office of Graduate Affairs, Brooke Noonan. I am also grateful for courses and interactions with Jessica Cattelino, Dipesh Chakrabarty, Mark Lycett, John Lucy, William Mazzarella, Kathy Morrison, and Michael Silverstein. Bambi Chapin offered an early model and encouragement, and has continued to be a cherished colleague. A stray comment from Tanya Luhrmann on a final paper—"Do consider Human Development!"—lured me into the interpretive social sciences as a college freshman, as did her explanation of anthropology as the social science that "writes books, rather than articles"; I've valued her support since.

One reason I am drawn to theories of social life that center the generative power of interaction is the fact that I think best in conversation with others. This book is the product of many thousands of hours of conversation about topics ranging from personhood, interaction, gender, and the lifecourse to the nature of ethnographic writing and analysis to coping with the challenges of academic life. In Chicago, my conversation partners included Elise Berman, Beth Brummel, Nadxieli Toledo Bustamante, Michael Chladek, John Davy, Christine El-Ouardani, Allison DiBianca Fasoli, Lainie Goldwert, Hallie Kushner, Margaret Mass, Erin Moore, and Talia Weiner, all of whom were members of various writing groups over the years. While a fellow at the Center for the Study of Gender and Sexuality (CSGS) at the University of Chicago, I had the good fortune to overlap with Sarah Luna, George Paul Meiu, and Monica Mercado, and benefitted from the support and leadership of Linda Zerilli, Sarah Tuohey, and Gina Olson. At CSGS my office mate was Carly Schuster, who quickly became a valued friend and interlocuter, crucially shaping this work at its early stages.

Other sources of support, provocation, and inspiration in Chicago (and beyond) include Les Beldo, Amy Cooper, Kathryn Goldfarb, Allison Gray, Pinky Hota, Katie Jenness, Jocelyn Marrow, Kathryn McHarry, Lauren Osborne, Adam Sargent, Amy Sousa, Kim Walters, and Sarah Yardney. Kristel Clayville and Mandy Burton blended being good neighbors, good colleagues, and wonderful friends. Erin Moore offered both intellectual and social joy as a fellow traveler throughout the life of this project.

The Academic Writing program at the University of Chicago offered not only stable and meaningful employment during graduate school but a powerful toolkit for thinking about writing, audience, and argument that continues to inform my approach to both writing and pedagogy (and helps me see the many remaining flaws in this book). I am grateful to Kathy Cochran and Tracy Weiner for the education in writing they provided in this space.

The Oakley Center at Williams College generously supported a manuscript conference for an early draft of the this volume in 2016, ably organized by Krista Birch. The careful reading and comments from Sarah Lamb, Olga Shevchenko, and Saadia Yacoob profoundly shaped the book that emerged. Olga and Saadia were also central to the supportive community I found during my year at Williams, along with Zaid Adhami, Ashley Barnes, David Edwards, Stacy Fahrenthold, Antonia Foias, VaNatta Ford, Kim Gutschow, Jacqueline Hidalgo, Jon Malesic, Gregory Mitchell, Grant Shoffstall, and Christina Simko. Participants in the 2015 American Institute of Indian Studies Dissertation to Book Workshop, hosted at the Annual Conference on South Asia, also provided valuable feedback on the future shape of the book, under the able guidance of Susan Wadley.

In my years at North Dakota State University, this book took shape in the context of a rich community that offered intellectual and social support as well as valuable mentorship. In addition to financial and intellectual support from the office of the Dean of the Arts, Humanities, and Social Sciences, I am grateful for the mentorship of Betsy Birmingham, Carrie Ann Platt, Christina Weber, and Christopher Whitsel. John Creese and Kristen Fellows provided a model of collaborative collegiality and community building that I continue to emulate. Sarah Boonstoppel made Fargo a warm home in spite of frigid temperatures, alongside Bradley Benton, Sean Burt, Gordon Fraser, Jake Friedman, Don Johnson, and Heath Wing.

At the Keough School of Global Affairs at the University of Notre Dame, I've encountered lively interdisciplinary dialogue that cast the findings of this book in new light. The Dean's Office at Keough has provided crucial material support, including funds to work with Chris Lura on the final version of the manuscript. Leadership from Scott Appleby, Ted Beatty, Caroline Hughes, and Michel Hockx gave me the space and fortitude to finish the book, along with incredible administrative support from Denise Ayo, Anne Bax, Chris Cox, Patrick Deegan, and Megan McNichols. Cat Bolten and Susan Blum have been welcoming and inspiring anthropological colleagues on campus. Susan Ostermann has been a keen interlocuter across disciplinary difference. I am also grateful for Pam Butler, Katlyn Carter, Tarryn Chun, Abby Córdova, Amitava Dutta, Jennifer Huynh, Lakshmi Iyer, Kyle Jaros, Tamara Kay, Mahan Mirza, Nikhil Menon, Anne Mische, Abigail Ocobock, Harold Toro Tulla, Tom Tweed, and Sharon Yoon, who have provided conversation, writerly support, and community in South Bend.

Beyond institutions, I have learned so much from interactions large and small with Srimati Basu, Tarini Bedi, Laura Brown, Erica Bornstein, Susan Johnson-Roehr, Ann Grodzins Gold, Matthew Hull, Katherine Martineau, Megan Moodie, Sameena Mulla, Claire Snell-Rood, and Andrea Wright. Sameena Mulla provided brainstorming support toward the final title of this book. Sarah Pinto has provided longstanding support and encouragement, both in person and through her own brilliant writing on kinship, marriage, and gender in India. Sarah Lamb has also been an important source of intellectual and writerly inspiration, and the traces of her work will be clear to readers.

Over the years of revising this book, I was also working with fabulous, curious students. Seeing the themes and methods of anthropology anew through their eyes provided motivation and many new insights. I want to especially thank students in my seminars Paradoxes of Human Rights and Gender, Sexuality, and Development, taught at Williams College and the University of Notre Dame. In trusting me with their own research interests and provocations, I am particularly grateful to Bushra Ali, Rubén Flores, Rana El-Beheiry, Benjamín Rascon Gracia, Tyrel Iron Eyes, and Jacqueline Shrader.

I presented elements of this work at numerous conferences over the years. For providing opportunities to present or offering discussant commentary, I thank Maggie Dickinson, Jennie Doberne, Michele Friedner, Katherine Fultz, Charlotte Haney, Pinky Hota, Gabriele Koch, Mindie Lazarus-Black, Gayatri Moorthi, Greg Morton, Shaylih Muehlmann, Sarah Pinto, Llerena Searle, Lisa Stevenson, Sonali Thakkar, Thomas Trautmann, and Stanton Wortham.

This book would not exist without the collaborative feedback, encouragement, and inspiration of Care and the Life Course Writing Group. Elana Buch, Laura Heinemann, Jessica Robbins, Aaron Seaman, and Kristin Yarris saw this work through the transition from student to professor, providing intellectual and emotional continuity over the past seven years. I have learned so much about interdependent relations not only from the content of their research but from the models they provide as colleagues, mentors, and friends.

This analysis was made possible by the groundbreaking scholarship of two scholars who have since passed on. The work of Saba Mahmood, on one hand, and Sally Engle Merry, on the other, provided the two poles this book strives to move between. Although our paths did not cross, I continue to draw inspiration from their fierce thinking. While both are cited extensively here, citations alone do not fully capture the influence their ideas have had on this work.

This research was carried out with funding from Fulbright-Hays, the University of Chicago's Committee on Southern Asian Studies, the American Institute for Indian Studies, a Dean's Challenge Grant at North Dakota State University, and Foreign Language and Area Studies grants for language study in India as well as Chicago. The writing and analysis were supported by a Woodrow Wilson Women's Studies Dissertation Fellowship and a dissertation fellowship from the University of Chicago's Center for the Study of Gender and Sexuality affiliated with their 2011–2012 Sawyer Seminar, International

Women's Human Rights: Paradigms, Paradoxes, and Possibilities, and funds from the Keough School of Global Affairs at the University of Notre Dame.

Portions of this book appeared in earlier publications. Portions of Chapters 4 and 5 appeared in "Ordering Dependence: Care, Disorder, and Kinship Ideology in North Indian Antiviolence Counseling," published in *American Ethnologist,* 43, no. 1 (2016): 63–75. Portions of the introduction appeared in "Between Gender and Kinship: Mediating Rights and Relations in North Indian NGOs," published in *American Anthropologist,* 123, no. 2 (2021): 330–342.

At the University of Pennsylvania Press, Jenny Tan has been a phenomenal editor and patient guide through the process of completing a book. Two anonymous reviewers provided constructive, thoughtful feedback, drawing wide ranging theoretical connections that I look forward to continuing to explore.

My in-laws, Hsiao-Shu Hsu, Maria Hsu, Adam Hsu, and Danielle Zheng have been unwavering in their support, and forgiving of the unpredictable demands fieldwork and academic life make on our time.

My parents made this possible through many forms of support over a lifetime. My father, Gregory Kowalski, models a boundless enthusiasm for figuring out how things work, and a propensity for patient, stubborn tinkering. My mother, Kathryn Kowalski, encouraged me to reflect on what I noticed about the social world, particularly about gender, from an early age, teaching me that it was a worthwhile effort even when it occasionally got me into trouble.

My spouse, Alexander Hsu, lived with this project from graduate school tears to 117-degree Rajasthani heat to all-consuming revisions, hopping from institution to institution over many years. His own insights, both lived and scholarly, about skillful means and scriptural economy have had a profound impact on the process and product of this project, though far less of an impact than his care and companionship.

Lightning Source UK Ltd.
Milton Keynes UK
UKHW041826030922
408285UK00002B/186